Andrew LYTLE
Walker PERCY
Peter TAYLOR

a reference guide

A
Reference
Guide
to
Literature

Ronald Gottesman
Editor

Andrew LYTLE
Walker PERCY
Peter TAYLOR
a reference guide

VICTOR A. KRAMER
PATRICIA A. BAILEY
CAROL G. DANA
CARL H. GRIFFIN

G.K.HALL&CO.
70 LINCOLN STREET, BOSTON, MASS.

2/1984
Am. Lit.

Library of Congress Cataloging in Publication Data
Main entry under the title:

Andrew Lytle, Walker Percy, Peter Taylor : a reference guide.

   Includes index.
   1. American literature—Southern States—Bilbiography.
2. American literature—20th century—Bibliography.
3. Lytle, Andrew Nelson, 1902-   —Bibliography.
4. Percy, Walker, 1916-   —Bibliography. 5. Taylor,
Peter Hillsman, 1917-   —Bibliography. I. Kramer,
Victor A.
Z1229.S6A5   1983   [PS261]   016.81'09'975   82-15748
ISBN 0-8161-8399-6

This publication is printed on permanent/durable acid free paper
MANUFACTURED IN THE UNITED STATES OF AMERICA

Contents

The Authors

Victor A. Kramer is Professor of English at Georgia State University in Atlanta where he teaches literary criticism and American literature. He received his bachelor's degree from St. Edward's in Austin, Texas, and his Ph.D. from the University of Texas, Austin. He is the author of James Agee (1975), a forthcoming book about Thomas Merton, and co-editor of Olmsted South (1979).

Patricia Ann Bailey attended Auburn University and graduated from the University of Houston with a B.A. degree in English. She is currently in the graduate program at Georgia State University, where her M.A. thesis is a study of James Agee's Let Us Now Praise Famous Men. While at Georgia State she has been a graduate research assistant and plans to do additional work on Southern writers.

Carol Dana teaches English at DeKalb Community College in suburban Atlanta. She received her B.A. degree from Tulane University in New Orleans, and her M.A. and Ph.D. degrees from Georgia State University. In her doctoral dissertation, she explored the convergence of the American Dream and spiritual quest in Walker Percy's novels. Additionally, she has presented papers on Percy at several professional conferences.

Carl H. Griffin is chairman of the humanities division of DeKalb Community College, North Campus. He received his B.A. degree from the University of North Carolina, Chapel Hill, and his M.A. degree from the University of Florida, where he studied with Andrew Lytle. He taught for six years at Shorter College, Rome, Georgia. Recently he served as chairman of the South Atlantic Modern Language Association-Southeastern American Studies Association section.

Preface

These surveys of commentary about the writings of Andrew Lytle, Walker Percy, and Peter Taylor provide an analysis of the significant scholarship and reviews through 1979. Insofar as possible, materials for 1980 are also included. Some forty different bibliographical sources were used to find citations for these bibliographies, and while we are aware that for recent years there may be omissions because some indexes have not yet been published, we think that our listings are substantially complete. We are appreciative of the work that has been done by other scholars who have provided bibliographies for these writers. The checklists by Noel Polk on Lytle (1978.10 and 1973.7), by Joe Weixlmann and Daniel H. Gann on Percy (1980.58), and by James Penny Smith on Taylor (1967.6) were especially helpful.

It should be emphasized that we have been selective in our inclusion of reviews, for many more were located, especially in newspapers. We have not sought to read all the reviews in newspapers. Materials excluded were limited to regional newspaper reviews that we thought would be repetitious. Reviews were annotated from New York, Washington, Chicago, and Los Angeles newspapers. No scholarly articles or essay-reviews were knowingly omitted. A student who seeks thorough coverage of newspaper commentary about these writers will perhaps want to investigate newspapers such as the Nashville, Memphis, New Orleans, Atlanta, and Chattanooga papers. Also, we have frequently chosen to omit extremely brief reviews if these are of little significance. This is especially true of the numerous repetitive reviews of Percy's fiction. Similarly, we have not attempted to locate all the places where stories or essays are anthologized and which might also be accompanied by brief critical commentary. We realize that inclusion of such material would in a limited way be of value, yet no major scholarly work has been lost. Cross-references between the three parts of this book are incorporated when an article or review refers to more than one of the three writers whose work is surveyed. Asterisks are used to indicate that a particular entry has not been seen. In a few places in the Lytle guide we have incorporated the substance of the annotation provided in the Noel Polk bibliography on Lytle in <u>Mississippi Quarterly</u> (1970.2, 12), and have so indicated. Abbreviations used for the table of abbreviations are regularlized to conform with the master list of abbreviations in the bibliography of Publications of the Modern Language Association.

A fundamental reason for doing these reference guides was our conviction that these writers deserve wider recognition. Each of the three has sustained a large body of work over a period of decades. They have been grouped together for this study because they share in a world view that honors the individual in a society where the traditional world is so rapidly changing. It is significant that these writers sometimes share literary friends, and in some instances even influences, as is the case with John Crowe Ransom for Lytle and Taylor, and Caroline Gordon for Lytle and Percy. These writers also share a continuing interest in the developing traditions of Southern life and letters. This grouping of guides should serve both as a means of adding critical attention to writers well received by critics but who today retain a relatively small readership, and as a way of stimulating a wider audience. Percy's reputation, in just the few years that we have been engaged in this project, has increased considerably. Three books about him recently appeared, and undoubtedly there will be more study of Percy who now has a national reputation. The writings of Lytle and Taylor, however, demand more attention. Lytle's books are out of print, and while his fiction has received serious investigation during the past decade, critical acceptance of his work and public recognition are hardly wider today than just after his masterpiece, The Velvet Horn, was published in 1957. We recall the hopeful words of Robie Macauley, who reviewed that novel in Kenyon Review (1957.8) almost twenty-five years ago:

> A combination of unfortunate circumstances has made
> Andrew Lytle too long overlooked and his books ignored.
> I should imagine that the situation will change after
> the publication of The Velvet Horn. This is a novel of
> unique setting and feeling and of intricate artful tell-
> ing. Without the least bit of cant it arrives at a
> hopeful and positive conclusion. In short it should
> assure Mr. Lytle of his rightful place among the first
> rank of American novelists practicing today.

In a quiet way recognition has come for Lytle's writing, but only for a very small number of readers, and usually in academic circles. The same must be said of Taylor, whose beautiful stories continue to appear at regular intervals, but whose career as a whole has yet to be fully assessed. Percy now commands a wide audience, but neither Lytle nor Taylor has ever had large numbers of readers.

One of the reasons for this neglect, or misunderstanding, is that Lytle and Taylor have often been dismissed as "Southern" writers; yet they are writers who are beyond the scope of a particular region. Percy has openly resisted the regional label. While all three can be classified as "Southern" and they would indeed not object to such a designation if it were properly qualified, perhaps the most important

thing about their work and the scholarly commentary which it has
generated is that it is successful precisely because it transcends
regional writing. Place is surely important for all three of these
writers, but the human condition and its implications are the core of
their concern, not some stereotype of Southern character, or worse,
some nostalgia for a time past. Lytle's classic, A Wake for the
Living, and the most recent stories published by Taylor in the New
Yorker in 1980 and 1981, clearly validate these facts. Just as we
have recently seen an increase of interest in Percy's writings, we
hope that there will be a corresponding resurgence of interest in
Lytle and Taylor, too. Critics have been consistently enthusiastic,
about the accomplishment of both for decades. Readers are too when
they know of these writers.

Two sets of conferences and readings that were held at Georgia
State University and at DeKalb Community College, North Campus, in
1980 and 1981 are perhaps an indication of contemporary interest.
Lytle and Taylor both graciously attended those conferences, and
papers about their work were presented. The focus of the conferences
was upon the fictional worlds created by these two writers, as well
as Percy. Eventually the papers presented at those conferences will
be published. Among them were two that were especially valuable as
demonstrations of the scope of Lytle and Taylor's work. Jane Barnes
Casey spoke about "What Happens to the Happy Family in Peter Taylor's
Work." She stressed how the subject of Taylor's art has changed, and
how his art reveals a growth in the artist. Thomas Carlson presented
a paper on Lytle's fiction which he entitled "An Overview of Lytle's
Work: In Pursuit of Natasha or Uncle Jack's Dream." Carlson's lecture stressed that Lytle's vision of mankind is not just one of iso-
lated moments, but a vision of man's continuing adventure as part of
an ever widening community. It was also a pleasure to have presenta-
tions given at these conferences by three additional scholar-critics
who have over the years made substantial contributions to our knowledge about Lytle, Percy, and Taylor. David McDowell was a participant in both conferences. His work as editor of books by both Lytle
and Taylor, and his close friendship with these writers, allowed him
to make perceptive comments. Professors Ashley Brown and Lewis A.
Lawson, who have written about Taylor and Percy over a long period of
time, also gave insightful lectures. In the success of the conferences held in 1980 and 1981, we see a symbol of ongoing concern which
will continue as we develop a fuller understanding of these writers.
We are appreciative of the support that George State and DeKalb
Community College provided to make these gatherings possible.

Thanks must also be extended to many people who assisted in the
work of preparing this volume. We especially want to thank the reference and interlibrary loan departments of Georgia State University,
and most of all Jane Hobson. We are also appreciative of the assistance provided by the Emory University libraries: the Woodruff
Library, the Pitts Theology Library, and the Library School Library;
and by the De Kalb Community College Libraries.

We are also appreciative of the support provided in the completion of this project by Dewey Weiss Kramer, who read, commented upon, sometimes translated, and occasionally revised abstracts written by others, and who encouraged the writers of these abstracts during the course of the project.

P.A.B.
V.A.K.

Abbreviations

ABC	ABC Book Collector	JSH	Journal of Southern History
AL	American Literature	KanQ	Kansas Quarterly
AR	Antioch Review	KR	Kenyon Review
BB	Bulletin of Bibliography	LaS	Louisiana Studies
Books	New York Herald Tribune Book Review	LJ	Library Journal
		MFS	Modern Fiction Studies
BS	Best Sellers	MissQ	Mississippi Quarterly
BW	Washington Post Book World	MQR	Michigan Quarterly Review
CC	Christian Century	Nat	Nation
Crit	Critique: Studies in Modern Fiction	NatR	National Review
CSM	Christian Science Monitor	NConL	Notes on Contemporary Literature
Expl	Explicator	NewR	New Republic
FQ	Florida Quarterly	NL	New Leader
GaR	Georgia Review	NMW	Notes on Mississippi Writers
HC	Hollins Critic	NoAm	North American
HudR	Hudson Review	NW	Newsweek
JMH	Journal of Mississippi History	NY	New Yorker

NYRB	New York Review of Books	SLJ	Southern Literary Journal
NYTBR	New York Times Book Review	SoQ	Southern Quarterly
ORev	Occasional Review	SoR	Southern Review (Baton Rouge, La.)
PR	Partisan Review	SR	Sewanee Review
Prospects	Prospects: An Annual Journal of American Cultural Studies	SSF	Studies in Short Fiction (Newberry, S.C.)
PW	Publishers Weekly	SWR	Southwest Review
RALS	Resources for American Literary Study	TLS	Times Literary Supplement (London)
RANAM	Recherches anglaises et américaines	VQR	Virginia Quarterly Review
SAB	South Atlantic Bulletin	WP	Washington Post
SAQ	South Atlantic Quarterly	WR	Western Review
		WSCL	Wisconsin Studies in Contemporary Literature
SatR	Saturday Review of Literature	YR	Yale Review
SHR	Southern Humanities Review		

Andrew Lytle

Introduction

Andrew Nelson Lytle was born on December 26, 1902, in Murfreesboro, Tennessee. Both his parents, Robert Logan Lytle and Lillie Belle Nelson, were members of families long prominent in middle Tennessee. His memoir and family chronicle, A Wake for the Living (1975), is Lytle's memorial to his family and a reminder to readers of the fundamental facts of human continuity, facts he believes a modern industrialized society that emphasizes freedom of the individual can too easily forget. Lytle's writing, which spans a fifty-year period from his contribution to I'll Take My Stand to the present, stresses man's Christian heritage, a heritage often abused as Western man's adventure in the New World has unfolded. Lytle's art emphasizes the unhappiness of the displaced in a world that seeks to ignore man's fundamental responsibilities to himself and to others. He has been called a "writer's writer," but this is true only if we say that careful assimilation of Flaubert, James, and Tolstoy results in such a writer. Lytle has been insistent on making the point that man must not live in isolation from the land and from others, yet to be honest in the production of his art he has had to deal with the fact that it appears to him that a narrowness of vision has been responsible for much of man's unhappiness. All of this is basic, while it also must be stressed that Lytle's career as artist, critic, and editor has been one with integrity at its core--a career with a singleness of vision that rejoices in the complexity of man. For Lytle that complexity blends good and evil, and this fundamental vision unites his best work.

Lytle has never sought to cultivate a large audience: he has chosen instead to cultivate his art, yet in that choice he has produced nine books that have permanence. It is unfortunate that these books should be out of print, yet it is certain that for serious readers they will not be forgotten. Each of these books stands as a reflection of an artist who has had the patience to write carefully about subjects that interested him.

Andrew Nelson Lytle's literary career has been a happy one, as indeed has been his life. He seems always to have chosen to do what he knew was best at the moment. The result is a career full of accomplishments spanning half a century. A true man of letters, Lytle's work is crafted to stand the test of time. Yet apparently he never thought of his life's work as a literary "career." Each piece, each story, each essay, each performance stands by itself; for Lytle would have us remember as we look at his work, what impresses us when we meet him: that the important, indeed civilized, thing is to live well each particular moment and yet recognize, of course, that all moments do fit together.

Lytle was fortunate to be a student at Vanderbilt in the 1920s. Likewise, he was fortunate to make friendships early which he has maintained for a lifetime. His contribution to I'll Take My Stand can now be seen clearly, in retrospect, as valuable because of its metaphorical approach. Many reviews and essays that trace the development of his work observe this ability, which is united with Lytle's attention to specific detail. These facts can be traced to his sure love of the particular--places, people, and their interaction. It is, perhaps, his love of the particular, his respect for the conjunction of a particular time and place as imagined by the artist and brought alive through language, that gives a timelessness to his best writing.

Lytle also was fortunate in having as mentor John Crowe Ransom, and as friends Robert Penn Warren, Allen Tate, and Caroline Gordon from whom he received encouragement over the years; yet he has always been very much his own man. His work has sometimes been compared to that of others who grew out of the Southern Renascence. But finally it is his ability as story teller that makes his work valuable, for it is here that Lytle always seems to be sure of his gifts. Yet to be sure of one's self, one has to know how the individual fits into a particular story, tradition, and history; in large part, Lytle's career has been a chronicle of his awareness of what can go wrong if man tries to step out of his proper place.

Lytle was lucky to be born into his family and to have the gift of being able to listen and to write. But more importantly, he is to be commended for his ability to cultivate gifts which arose because of the synchronicity of time, place, and circumstance in his life's work. Lytle's critical pieces indicate his awareness of myth and of the fact that all stories reflect the larger patterns of the culture as a whole. This fact is what his critics are slowly coming to realize.

Lytle's total production has been modest, but the total body is impressive. The biography of Forrest appeared in 1931; the first novel, The Long Night, was published in 1936. Both have been highly praised, yet neither ever attained a large readership. Five years later At the Moon's Inn appeared. But, just as James Agee's Let Us Now Praise Famous Men which appeared in 1941, Lytle's ambitious work about de Soto was eclipsed by other events. In 1947 A Name for Evil received favorable comments, yet the book was not seen as part of a

developing pattern. Only with the publication of The Velvet Horn ten
years later did Lytle begin to receive some systematic critical attention. The collection A Novella, A Novel, and Four Stories followed quickly, and in 1960 Bedford Forrest was issued. In addition,
there were years of teaching and then editing The Sewanee Review
documented in part by the anthology Craft and Vision. With A Wake
for the Living this makes nine valuable books.

Lytle's fiction and storytelling is that of a mastercraftsman,
and yet because these books seem so different, proper connections are
not quickly made among them. It is almost as if each time Lytle published a book from 1931 to 1957, he was starting over. Yet in all
the work there is a common theme, perhaps best described as the unhappy development of western civilization resulting from man's attempt to control his world. This theme provides a focus for many
critics, but it is hardly a vein that has been exhausted.

Reviews of his writing have usually consisted of high praise, yet
Lytle has never had the body of readers that he deserves. Each book,
from 1931 to 1957, has been deemed a success, but except for doctoral
dissertations, we have yet to assess the entire body of the work from
the first book, Nathan Bedford Forrest and His Critter Company (1931),
to A Wake for the Living (1975). Clearly there would be enough material in each of these books alone for an extended analysis. Forrest
was announced as the best biography written about the confederate
general when it was published, but it has never been seriously compared to other works, or to primary sources. It has not, to date,
been examined as a biography that relies heavily upon novelistic
techniques. Similarly, except for its treatment within a recent dissertation, there is yet to be an extended study of A Wake for the
Living, a work that is in a fundamental way a gloss on all Lytle's
writing. Part fact, part tale-telling, part just plain fun, part
history, A Wake is Lytle's overview and an essential means to appre-
ciating his other works.

A study of Lytle falls into a distinct pattern and, as has been
indicated, the longest time period is the first. From 1931 to the
publication of The Velvet Horn in 1957, the books were favorably
reviewed, but Lytle had little visibility as a writer. He did, however, have encouragement from his fellow writers and artist-friends
during that long period.

Some of the early commentary that stands out was done by those
closest to Lytle. Already in the thirties, Ranson (1936.5), while
expressing some doubts about The Long Night, was not afraid to com-
pare it to Shakespeare. Allen Tate (1936.7) also wrote a perceptive
review of the novel when it appeared. Many years later, when the
book had been largely forgotten, it was Robert Penn Warren (1971.6-7)
who wrote an introduction for a reprint of it. In such scattered
pieces that appeared over the years we are able to see some of the
reasons that account for Lytle's patience as an artist. His fellows

had confidence in his work. Yet it can be said of few artists that
they would have the patience to wait a quarter of a century for recognition. This is precisely what Lytle had to do, for it was only
in 1957, when The Velvet Horn appeared, that he began to receive wide
recognition, and thereby the second phase of critical interest in his
work began.

When The Velvet Horn was published, Lytle's skill was finally
recognized by a larger audience. In the years following, when his
editor, David McDowell, perceptively arranged for the publication of
A Novel, A Novella, and Four Stories, as well as the reissue of
Bedford Forrest, Lytle began to develop a national reputation. When
the history of Lytle's literary career is written it will have to include a significant chapter about David McDowell who edited these
three books. McDowell is also the person who urged Lytle to write A
Wake. With the success of The Velvet Horn and the publication of
three additional books, critical interest in Lytle developed system-
atically so that the years 1957-1960 can be described as the second
phase in the development of Lytle's reputation.

By 1960, Lytle's work had become the subject of academic curios-
ity, as signified by the Lytle checklist compiled by Jack DeBellis
(1960.4). In the opening years of the 1960s, several excellent articles about his work also appeared. This period, 1960-1965, consti-
tutes the third phase that followed in the wake of his recognition in
the later 1950s. It is also significant that I'll Take My Stand was
reissued (1962.3), and during these years careful studies were being
made about the implications of the Agrarian Movement. Still other
scholars were beginning to look carefully at the nature of Lytle's
work as an artist. The early sixties therefore constitute a third
phase in Lytle's recognition.

Thus, after a long period of neglect, Lytle was recognized with
the appearance of The Velvet Horn, and soon after serious critical
examination began. A fourth period was to follow the publication of
Lytle's critical essays in 1966. Lytle's own criticism has been
examined by various critics, and such examination provides a clearer
understanding of his goals and accomplishments as a fiction writer.
Several critics have demonstrated that we can understand Lytle best
by studying his criticism with care. With the publication of The
Hero with the Private Parts, then, still another phase of recognition
and appreciation of Lytle began. It was also during this time (the
middle sixties) and partly because of Lytle's own recently published
critical insights that careful assessment of The Velvet Horn began.
This led to interest in other aspects of his work and gave rise to
the special issue of Mississippi Quarterly devoted to his work
(1970.2-12).

The 1970 Mississippi Quarterly devoted to Lytle's fiction provides ten essays that examine much of the major writing. These
studies, which are for the most part explications, along with

additional essays, were made into a book called <u>The Form Discovered</u> (1973.3). With the appearance of <u>The Form Discovered</u>, and with Lytle's editing of <u>Craft and Vision</u>, his work as artist and as editor clearly was recognized on a wide scale. <u>Craft and Vision</u>, Lytle's edited collection of fiction from <u>The Sewanee Review</u>, appeared in 1971, and this was also the year of the first doctoral dissertation about his work. The two collections of essays of the 1970s are in-dications that Lytle had become a subject for serious academic criti-cism. However, Melvin Bradford's <u>The Form Discovered</u> is still the only book published about Lytle. Thus, it remains the best single place to begin a systematic study of his work.

Lytle's latest book, <u>A Wake for the Living</u>, appeared in 1975 and signals still another phase of interest in his work as well. As in-dicated earlier, it is a book that speaks to the present about the living past. The reviews of <u>A Wake for the Living</u> are important in reminding us of the need for still more systematic study of Lytle. His unusual tour de force reminds us that above all he remains a magnificent storyteller, yet we also are reminded of the unity of his vision. There is no doubt that one day we will have a study of Lytle as raconteur.

It has been established that each of Lytle's novels is a separate experiment. That fact has provided a basic subject for much of the better criticism; yet what is needed is a greater vision of the whole. His craft allows him to be Lytle the Christian artist, Lytle the myth-maker, Lytle the crafter of individual texts, and all of these sub-jects need critical attention; but ultimately they need attention as they work together to give us a picture of Western man. Criticism about Lytle's work has been helpful in allowing us to see him as a craftsman, and also as one who is fully aware of Western history. Critics have shown us how Lytle, the artist, builds fiction on an awareness of the particular, often with the reinforcement of knowl-edge from literary sources--whether a Spanish chronicle, or Henry James, or the Old Testament. Still other essays about his work stress his uses of myth and his respect for technique. We need to have more examination of Lytle's fiction as individual works, and studies of how the body of his work fits together. Several interest-ing studies have appeared since 1973. Perhaps the most important essay is by Robert V. Weston (1978.3). Articles in French by Anne Foata (1974.4; 1976.1; 1978.2) indicate that there is a European audience. Recent articles by Charles C. Clark (1970.5; 1972.7; 1974.2; 1977.1) and Nancy Joyner (1974.5) are also provocative. A considerable number of theses have been completed on Lytle's fiction; doctoral dissertations have been cited chronologically in the guide, and an appendix has been added which lists master's theses.

V.A.K.

Writings by Andrew Lytle

"The Hind Tit." In I'll Take My Stand: The South and the Agrarian Tradition. New York: Harper & Brothers, 1930.

Bedford Forrest and His Critter Company. New York: Minton, Balch & Co., 1931. Reprints. New York: G.P. Putnam's Sons, 1935; London: Eyre & Spottiswoode, 1938; London: Eyre & Spottiswoode, with a foreword by B.H. Liddell Hart, 1939; New York: McDowell, Obolensky, 1960.

The Long Night. Indianapolis and New York: Bobbs-Merrill Co., 1936. Reprints. New York: Grossett & Dunlap, 1938; London: Eyre & Spottiswoode, 1937; New York: Avon, 1973.

At the Moon's Inn. Indianapolis and New York: Bobbs-Merrill Co., 1941. Reprints. London: Eyre & Spottiswoode, 1943; Stockholm: Förlagsaktiebolaget A. Sohlman & Co., 1943.

A Name for Evil. Indianapolis and New York: Bobbs-Merrill Co., 1947. Reprint. New York: Avon, 1969.

The Velvet Horn. New York: McDowell, Obolensky, 1957.

A Novel, A Novella, and Four Stories. New York: McDowell, Obolensky, 1958.

The Hero with the Private Parts. Baton Rouge: Louisiana State University Press, 1966.

Craft and Vision: The Best Fiction from "The Sewanee Review." Edited and with a foreword by Andrew Lytle. New York: Delacorte Press, 1971.

A Wake for the Living: A Family Chronicle. New York: Crown Publishers, 1975.

9

Writings about Andrew Lytle, 1931-1980

1931

1 ANON. Review of <u>Bedford Forrest</u>. <u>Pittsburgh Monthly Bulletin</u>
   36 (October):66.
      Essentially a restatement of the thesis of the book as
   stated in 1931.6.

2 COMMAGER, H.S. "The Terror of the Damyankees." <u>NewR</u> 67
   (22 July):266.
      Review of <u>Bedford Forrest and His Critter Company</u>. The
   Agrarian theme which Lytle emphasized in <u>I'll Take My Stand</u>
   stressed the virtues of the plain people; as the central theme
   of this biography, philosophical significance is given to an
   "excellent but unoriginal military study." <u>Bedford Forrest</u> is
   infused with an "admirable unity," its style a "happy vehicle."
   Forrest is a medium for "social and historical interpretation,"
   and while many of Lytle's assumptions about the potential success
   of Forrest, had he been properly recognized, are questionable,
   the book is the most readable of various biographies of Forrest.

3 CRAVEN, AVERY. "General Lee's Greatest Soldier." <u>Books</u> 7
   (28 June):7.
      Lytle's understanding of dramatic values in writing and his
   intimate knowledge of the Southern landscape give this book "real
   distinction." He convinces the reader that Forrest was a military genius by providing specific details of actions as soldier
   and leader. This account reveals "the lengths to which human
   endurance can go"; "more than a biography," it makes good reading
   for many reasons.

4 MENEELY, A.H. "Old Forrest." <u>SatR</u> 8 (25 July):4.
      Reviewed with Eric William Sheppard's 1930 biography of
   Forrest which sometimes resorts to "impressionism," Lytle's book
   shows a much more "discriminating sense of emphasis" for he tells
   his story with clarity. The main points of both books are emphasized: Sheppard giving credit to Forrest as a "rough and ready

raider"; Lytle stressing that Forrest's skills included tactical
abilities both in particular maneuvers and in the large aspects
of the war.

5   SEITZ, DON C. Review of Bedford Forrest. Bookman 74, no. 2
     (31 October):206.
         Lytle "has written the first epic of the 'poor whites.'"
Forrest stood first among those who "fought in the interests of
the slave magnates," and Lytle's portrait is one which makes the
reader believe in Forrest's ability. "A redblooded biography of
a first-class fighting man!"

6   THOMPSON, C.W. Review of Bedford Forrest. NYTBR, 5 July,
     p. 3.
         A detailed case is made in Bedford Forrest and His Critter
Company that Forrest, though uneducated and not a military man by
training, was the military genius capable of altering the outcome
of the Civil War. Admired by the opposing Union generals for his
abilities, Forrest, however, incurred the wrath of Braxton Bragg,
who later as chief of staff for Jefferson Davis, was instrumental
in undermining Forrest and destroying the Confederacy.

7   WHARTON, DON. Review of Bedford Forrest. Outlook 158, no. 7
     (17 June):216.
         Provides background about Forrest, and his ability as an
"excellent cavalry leader"; asserts Lytle takes the reader along
with the Army of Tennessee, but does not succeed in taking the
reader "into the heart of Forrest." Lytle does not even come
close to "Old Bedford."

1932

1   MILTON, GEORGE FORT. "Forrest Against Sheridan." VQR 8
     (January):127-32.
         Bedford Forrest reviewed with Joseph Hergesheimer's
Sheridan: A Military Narrative. Lytle uses "amplitude of detail"
far more advantageously than Hergesheimer; Lytle's searching for
"new verbal coinages" also meets with more success than
Hergesheimer; finally Lytle destroys the myth that Forrest was
unlettered. The two subjects are opposites: Forrest was the
strategist; Sheridan seems to be second-rate. Includes letter to
reviewer by B.H. Liddell Hart, a well-known English military
critic, who enthusiastically endorses Lytle's work. Forrest makes
an excellent case for the fact that his hero is a genius. See
1939.1.

1935

1   DAVIDSON, DONALD. "I'll Take My Stand: A History." American
     Review 5 (Summer):301-21, esp. 307, 312, 315.

12

Lytle mentioned in relation to the origins of the book; in relation to the aim of Lytle's essay "to show the merits of an agrarian life"; and in relation to his, Tate's, and Warren's wish to entitle the book A Tract Against Communism.

1936

1   ANON. Review of The Long Night. Booklist 33 (October):53.
    Brief review of a "hair-raising psychological story." The Civil War and the battle of Shiloh "rather over-balance the story." The combination of the brutality of war and the growth of the protagonist lead him to forego revenge.

2   BASSO, HAMILTON. "Orestes in Alabama." NewR 88 (30 September):231.
    The Long Night "will probably rank with John Peale Bishop's Act of Darkness as the best fictional performance of the Southern Agrarians." Its importance derives from its reconstruction of a vanished way of life. Lytle makes it clear that life on the frontier was hard, "even brutal." His is a "very well done picture" of the South around 1860, even though this very good story of revenge sometimes seems to echo The Count of Monte Cristo.

3   DAVIS, ELMOR T. Review of The Long Night. SatR 14 (12 September):11.
    Approves of the work as "one of the finest first novels of recent years." In the chapters set in the wilderness Lytle "displays either superb woodcraft, or more probably, a superb imagination." Visualization of earlier culture is powerfully evoked. As for the chapters on army life, concern is expressed about the proportion taken up by the battle of Shiloh, but Lytle invites comparisons with Tolstoy. In comparison with Gone with the Wind the book is also "unquestionably better."

4   MARSH, F.T. Review of The Long Night. NYTBR, 6 September, p. 9.
    Much of the novel moves on "the plane of story-telling of another day . . . the 'making your peace with God' kind of thing so familiar to romantic mystery." Considerable virtuosity is achieved through several styles and moods leading to several effects. Parts are regional and parts historic realism; some of the war scenes seem almost to be taken directly from Evelyn Scott's The Wave. However, there is no "totality of effect," thus the work is unconvincing.

5   RANSOM, JOHN CROWE. "Fiction Harvest." SoR, o.s. 2, no. 3 (Autumn):399-418, esp. 403-405.
    Within this review-essay of twenty-one novels, The Long Night is called "an original and amazing book." While the reviewer believes there are "technical blunders," because of the

shift in point of view, Lytle has a gift for narrative. He sees "life sharply under its specific images." The novel is epical and parallels can be drawn between Lytle's method here and that of Shakespeare in <u>Hamlet</u>: "Finally Pleasant must acknowledge that he has no more heart for blood-feud." But he does not lapse into just a soldier who "has suffered a personal defeat and betrayed the father's ghost." Lytle's character deserts to live in a remote part of the frontier; his Hamlet seems less human than Shakespeare's, but the novel is a success.

6   STILLMAN, CHAUNCEY. Review of <u>The Long Night</u>. <u>NoAm</u> 242, no. 2 (Winter):438-41.

     Lytle's novel has cumulative force and his greatest power, to be compared to Tolstoy's, is in his handling of the relationship of the individual to the mass. Incidental to the plot, Lytle provides "color and relief" of the middle South one generation removed from the frontier. While there are "narrative obstructions" the novel succeeds because it drives "the wild team of history and fiction with such sure swiftness."

7   TATE, ALLEN. "A Prodigal Novel of Pioneer Alabama." <u>Books</u> 13 (6 September):3.

     Finds <u>The Long Night</u> "consistently objective and dramatic," and because of the control of a "genuine historical imagination" every scene is purposive. Provides insight into Lytle's method; compares it to the Greek dramatists; and suggests that Lytle is successful because his approach is "not the least literary." While expressing some reservations about the narration's abrupt shift, thinks the book is successful because suspense about Pleasant McIvor is built up gradually, especially in relation to the depiction of the battle of Shiloh.

1937

1   ANON. Review of <u>The Long Night</u>. <u>Pratt Quarterly Booklist</u> 5, no. 100 (Winter):40.

     Brief comment on the novel: "Story of revenge leading to scenes in the Civil War and later in Alabama and Tennessee."

2   COUCH, W.T. "The Agrarian Romance." <u>SAQ</u> 36 (October):419-30, esp. 427-28.

     Text of a paper read at the 1936 Southern Historical Association Meeting that refers to Lytle's articles on John Taylor, but expresses view that Lytle may not have read Taylor's <u>Inquiry</u>. While Lytle, along with other Agrarians, makes an appeal for, and places faith in, authority, Taylor emphasized the possibility of the abuse of authority.

3   DeVOTO, BERNARD. "Fiction Fights the Civil War." <u>SatR</u> 17
    (18 December):1, 4, 15-16.
         Condensed version of a lecture. The author speculates
    about the social meaning of fiction's preoccupation with the
    Civil War. The initial move of Civil War fiction was shaped by
    Howells, James, and Twain and phrased in moral terms. Later, the
    "censorious but forgiving North had been displaced by the glam-
    orous Southland," yet to that point Civil War fiction had had
    only "such elementary psychology as gets into oratory." A new
    cycle, largely devoted to the Confederacy, has now appeared.
    These novels often stress the tragic loss of the earlier agrarian
    order. Further, with a shift toward the individual experiences,
    the Civil War novel has been democratized; yet Lytle's <u>The Long</u>
    <u>Night</u> itself is an ironical comment upon such a theory of history
    propounded by intellectuals in the South. Lytle accepts the
    dogmas of a society tragically lost, but provides a story which
    is a "blood vendetta." Nevertheless his novel is successful be-
    cause it "taps the history folk literature." Comparisons to
    novels by Caroline Gordon, MacKinlay Kantor, and others illumi-
    nate the meaning of the historical imagination.

4   PARKS, EDD WINFIELD. "Six Southern Novels." <u>VQR</u> 13 (Winter):
    154-60, esp. 157.
         <u>The Long Night</u> is "impressive and interesting"; and while
    there are problems with pace and change of character, the "sus-
    tained drive" of the first part of the book carries over into the
    second. Lytle "knits his episodes" together and proves to have a
    "communicable gusto" and "idiomatic prose" which gives the book
    distinction.

1939

*1 HART, B.H. LIDDELL. Foreword to <u>Bedford Forrest</u>. London:
    Eyre & Spottiswoode, pp. vii-viii.
         Source: 1973.3, p. 105. See also 1932.1.

1941

1   ANON. "Briefly Noted Fiction." <u>NY</u> 17 (22 November):94.
         <u>At the Moon's Inn</u> is described as a novel in which Lytle
    "has an extraordinary feeling for the sound and shape of the
    period." He has recreated the complexity of the conquistadors
    and has told "a credible and exciting tale of human endeavor and
    defeat."

2   FIELD, LOUISE MAUNSELL. Review of <u>At the Moon's Inn</u>. NYTBR,
    23 November, p. 7.
         This novel graphically recreates de Soto's visit to Florida,
    a period many know little of. Some reservations expressed about

the writing, but the novel is exciting, with dramatic and picturesque scenes, especially such "notable events as the battle
of Mauvilla . . . or Tovar's visit to the accursed town of
Talimeco."

3   PRESSLY, THOMAS J. "Agrarianism: An Autopsy." SR 49 (April-
     June):145-63.
         Lytle is discussed in several scattered references within
this examination of practical effects of the Agrarian Movement.

4   RUGOFF, MILTON. "New Novels: Historical and Present-Day."
     Books 18 (30 November):10.
         At the Moon's Inn has quite a number of good things in it.
Re-creations of atmosphere and scene pass, however, "without
introduction or farewell" and are in danger of being "blown to
the winds by sheer impressionism." Lytle omits the seventeen
years when de Soto "won glory" in South America, and presents him
"craving--to pacify mysterious Florida." Individual scenes are
"brilliant and dramatic." One regrets that Lytle did not make a
few basic concessions in the way of chronological sequence.

                              1943

1   PRESCOTT, ORVILLE. "A Handful of Rising Stars." NYTBR,
     21 March, p. 13.
         A paragraph-long comment about Lytle's At the Moon's Inn in
comparison with Edgar Maass's Don Pedro and the Devil, "two of
the finest historical novels of our time."

                              1947

1   ANON. "The Criminal Record." SatR 30 (23 August):24.
         Review of A Name for Evil. Two sentences under the sub-
title "The Saturday Review's Guide to Detective Fiction":
"Begins as out-and-out ghost story, then undergoes some strange
changes and winds up spookier than ever."

2   BARRY, IRIS. Review of A Name for Evil. Books 23 (10 August):
     6.
         Lytle "artfully leaves it to the reader to surmise for him-
self the true nature of Brent's predicament"; yet while the course
of events is recounted by Brent as narrator, it is apparent that
the mounting distress of the young wife is due to the irrational
behavior of Brent. Implications are left "deliberately indefi-
nite" but in an effective manner.

3   BOUCHER, ANTHONY. Review of A Name for Evil. San Francisco
     Chronicle This World Magazine 165 (10 August):14.
          A very brief, unfavorable review. "Miasma of evil sur-
     rounds old southern mansion in what may be either a ghost story
     or the study of a mind's disintegration. Whichever it is, it is
     recounted in some of the most distinguished bad prose that I have
     ever met with." See also 1974.6.

4   FARRELLY, JOHN. "Ghost Story." NewR 117, no. 1703
     (25 August):31.
          While there are good things in A Name for Evil, the "'hor-
     ror'" is described rather than conveyed, and is not "sufficiently
     associated with the commonplace which would beguile the reader's
     attention." The real flaw, however, seems to be in Lytle's in-
     tentions, for he brings to a ghost story (by its nature something
     of a tour de force) the critical attitude of a serious novelist.

5   HENDRY, IRENE. "Fiction Chronicle." SR 55 (Autumn):700-707.
          Brief review of a "first-person ghost story of equivocal
     meaning" which is "quite successful" within its limits. The
     unavoidable "Gothic" tone and the occasional reminder of the
     "psychological" thrillers of Hollywood tend to blur Lytle's point
     about the "disguised death-wish" of a present that yearns for the
     past.

6   McKAY, M.P. Review of A Name for Evil. LJ 72 (August):1108.
          Extremely brief description of the tale: "Husband and wife
     work hard to restore their property but the apparitions defeat
     them in the end." A book of "limited appeal."

7   TERRY, C.V. Review of A Name for Evil. NYTBR, 17 August,
     p. 17.
          After the first few paragraphs, the "Poesque conceit goes
     wan . . . and lumbers on forever thereafter." The ingredients do
     not coalesce; ghosts can be as uninteresting as people if they
     are unable to start a story and keep it moving.

8   WILSON, EDMUND. "Miscellaneous Recommendations." NY 23,
     no. 31 (20 September):97.
          A Name for Evil does not quite achieve what it attempts.
     It leans "a little too obviously on The Turn of the Screw," and
     events are "not always handled in such a way that we believe
     them." Yet the book has psychological interest and a point which
     is not merely dramatic, "a not undistinguished performance." The
     general atmosphere of a "return to the country" that does not
     succeed, is well done.

1949

1   HARKNESS, DAVID J.   "Tennessee in Literature."   Newsletter,
    The University of Tennessee [Knoxville] 28, no. 11 (November):
    14.
        Lytle is identified as "Andrew Nelson Lytle of 'Cornsilk'
    Farm" near Portland and as a "writer of historical novels."
    Basic facts about the settings of each book are provided.

1950

1   LEISY, EARNEST E.   The American Historical Novel.   Norman:
    University of Oklahoma Press, pp. 224, 251.
        Brief comments in the bibliography on Lytle's work.   See
    1973.3.

1951

*1   WARFEL, HARRY R.   "Andrew Lytle."   In American Novelists of
     Today.   New York: American Book Co., p. 273.
         Warfel quotes from what is apparently a letter from Lytle
     to him.   Source: 1973.3, p. 108.

1952

1   RANSOM, JOHN CROWE et al.   "A Symposium: The Agrarians Today."
    Shenandoah 3, no. 2 (Summer):14-33.
        Answers questions about "The Agrarian Today" submitted to
    John Crowe Ransom, Donald Davidson, Frank Owsley, Allen Tate,
    H.C. Nixon, and Lytle.   Owsley notes the differences of economic
    opinion between men such as himself who thought more in terms of
    a balanced economy and the more idealistic Ransom, Tate, Lytle,
    Fletcher, and Stark Young.   These replies cumulatively provide an
    overview of how the Agrarians viewed changes in society in rela-
    tion to the book of two decades earlier.

1953

1   O'CONNOR, FRANK.   "The Novel Approach."   NYTBR, 23 August,
    p. 5.
        Laconic report of a conference on the contemporary novel
    held at Harvard and attended by Lytle, whose comments about the
    need for an "aristocratic" audience seemed (in retrospect) some-
    what characteristic of changing attitudes of the various dis-
    tinguished participants.

2   SULLIVAN, WALTER. "Southern Novelists and the Civil War."   In
      Southern Renascence: The Literature of the Modern South.
      Baltimore: Johns Hopkins, pp. 117-19.
         Within a discussion of novels by Tate, Stark Young and
      others, The Long Night is summarized and described as "constructed
      with a great deal of subtlety." The unifying element is the
      thematic structure which combines elements of family responsibil-
      ity and revenge. Finally the war changes the patterns of Pleasant
      McIvor's action and "the traditional order by which he had lived"
      is renounced.

1957

1   ANON. "The Cropleigh Saga." Time 70 (26 August):88.
         While many Southern authors are in danger of drowning
    readers in words, Lytle's novel strikes a balance between immer-
    sion of the reader and "coming up for air" in distinct scenes.
    The eight years of writing which went into this book results in
    the "loving re-creation" of events and places. After readers
    have forgotten the "flamboyant Cropleighs," the marriage of Julia,
    the wake, and sketches of mountain people will be remembered.

2   ANON. Review of The Velvet Horn. Booklist 54 (1 October):76.
         Brief review of the novel which includes a "kaleidoscopic"
    presentation of past events in the lives of the Cropleighs and
    the Crees of the Tennessee wilderness. The "lush" descriptions
    of the wilderness accentuate "the timeless quality of a novel
    populated by wonderfully human persons."

3   ANON. Review of The Velvet Horn. Kirkus 25, no. 12 (15 June):
    422.
         Brief review which draws comparisons to The Long Night.
    Each of the main characters is mentioned; the fact that stories
    within stories weave back and forth and that there are "moments
    of superb writing" contribute to the success of a novel which,
    while it may not "quite sustain the heights," is nevertheless a
    novel that has its heights.

4   BLACKMAN, RUTH C. "Lytle's Novel of the South as First Book
    from New Publisher." CSM, 15 August, p. 7.
         The Velvet Horn--the first book of the publisher, McDowell,
    Obolensky, Inc.--reveals an author shaped by his past. Positions
    stated in I'll Take My Stand, 1930, reemerge in the novel, and
    the novel's dramatic structure, with its well-placed suspenses,
    may be the result of Lytle's earlier involvement with the Baker
    Drama Workshop at Yale. While the novel is entirely successful,
    its originality is diminished by its recurring stereotypes and
    its echoes of Wolfe, McCullers, and Faulkner. The Adam myth fig-
    ures predominantly, and the novel's main theme is the inseparable
    mixture of the spiritual and the physical.

5   BOWEN, R.O. "Sons of the Soil." SatR 40 (17 August):13.
        The Velvet Horn contains the "ranging profundity and rich
life" found only in current American fiction in the South. As a
family tale, the novel moves outward from Lucius Cree. Left to
the puzzle of his parentage, Lucius, the hero, finally deals with
much more than family enmity. A lesser writer might make this
melodrama; Lytle provides "a solid, moving, and readable book."
The prose resembles Faulkner, though the similarity indicates a
common source, not a borrowing. See also 1974.6.

6   GHISELIN, BREWSTER. "Trial of Light." SR 65, no. 4 (Autumn):
        657-65.
        The Velvet Horn shares characteristics with Lytle's short
story "The Guide," yet is more complex in meaning and goes far
beyond initiation to reveal meaning about the moral condition of
an earlier society. The use of the oak as a symbol which concentrates meaning is basic because we seize meaning beyond words;
thus the tree of life is as well the tree of blood, and the death
of Captain Cree reflects "the central knowledge that emerges
. . . to place anything first except life is to fell the tree of
life." This is not expounded, but "realized" in the "experience
and action of the characters" offered to the imagination. Each
of the main characters' actions is traced, and Lucius Cree is de-
fined as the "inheritor of consequences" of those who either
tried to escape the world or who were too much committed to it.
Jack Cropleigh alone tried to understand. While no attempt is
made to examine the intricate symbolic form of The Velvet Horn,
many valuable insights about symbolism are provided as well as
insights about the "discipline of sound" which contribute to the
success of individual images.

7   HOLLAND, ROBERT B. "The Agrarian Manifesto--a Generation
        Later." MissQ 10 (Spring):73-78.
        Lytle's "The Hind Tit" is characterized as a piece which
sees industrialization as "the inevitable road to empire and war"
within an essay that examines the continuing importance of the
ideas in I'll Take My Stand.

8   MACAULEY, ROBIE. "Big Novel." KR 19, no. 4 (Autumn):644-46.
        The Velvet Horn is not a "Southern book," but rather an
extremely "individualistic" piece of work. If anything, it is
"a highland novel with a dour, ribald, violent, poetic view of
life." Lytle's skill is evident in his use of compression ("the
problem of the miniature insert"); descriptive style; and in his
fitting the two parts of the story together. The introductory
monologue by Jack Cropleigh is a discouragement to the reader,
but as the story is underway, Lytle calculates each successive
move and alternation forward.

9   NEMEROV, HOWARD. "The Nature of Novels." PR 24 (Fall):
      597-607, esp. 601-2.
          Objects to "somewhat windy sentences," and to abrupt tran-
      sitions which disturb the opening parts of the book. The Velvet
      Horn, nevertheless, must be recognized as a work of art which in
      "many places reaches a major solidity." Other strictures include
      an objection to too great a reliance on Lucius's uncle and ob-
      jections to some of the "macabre comedy." Such problems exist
      because this book is not facile, but serious art.

10   PHELPS, ROBERT. "Dust for an Adam." NatR 4, no. 7
      (24 August):162-63.
          Lytle's luck has been to live in a world as "richly phenom-
      enal" as Elizabethan England and The Velvet Horn reflects the
      author's "precise, loving knowledge of life." He writes about
      details felt and observed and he knows "more about manliness"
      than any other contemporary American writer, a rare subject when
      so many Americans write about adolescents. The Velvet Horn is
      about a change "as mysterious and majestic as anything in Ovid."
      One of the reasons Lytle has accomplished so much is that he
      writes about a world where people lived in immediate relation
      with "animals, crops, seasons." The novel has none of the didac-
      tic tone of Lytle's essay in I'll Take My Stand. Instead he sings
      of the things he loves.

11   ROSENBERGER, COLEMAN. "In Search of His Identity." Books 34,
      no. 1 (18 August):3.
          The Velvet Horn is primarily concerned with the theme of
      identity. This is a "major novel" which can be read "for its
      sheer verbal delight, for its rhetoric . . . symbols . . . and
      allusiveness." A difficulty in the first half is that it seems
      "erratic and episodic" and even the attentive reader may have
      difficulty with sequence. Only in the final third does the nar-
      rative possess sustained interest.

12   SULLIVAN, RICHARD. "Tormented Prose in this Rewarding Novel."
      Chicago Sunday Tribune Magazine of Books, 18 August, p. 6.
          While The Velvet Horn is to be admired for its lyrical
      style, its fidelity of characterization, its depths and complexi-
      ties, it is also a difficult book. Flashbacks and time switches,
      as well as certain typographical novelties, can scare off the
      most dedicated admirer. Yet for that diligent reader who per-
      severes to the novel's resolution, there is the reward of some-
      thing like "ancient catharsis," an effect seldom produced by
      modern fiction.

1958

1   ANON. Review of A Novel, A Novella, and Four Stories.
      Booklist 55, no. 4 (15 October):99.
        The Velvet Horn and A Name for Evil share a common back-
country landscape. These other pieces demonstrate Lytle's
"perceptiveness and wide versatility." The most effective of
this shorter fiction is "Alchemy," while the ghost story is less
so.

2   ANON. Review of A Novel, A Novella, and Four Stories. Kirkus
      26, no. 13 (1 July):469.
        Brief description of the volume's contents. Remarks on
Lytle's ability to provide "a tangible texture," and on the value
of his preface, which provides "interesting background" for the
book as a whole and which "invokes provocative reading."

3   BRADBURY, JOHN M. "The Minor Fugitives." In The Fugitives:
      A Critical Account. Chapel Hill: University of North
      Carolina Press, pp. 265-71.
        Bedford Forrest is a "frankly partisan account"; its gen-
eralizations are indebted to Tate's Jefferson Davis and already
it is clear that Lytle's talents are narrative. The Long Night,
inevitably episodic, does not survive the "contrived quality" of
its central action. At the Moon's Inn is successful because of
detailed descriptions of the Indian way of life. "Alchemy" functions well because it is all of a piece. Of other stories which
preceded these Spanish pieces, two are slight; "Jericho, Jericho,
Jericho" seems to owe something to Warren's "When the Light Goes
Green," and perhaps more to Katherine Anne Porter. "Guide" seems
Faulknerian. A Name for Evil is dismissed as Lytle's "least
effective" work. Lytle's criticism is valuable for its close
reading. His most recent work ("What Quarter of the Night")
seems Faulknerian, yet the texture and particularity of vision
are distinctly Lytle's.

4   BRYANT, J.W. Review of A Novel, A Novella, and Four Stories.
      LJ 83, no. 1 (15 October):2842.
        Brief review which alludes to the "perceptive" novel, The
Velvet Horn, and which describes each of the new pieces--"entertaining short stories," a novel, and a "thought-provoking
novella." All the stories "are successful and well done." They
evoke the work of Eudora Welty and "to some extent" Truman
Capote, while all have a distinctive style of their own.

5   CABANISS, ALLEN. "The Lady of Dogwood Town." JMH 20, no. 3
      (January-October):99-106.
        A retelling of the Cofitachequi story, an incident related
by de Soto's chroniclers and used by Lytle in At the Moon's Inn.
The story is presented as history by an anonymous gentleman of
Elvas; in the journal of de Soto's secretary Rodrigo Ranjel; and
in a quasi-official report of Luys Hernandez de Biedina.

6 DAVIDSON, DONALD. <u>Southern Writers in the Modern World</u>.
   Athens: University of Georgia Press, 87 pp., esp. 52-53.
   Lytle mentioned in relation to <u>I'll Take My Stand</u>; bio-
   graphical details about Lytle once standing on same point on
   Monteagle Mountain as Forrest confirmed.

7 GEISMAR, MAXWELL. "Mostly about the South." <u>SatR</u> 41
   (30 August):12.
   Lytle's introduction is a rather strict lecture "on the
   true meaning of fiction, the processes of the creative act, the
   present corruption of democracy, the real values of Southern
   literature," etc., something which takes "audacity when the
   object of the sermon is the writer's own work." However, Lytle's
   stories about the South do not seem to be as effective as the
   material about Spanish explorers where there is more "fictional
   authenticity." There is, however, a "literary spirit . . . beneath the Southern pedagogue and Southern apologist."

8 HOLZHAUER, JEAN. "Utterly Unique." <u>Commonweal</u> 68 (12 September):598-99.
   In a review of <u>A Novel, A Novella, and Four Stories</u> a
   prejudice "against some of the trappings of Southern fiction" is
   admitted. In these pieces Lytle "has extended his range [beyond
   <u>The Velvet Horn</u>] and writes in the leisurely pace of a man con-
   vinced he has a subtle story to tell." The most effective of the
   six pieces here is "Ortiz's Mass."

9 LYELL, FRANK H. Review of <u>A Novel, A Novella, and Four Sto-
   ries</u>. <u>NYTBR</u>, 31 August, p. 6.
   Brief review which praises Lytle's work, the best pages of
   which are "happy reminders" that no other contemporary writer
   excels him in projecting "through a single episode the larger
   patterns of Southern domestic life and thought." "Jericho,
   Jericho, Jericho," "The Mahogany Frame" and "Mr. McGregor" are
   described as "marvels of compression and psychological subtlety,"
   while reservations are expressed about the longer works. [Al-
   though Lytle's spelling is "MacGregor," the story has been reprinted as "McGregor."]. See also 1974.6.

10 MAGILL, FRANK N., ed. "<u>The Velvet Horn</u>." In <u>Masterplots 1958
   Annual</u>. New York: Salem Press, pp. 255-58.
   Essay-review: compared to Faulkner's <u>Absalom, Absalom!</u>,
   Lytle's <u>Velvet Horn</u> exemplifies his interest in the "double problem of continuity and identity," a theme basic to his other novels. The same theme appears in "The Guide," which can be compared
   to Faulkner's "The Bear." Lucius Cree's story is a search for
   "identity and wholeness," but Lytle is dealing with more than
   this--finally he treats a society's social confusion and guilt as
   it relates to the heritage of the past. The method may appear
   confusing at first, but Lytle's strategy with metaphor and symbol
   allows him to invest this tale with the "haunting qualities of an
   old ballad."

11   ROLO, CHARLES. "Reader's Choice." Atlantic 202, no. 3
     (September):81-82.
          Commenting on A Novel, A Novella, and Four Short Stories,
     and remarking that "the quality of the writing is so good, and
     the storytelling so compelling," the reviewer describes how he
     checked into Lytle's publishing history to find that the first
     book had been eclipsed by the simultaneous publication of Gone
     with the Wind, and often landed on the reviewing circuit with
     murder mysteries. Yet Lytle's range here is varied, a combina-
     tion "of fine artistry and considerable force." See also 1974.6.

12   ROSENBERGER, COLEMAN. "Six Stories from the South." Books
     35, no. 8 (28 September):12.
          This generous selection brings important examples of
     Lytle's work to hand. Placing the stories within Lytle's career,
     the reviewer relates them to the developing career. Both
     "Jericho" and "Mr. MacGregor" are powerful because of their
     implicit criticism of an agrarian way of life. The Spanish
     exploration material provides a perspective "more rewarding than
     the stories in which Lytle's own judgments seem . . . engaged."
     The introduction is provocative; Lytle is "always stimulating."

13   SULLIVAN, RICHARD. "Six Pieces of Fine, Sound Writing."
     Chicago Sunday Tribune Magazine of Books, 17 August, p. 3.
          Three of the stories in A Novel, A Novella, and Four Sto-
     ries are representatives of southern fiction, defined as "a new,
     intense, troubled, often anguished, often poetic, always clearly
     regional realism." The fourth story and the novella, set in the
     times of the conquistadores, reveal a talent uncorrupted by fads
     and trends. The novel, ostensibly a ghost story, has as its
     theme, evil and its malevolent and mysterious influence on men.
     The volume in its entirety is a "most honorable work."

*14 WARD, C.A. "The Good Myth"; "Myths: Further Vanderbilt
     Views." University of Kansas City Review 25 (Summer-Fall):
     53-56, 272-76, esp. 55-56.
          Source: 1973.3, p. 108.

                              1959

1   COWAN, LOUISE. "The End of The Fugitive: 1925." In The
     Fugitive Group: A Literary History. Baton Rouge: Louisiana
     State University Press, pp. 200-201.
          Within a discussion of Ransom's concept of irony, "the
     rarest of the states of mind because it is the most inclusive,"
     Lytle is mentioned as one of Ransom's "most able students and
     disciples." Ransom's phrase "the most inclusive" can be taken as
     a key to the whole modern Southern school of writing.

2   MAGILL, FRANK N., ed. "<u>A Novel, A Novella, and Four Stories</u>."
     In <u>Masterplots 1959 Annual</u>. New York: Salem Press,
     pp. 179-82.
         Essay-review: Lytle's development as a writer "has been
     gradual and oblique"; his work has also paralleled that of Tate
     and Warren, but it is now clear that he succeeds in providing a
     reflection of a Southern and modern sensibility. His writing is
     "both ancestral and prophetic"; and his theme is "a dying society"
     caught in entanglements "of its moral code." A basic overview of
     earlier books is provided. Of the pieces in <u>A Novel, A Novella,</u>
     <u>and Four Stories</u>, reservations are expressed about <u>A Name for</u>
     <u>Evil</u> because its many elements never quite join. The shorter
     stories are a success. The novella, "Alchemy," is "beautifully,"
     "unobtrusively" done. This book should contain more of Lytle's
     criticism.

3   PEDEN, WILLIAM. "On the Short Story Scene." <u>VQR</u> 35, no. 1
     (Winter):153-60.
         Reviews <u>A Novel, A Novella, and Four Stories</u> briefly from
     the viewpoint of the stories' presentations of the "archetypal
     experiences"; ordeal by violence ("Alchemy"); initiation into
     manhood ("The Mahogany Frame"); and death ("Jericho"). Praises
     Lytle's artistry, especially the reality of his characters; con-
     siders the Southern stories superior to others which betray some
     overrefinement of technique.

4   PURDY, ROB ROY, ed. <u>Fugitives' Reunion: Conversations at</u>
     <u>Vanderbilt</u>, May 3-5, 1956. Introduction by Louis D. Rubin, Jr.
     Nashville, Tenn.: Vanderbilt University Press, 224 pp.,
     passim.
         Conversations recorded during four private sessions of the
     reunion of the Nashville Fugitives which took place May 1956.
     Ten critics and observers also participated, among them Lytle.
     Major topics of conversation included the absence of the epic in
     American literature, the proper strategy of poetry, and problems
     concerning the Agrarians. Lytle's remarks are passim.

                              1960

1   AMACHER, A.W. "Myths and Consequences: Calhoun and Some
     Nashville Agrarians." <u>SAQ</u> 59 (Spring):251-64.
         In the writings of Tate and Lytle an image of John C.
     Calhoun is projected of "a prophet lamenting the doom of feudal-
     ism." Both have equated Calhoun with "responsible paternalism."
     Asking if such an image is well-documented, and if it stands up
     in comparison with Calhoun's writings, the conclusions are
     reached--that Tate and Lytle's views may have as much to do with
     Oswald Spengler's "romantic medievalism" as it does with
     Calhoun's writings. Lytle's presentation of Calhoun's ideas does
     not reveal Calhoun's essential materialism. Tate and Lytle are

far too selective in their choices of materials. Questions are
raised about usefulness of these images either for new conserva-
tives or for those seeking assistance for the Negro.

2   BROWN, D.A. Review of Bedford Forrest. JSH 26, no. 4
    (November):558-60.
        Forrest is described as one of the actors on the vast
    stage of the Civil War who "approaches but never quite achieved
    real greatness." Yet Lytle admits that Forrest symbolizes "the
    Hero" and in the end the Hero always fails. Lytle's book, a
    literary, not a documented biography, reflects the fact of its
    being written when the author was young. The "somber" introduc-
    tion looks back over the thirty years since the book was first
    published and laments the loss of individualism for which Forrest
    stands as a symbol.

3   CURRENT, RICHARD N. "Some Soldiers and a Spy." Books 36
    (10 April):12.
        Bedford Forrest has its merit as literary, not historical
    material. "A frankly hero-worshipping yarn," it is somewhat care-
    less as to facts and dates. Judged "merely as narrative, it is
    hard to beat." The book will "especially delight professional
    Southerners."

4   DeBELLIS, JACK. "An Andrew Lytle Check List." Secretary's
    News Sheet, Bibliographic Society, University of Virginia,
    no. 46 (June):3-15.
        Introduction states that "careful study of the way Mr.
    Lytle has achieved his effects by skillful handling of point of
    view, imagery, symbolism, etc. will reveal not only the methods
    of a skilled craftsman but the evolution of a mature artist."
    The purpose of the checklist is to invite reappraisal of all of
    Lytle's work. Includes articles, articles in anthologies, books,
    poetry, and reviews as well as short stories (original appearance
    and reprinting) and is complete for the years 1923-1959.

5   HARWELL, RICHARD B. Review of Bedford Forrest and His Critter
    Company [Rev. ed.]. Chicago Sunday Tribune Magazine of Books,
    15 May, p. 10.
        Lytle is seen as forerunner of such popular historians as
    Bruce Catton, Clifford Dowdey, and George Stewart. His new edi-
    tion of Bedford Forrest is favorably reviewed. Although the new
    introduction is "charmingly written," the reviewer finds in it "a
    large element of Bourbonism" which seems anachronistic.

6   HOOGENBOOM, ARI. "Appomattox Was Not the End." SatR 43
    (16 July):21.
        Within a review of several books about the Civil War,
    Lytle's Bedford Forrest is described as a "book for the unrecon-
    structed Southern agrarian." Lytle "worships" his hero "as a
    symbol of the Southern cause," fighting against the "'powers of

darkness'"--otherwise known as Yankees. While acknowledging
Forrest's genius, Yankees will object to this "idolatrous"
treatment.

7   McFADDEN, J.P. "Books in Brief." NatR 8 (2 July):432, 436.
        Overview of Bedford Forrest, a book which Mr. Lytle makes
    "as fast-moving as one of Forrest's raids." While Lytle has made
    few changes in the revised edition, he is willing to let it stand
    on its own merits "which are considerable." The new preface is
    valuable, and while there are opinions in the book which Lytle no
    longer holds, the book stands as one of the better ones reissued
    for the Centennial of the Civil War.

8   MIERS, EARL SCHENCK. Review of Bedford Forrest. NYTBR,
        3 July, p. 7.
        Brief mention of Forrest, originally published in 1931:
    "It endures as a pleasant companion volume to place beside John
    A. Wyeth's That Devil Forrest. . . ."

9   W., C.W. Review of Bedford Forrest. San Francisco Chronicle
        This World Magazine, 7 August, p. 19.
        Notes the revised reprint of Bedford Forrest. Although
    Lytle's biography reflects his hero-worship of Forrest, "that
    does not prevent it from being an absorbing, accurate portrayal
    of a cavalry man and genius."

                            1961

1   MAGILL, FRANK N., ed. "Bedford Forrest and His Critter Com-
        pany." In Masterplots 1961 Annual. New York: Salem Press,
        pp. 16-18.
        Essay-review: approval of the "vividness and vigor" of the
    style and the manner in which Lytle tells his story in the ver-
    nacular. The book sometimes appears to be guilty of over-
    simplification, but its merits outweigh any weaknesses. It
    abounds in anecdotes "well chosen, well placed, well proportioned,
    and well related."

2   STERLING, ROBERT. Review of Bedford Forrest. Journal of the
        Illinois State Historical Society 44, no. 1 (Spring):89-90.
        Lytle's book is the story of the "Confederate cavalry
    wizard" who went virtually unrecognized by Southern leaders for
    three years. This new edition "contains practically no changes
    in the text" from the 1931 edition. The author does go to ex-
    tremes in excusing Forrest's conduct after the war. Interrup-
    tions, which amount to complaints about the mistreatment of
    Forrest by President Davis, and a lack of documentation weaken
    the book; still a "rather comprehensive study" of the war years.

1962

1   CARTER, T.H. "Andrew Lytle." In South: Modern Southern
     Literature in Its Cultural Setting. Edited by L.D. Rubin and
     R.D. Jacobs. New York: Doubleday, pp. 287-300.
        Providing background about Lytle's development as artist,
     the essay outlines how he is an artist, yet an individual. As an
     artist he is concerned that fiction "find its form"; "cut-and-
     dried Agrarianism has never been his subject." Surveying each of
     the novels that trace Lytle's development, the first novel uses a
     variety of skills to make its points and is especially successful
     in presenting concrete scenes; while imperfect, it demonstrates
     skill at "rendering." Technical control grew in At the Moon's
     Inn, and there the modern dilemma "in which spiritual and tempo-
     ral authorities . . . usurp one another's realm is prefigured."
     A Name for Evil is stylistically Lytle's weakest work while The
     Velvet Horn is technically smooth. Love is a central theme in
     much of Lytle, and Velvet Horn is especially successful through
     dramatization of the human condition. While the superficial
     reader might assume a resemblance between Faulkner and Lytle,
     their attitudes toward life are almost at opposite poles.
     Lytle's works stress the need to be oneself, and like his charac-
     ter Lucius Cree, his novels emphasize that Lytle is his own man.
     Reprinted: 1968.1.

2   HURT, JAMES R. "Lytle's 'Jerico, Jerico, Jerico' [sic]."
     Expl 20 (February): Item 52.
        Discusses the significance of the title by retracing the
     Joshua analogy (X:12) through the story which concerns the "vio-
     lent acquisition of the land" and ascertains that the analogy is
     reversed: the protagonist, Mrs. McCowan, is not Joshua, but his
     enemy; chapter 24 echoes a situation in the story where Joshua is
     death, who defeats Mrs. McCowan, and the walls of Long Gourd come
     tumbling down. Read in this context the story is deeply ironic.
     Reprinted: 1968.5. See also 1970.1.

*3   RUBIN, LOUIS D. Introduction to I'll Take My Stand: The
     South and the Agrarian Tradition, by Twelve Southerners.
     Edited by John Crowe Ransom et al. New York: Harper. Re-
     printed. Baton Rouge: Louisiana State University Press,
     1977, pp. xxiii-xxxv.
        Lytle is only mentioned occasionally, but essay provides
     analysis of the vision of an agrarian South, best "considered as
     extended metaphor." Lytle's essay is quoted to substantiate the
     assertion that I'll Take My Stand "presented a critique of modern
     life." Such a vision has provided much of the imaginative appeal
     of the book for Southerners and non-Southerners. Reprinted:
     1977.4.

<u>1963</u>

1   BRADBURY, JOHN M. "The New Tradition." In <u>Renaissance in the</u>
     <u>South: A Critical History of the Literature</u>. Chapel Hill:
     University of North Carolina Press, pp. 65-67.
        Lytle's career outlined: He "emulated" Tate and Warren
     with a Civil War biography, but his "true quality" as novelist
     only became evident with <u>The Velvet Horn</u>. Parallels with
     Faulkner are suggested; the influence of James is acknowledged,
     something "especially strong among the Fugitive group in the
     Forties." The highly complex <u>The Velvet Horn</u> is influenced by
     Faulkner and Warren.

2   BROOKS, CLEANTH. "The Old Order: <u>The Unvanquished</u> as an
     Account of the Disintegration of Society." In <u>William</u>
     <u>Faulkner: The Yoknapatawpha Country</u>. New Haven: Yale
     University Press, pp. 93, 382-83.
        Brief discussion of Lytle's essay-review "The Son of Man:
     He Will Prevail" as a "discerning" account of the disintegration
     of society.

3   EISINGER, CHESTER E. "The Conservative Imagination." In
     <u>Fiction of the Forties</u>. Chicago: University of Chicago
     Press, pp. 193-96.
        Comments on <u>At the Moon's Inn</u> as bearing thematic similari-
     ties to Caroline Gordon's <u>Green Centuries</u>, but surpassing it.
     The Spaniards fail in relation to the natural world while the
     Indian maintains integrity. <u>A Name for Evil</u> is Lytle's parable
     for the South, for man may destroy himself if he tries too hard
     to reclaim the past.

4   GHISELIN, BREWSTER. "Automation, Intention, and Autonomy in
     the Novelist's Production." <u>Daedalus</u> 92, no. 2 (Spring):
     297-311.
        Accompanies five other articles in the same issue about the
     novel, including Lytle's "Impressionism, The Ego, and The First
     Person." Consideration of the artist's intention and the un-
     conscious element with examples from James, Conrad, Robert Penn
     Warren and Lytle. Lytle's essay from <u>A Novel, A Novella, and</u>
     <u>Four Stories</u> is examined, and the essay "The Working Novelist" is
     used to demonstrate the process of discovering "'hidden mean-
     ing.'" The artist may be unaware or inattentive to particular
     details, and to some degree it can happen as Lytle said of his
     writing of <u>The Velvet Horn</u>: "'It possessed me,'"; yet even a
     writer who works in "utmost certitude" is unconsciously at work.
     In the end if a novel works it does so because of the resources
     of the craftsman and artist.

5   MOORE, EDWARD M. "The Nineteen-Thirty Agrarians." SR 71,
     no. 1 (Winter):133-42.
         Discusses reasons for the reissue of I'll Take My Stand;
     foremost is the fact that several contributors have become lead-
     ing artists. The general introduction makes it clear why the
     volume has significance for the 1960s; most importantly the con-
     tributors realized that the welfare of the individual had been
     replaced by "'the hypothetical welfare'" of society. Summaries
     of each of the essays are provided, and Lytle's "The Hind Tit" is
     described as an example of "grand sentiment," yet not boring be-
     cause of his descriptive powers. An enduring value of the book
     is that it provides "a poet's image" of man, but one should also
     realize that it is a clear indication of protest against a so-
     ciety which only a few months later collapsed into The Great
     Depression.

*6   NEWBY, IDUS A. "The Southern Ag[r]arians: A View After
     Thirty Years." Agricultural History 37 (July):143-55.
         Scattered references to Lytle which attempt to place him in
     the context of his Fugitive/Agrarian peers. Source: 1973.3,
     p. 106.

7   RUBIN, LOUIS D., Jr. The Faraway Country: Writers of the
     Modern South. Seattle: University of Washington Press,
     pp. 155-56, 194-96.
         Mention of Lytle within chapters about the poetry of
     Agrarianism and on William Styron. Subsequent achievements, such
     as the fiction of Lytle, have helped to earn I'll Take My Stand
     lasting attention. The characters of Faulkner, Wolfe, Warren,
     Lytle are "inescapably a part of society," and these writers
     realized that "lasting isolation from society" constituted a
     tragic condition.

8   WEAVER, RICHARD M. "The Southern Phoenix." GaR 17, no. 1
     (Spring):6-17.
         Review of I'll Take My Stand upon its reissue in 1962.
     Terms it a landmark for students of American intellectual history
     and elucidates the theory of Agrarianism given there. Brief
     overviews of selected articles by Ransom, Davidson, Owsley,
     Fletcher, Lanier and Young are prefaced by a reference to John
     Taylor's 1814 An Inquiry into the Principles and Policies of the
     U.S. and the development of the South's agricultural and social
     order. Agrarianism, in distinction to other "isms" of recent
     date, is a comprehensive program, considers man in relation to
     creation, recognizes differences in people, considers the place
     of art in society, and recognizes humanizing potential of an
     agriculturally based economy. Shows that Agrarianism has prece-
     dents from classical antiquity to Tocqueville and Jacob Burckhardt
     and suggests that the proposals of Stand might still be able to
     "prevail."

1964

1   BENSON, CARL. Comments in The Deep South in Transformation.
     Edited by Robert Highsaw. University, Ala.: University of
     Alabama Press, pp. 161-66, esp. 163-64.
         Brief commentary on The Velvet Horn.

2   ROCK, VIRGINIA JEAN. "The Making and Meaning of I'll Take My
     Stand: A Study in Utopian-Conservatism, 1925-1939." Ph.D.
     dissertation, University of Minnesota.
         A study of the interplay of events, personalities and ideas
     which resulted in the publication of I'll Take My Stand in 1930.
     Three parts constitute the study: first, examination of the
     background of the Agrarians prior to 1930; second, the book and
     its effects, which includes an analysis of each of the essays;
     lastly a critique of this "stand" which is best described as
     organic and aesthetic. There is an appendix of interpretive
     biographies for eight of the contributors, including Lytle.

3   RUBIN, LOUIS D., Jr. "The Image of an Army: The Civil War in
     Southern Fiction." In Southern Writers: Appraisals In Our
     Time. Edited by R.C. Simonini, Jr. Charlottesville:
     University of Virginia Press, p. 62.
         Lytle's use of a Civil War setting in The Long Night is
     called "only a phase, albeit the climactic one"; while some of
     his battle scenes, notably Shiloh, are skillful, the war is but
     the culminating episode in a story not essentially about the
     Confederacy. Reprinted: 1967.9.

1965

1   STEWART, JOHN L. The Burden of Time, The Fugitives and
     Agrarians: The Nashville Group of the 1920's and 1930's and
     the Writing of John Crowe Ransom, Allen Tate, and Robert Penn
     Warren. Princeton: Princeton University Press, pp. 143,
     167-69, 196-97, and passim.
         While concern with Lytle is only incidental to this study
     he is mentioned many times: chiefly, comments about Lytle's
     "contentious" attitudes in relation to I'll Take My Stand; the
     tone of "The Hind Tit"; and the success of his "creative writing"
     are mentioned in relation to Lytle's relationship to the general
     development of Agrarianism.

1966

1   DeBELLIS, JACK. "Andrew Lytle's A Name for Evil: A Transfor-
     mation of The Turn of the Screw." Crit 8, no. 3 (Spring-
     Summer):26-40.
         A detailed comparison of Lytle's book with James's; plot
     summary and structural similarities provided; other

conventions--in plot, setting, point of view and minor charac-
ters--reveal similarities, but the connection between James's
Governess and Henry Brent are at the heart of the transformation.
Lytle appears to have methodically employed The Turn of the Screw
as a model. Analysis of the "underlying forces for Brent's insanity" reveals Lytle's reasons for using James's novel as model.
Brent is driven mad because he sees himself as "'failed in manhood.'" The Major serves as an agent by which Henry can "avoid
the problems posed by real or symbolic sexuality." Lytle's complex understanding of Brent's madness is an original development
from the "ambiguous adumbrations" in James. Lytle's use of symbol and myth extends the meaning and demonstrates that his model-
ing was far from mechanical.

2   KARANIKAS, ALEXANDER. Tillers of a Myth: Southern Agrarians
     as Social and Literary Critics. Madison: University of
     Wisconsin Press, passim.
        Scattered references to Lytle.

                              1967

1   ANON. Review of The Hero with the Private Parts. Choice 4
     (October):831.
        Describes contents and concludes on the basis of Lytle's
     introduction that a conscious use of literary craftsmanship was
     a major criterion for selection.

2   ANON. Review of The Hero with the Private Parts. VQR 43,
     no. 1 (Winter):xxii.
        A short notice of the "fugitive pieces," essays which in
     their juxtaposition illustrate the author's "acuity" and "vari-
     ety." Lytle manages with ease to be both informative and inter-
     esting.

3   DRAKE, ROBERT. Review of The Hero with the Private Parts.
     MissQ 20, no. 1 (Winter):59-61.
        Objects to the title and to the fact that many of the
     essays are too "programmatic or tendentious." What is even more
     disturbing to the reviewer is that Lytle's rationale for criti-
     cism seems "ultimately sociological or even theological, rather
     than aesthetic." Feels Lytle misreads Flaubert's Madame Bovary
     and asserts the prose is "tedious and obfuscated." While some
     of Lytle's critical observations about Faulkner, Crane and
     Tolstoy are "perceptive and sound," argues that Lytle seems to
     take "refuge in a wistful dream of medieval Christendom." Feels
     Lytle has erred by abusing "what is essentially a fine critical
     ability by adjudicating literary questions on the basis of extra
     or non-literary concerns."

4   HEDGES, WILLIAM L.   Review of <u>The Hero with the Private Parts</u>.
    <u>WSCL</u> 8, no. 4 (Autumn):556-67.
        Review-essay of <u>The Hero</u>, Susan Sontag's <u>Against Interpre-</u>
    <u>tation</u>, and John W. Aldridge's <u>Time to Murder and Create: The</u>
    <u>Contemporary Novel in Crisis</u>.   Contrasted with the lament for the
    passing of the American novel in Aldridge, and the "post-modern"
    approach of Sontag which is sometimes a polemic "'against inter-
    pretation'" and for fragmentation, Lytle's essays stand as "re-
    peated instances of modern academic criticism at its best."   They
    demonstrate how, through controlling image or point of view,
    "meaning" radiates through an entire system.   Lytle is one of the
    most able expositors of the James-Lubbock approach, however, be-
    cause of their consistency his readings stand as examples of what
    Sontag would oppose.   Lytle's "anti-liberal Christian bias" con-
    trols his sense of what a novel should be; his theory of history
    seems to support "a radically unreconstructed view of the
    Southern Past"; but what is missing is a sense of the South's
    responsibility for its tragic history.   See also 1974.6.

5   HOFFMAN, FREDERICK J.   <u>The Art of Southern Fiction: A Study</u>
    <u>of Some Modern Novelists</u>.   Carbondale and Edwardsville:
    Southern Illinois University Press; London and Amsterdam:
    Feffer & Simons, pp. 99-102.
        Within a chapter about society and history, Tate's <u>The</u>
    <u>Fathers</u> and Lytle's <u>The Long Night</u> are compared; Lytle's essay
    about the composition of his novels is summarized, and an over-
    view of <u>The Long Night</u> is provided.   Maintains that <u>The Velvet</u>
    <u>Horn</u> is "a much more subtle and complex achievement," but little
    more than plot summary is provided.

6   RAYFORD, JULIAN LEE.   Review of <u>The Hero with the Private</u>
    <u>Parts</u>.   <u>ABC</u> 17, no. 6 (6 February):6.
        Begins with reminiscences of meeting Lytle at Vanderbilt in
    the twenties and mentions stories of his brilliance at that time.
    This book, the product of a "critic of critics," confirms that
    brilliance.   Lytle's skill comes because he is, as artist, a
    "master among masters."   A real writer, such as Lytle, renews
    himself like a good swimmer, and this is what he does throughout
    this book as, for example, in his insights into mythology.

7   ROCK, VIRGINIA.   "Dualisms in Agrarian Thought."   <u>MissQ</u> 13
    (Spring):80-89.
        Lytle is referred to as representative of an approach which
    treated southern leaders in an analytical and "mythic" manner.

8   _____.   "The Fugitive-Agrarians in Response to Social Change."
    <u>SHR</u> 1 (Summer):170-81, esp. 174.
        Lytle's remark about the Dayton trial "as an overt action
    joining the issue between 'the old god and the new, the super-
    natural and the natural . . .'" is used as an example of the con-
    tinuing concern of men of letters associated with Agrarianism in
    opposition to science.

9   RUBIN, LOUIS D., Jr. The Curious Death of the Novel. Baton
     Rouge: Louisiana State University Press, pp. 147-61.
     Reprint of 1964.3.

                              1968

1   CARTER, T.H. "Andrew Lytle." In Essays and Reviews. Edited
     by James Boatwright. Lexington, Va.: Shenandoah, pp. 60-71.
     Reprint of 1962.1.

2   CORE, GEORGE. "A Mirror for Fiction: The Criticism of Andrew
     Lytle." GaR 22, no. 2 (Summer):208-21.
         Review of Hero as among the finest criticism on fiction and
     assesses Lytle's criticism as an avenue to reevaluation of the
     whole oeuvre. Gives the thrust of the individual articles and
     defines major aspects of Lytle's criticsm. Lytle is a "New
     critic" with differences: he reads text closely though relies
     little on criticism of others; is interested in the relation of
     technique to theme; is aware of historical dimension of a work of
     art and the religious and moral dimension of fiction; is more
     interested in "Myth criticism" than the New Critics. First four
     essays examine the way the author renews the reader's conscious-
     ness of his world and its moral dilemmas. "The Image as Guide to
     Meaning in the Historical Novel" is the best piece and is the
     heart of Lytle's method. Considers the criticism of Faulkner to
     be some of the best available. See also 1974.6.

3   DeBELLIS, JACK. "The Southern Universe and the Counter-
     Renaissance." SoR 4, no. 3 (Spring):471-81.
         Essay-review of The Hero with the Private Parts with John
     Donald Wade's Selected Essays and Southern Writing in the Sixties
     edited by John Corrington and Miller Williams. Lytle's method as
     a "second-generation" member of the Renascence allows him to
     achieve distance despite an occasional "Olympian tone." Lytle
     screens all levity from his style yet provides many valuable in-
     sights. His study of War and Peace retrieves historical fiction
     from disrepute. His approach to Madame Bovary through technical
     examination is typical of his criticism. "Command" is the word
     for these "disciplined investigations." Lytle's development has
     been similar to Warren and Tate and illustrates the changing
     character of the Renascence: he has moved in two compatible
     directions. The body of his work reveals a feeling for the South
     and the larger implications of myth and symbol.

4   DURHAM, FRANK. "The Southern Literary Tradition: Shadow or
     Substance." SAQ 67 (Summer):455-68, esp. 463.
         Lytle is mentioned with others associated with Vanderbilt
     who stressed "tradition" but not just Southern tradition, rather
     seventeenth century English writers such as Donne and Browne.

                              34

5   HURT, JAMES R. "Jerico, Jerico, Jerico [sic]." In The
    Explicator Cyclopedia. Vol. 3. Edited by Charles C. Walcutt
    and J.E. Whitesell. Chicago: Quadrangle Books, pp. 124-25.
        Reprint of 1962.2. See also 1970.1.

6   ROCK, VIRGINIA J. "Agrarianism: Agrarian Themes and Ideas
    in Southern Writing." MissQ 21, no. 2 (Spring):145-56.
        Checklist on Agrarianism which includes some titles by
    Lytle. This listing includes a variety of materials about
    Agrarianism as it relates to I'll Take My Stand; it does not
    include selections about fiction, drama, and poetry.

*7 SHAPIRO, EDWARD S. "The American Distributists and the New
    Deal." Ph.D. dissertation, Harvard University.
        Source: 1973.3, p. 107.

8   TOLEDANO, BEN C. "Savannah Writer's Conference--1939." GaR
    22, no. 2 (Spring):145-58, esp. 148, 152, 156, 158.
        Outlines the planning, development, and program for a 1939
    conference attended by Allen Tate, Caroline Gordon, Andrew Lytle,
    John Peale Bishop, Samuel Gaillard Stoney, and George Stevens.

9   TROWBRIDGE, CLINTON W. "The Word Made Flesh: Andrew Lytle's
    The Velvet Horn." Crit 10, no. 2:53-68.
        Velvet Horn is concerned with Edenic awareness and the
    paradoxical fact that man would like to return to Eden, yet for-
    get that Eden ever existed. As a Christian book it remains true
    to the paradox of man's condition while it fuses "pagan mythology
    and Biblical allusion." Jack Cropleigh, at the center of the
    novel, evolves from a Dionysius to a Christ figure, yet holds
    within himself the various tensions of the novel. Cropleigh,
    like the great tree at the beginning and end of the novel, "grows
    to his own balance" yet in death he "brings the hope of glory."
    Tracing patterns of Jack's vacillation, the pagan and Christian
    allusions are developed. Specific relationships to Ecclesiastes,
    and examination of the scene where Jack falls into the grave of
    Joe Cree illustrate the change in his character as he becomes the
    Christ-figure. Other Biblical parallels are noted in Jack's
    final words. See also 1974.6.

                                1969

1   BRADFORD, M.E. "A Gathering of Friends." Religion and
    Society 2 (June):35-39.
        Essays in The Hero with the Private Parts confirm Lytle's
    stature. While his performance has been often ignored, Lytle has
    never been concerned with the literary establishment, yet he is a
    critic "obviously in possession of the craft of his subject."
    His title suggests the fact that there should not be private life
    and public life as so many think, for "manners, customs, and
    'prejudices' are the requisites of civil existence."

2   BROWN, ASHLEY. "Andrew Nelson Lytle." In A Bibliographical
     Guide to the Study of Southern Literature. Edited by Louis D.
     Rubin, Jr. Baton Rouge: Louisiana State University Press,
     p. 243.
          Eleven items are listed, all of which are abstracted in
this Guide. DeBellis on A Name for Evil (1966.1), and Lytle himself on The Velvet Horn, are cited as "the most thorough studies"
of these novels.

3   CORE, GEORGE. "A Crossing of the Ways." In Southern Fiction
     Today: Renascence and Beyond. Athens: University of Georgia
     Press, pp. 92-93.
          Lytle's comment about the efforts of the "continuing
renascence" involving a considerable amount of criticism is
noted. Gordon, Tate, Davidson, Ransom, Warren, and Lytle have
turned some of their finest efforts to criticism.

                              1970

1   AVNI, ABRAHAM. "The Influence of the Bible on American Lit-
     erature: A Review of Research from 1955 to 1965." BB 27,
     nos. 1-4 (October-December):101-6.
          Within an article about recent scholarship, James Hurt's
Explicator article (1962.2) about "Jericho, Jericho, Jericho" is
summarized. See also 1968.5.

2   BRADFORD, M.E., ed. Special Issue on Andrew Lytle. MissQ 23,
     no. 4 (Fall):347-491.
          Includes essays by Thomas H. Landess (1970.8), Madison
Jones (1970.6), Charles C. Clark (1970.5), H.L. Weatherby
(1970.11), Edward Krickel (1970.7), M.E. Bradford (1970.3),
Sidney J. Landman (1970.9), Robert Weston (1970.12), and Noel
Polk (1970.10). See also 1974.6.

3   BRADFORD, M.E. "The Fiction of Andrew Lytle." MissQ 23,
     no. 4 (Fall):347-48.
          States rationale for the issue; notes omissions, especially
Lytle's criticism, and his work as historian, biographer, and
essayist. Explication of fiction was a priority because of its
complexity and because novels and fables have been admired but
seldom "read through." Hoped that these essays will call forth
additional studies and a reprinting of Lytle's works. See also
1970.2.

4   _____. "Toward a Dark Shape: Lytle's 'Alchemy' and the Con-
     quest of the New World." MissQ 23, no. 4 (Fall):407-14.
          "Alchemy" is a "touchstone" that gives access into the
thematic thrust of all Lytle's writing. The title suggests the
action and alludes to the frame of reference in which the plot
develops. In the narrative the discovery and possession of the

Indies is "an alchemy in men." The narrators of "Alchemy" and
At the Moon's Inn provide access to the manipulation of de Soto
and Pizarro. In Lytle's novella the actions of Pizarro provide
an image inclusive of the meaning Lytle earlier discovered in the
Southern experience. Reprinted: 1973.3. See also 1970.2.

5   CLARK, CHARLES C. "A Name for Evil: A Search for Order."
    MissQ 23, no. 4 (Fall):371-82.
        While A Name for Evil was written with The Turn of the
Screw as a frame, it is quite different from the James tale.
Lytle's depiction is of a perverted view of tradition. The narrator's sometimes "involuted" style allows Lytle to present a
narrator "who is unaware of his own solipsism." Lytle achieves a
Doppelgänger effect by allowing Henry Brent to become the Major
Brent he creates in his mind while he remains unaware of the evil
which he himself has caused. Brent's search for order is depen-
dent upon his regeneration of The Grove as a mark of material
success. Through careful delineation of action, it is shown that
the distorted view of tradition held by Brent leads to his interpretation of events as he imagines them and this leads to the
death of his wife. See also 1970.2. Reprinted: 1973.3.

6   JONES, MADISON. "A Look at 'Mister McGregor.'" MissQ 23,
    no. 4 (Fall):363-70.
        Lytle taught his students that fiction was an "exception-
ally difficult craft." His first published story "Mister
McGregor" is one in which the narrator is "all-important," for
the story has nothing to do with slavery as such. Mrs. McGregor
uses the slave Rhears "as the agent of her defiance." Her concluding words are arranged to suggest her submission, yet the
tragic dimension of the story is focused mainly through the narrator. The contrast in speech between the narrator's colloquial
and ungrammatical speech and his parents' "is the strategy by
which the reader is drawn . . . into the real center." The narrator, by implication, defines what he is, a lazy drunkard, a
sort of child--one who has rejected full manhood because of its
obligations. This thematic implication becomes of increasing
concern in the books which follow. See also 1970.2. Reprinted:
1973.3.

7   KRICKEL, EDWARD. "The Whole and the Parts: Initiation in
    'The Mahogany Frame.'" MissQ 23, no. 4 (Fall):391-405.
        Critical prejudice and ignorance has harmed Lytle's reputa-
tion; sometimes appreciation of his work has been limited to
those who know him personally. John Bradbury's reading of "The
Mahogany Frame" is inadequate for he emphasizes its Faulknerian
"influences." Reading the story as an archetypal situation (in
the manner of Joseph Campbell) this initiation story takes on
wider meaning. Traditional initiation--ceremonial transformation
of the hero which gives him new being, and thereby new knowledge
of self, life and his society are all elements in the story. The

artistic use of these elements reveal the complexity; through the
events experienced by the youth the boy sees himself in relation
to his two guides, and he also realizes that all men must learn
to confront knowledge of the sexual nature of men and women as he
must confront the changing role of matriarchy in the contemporary
moment. See also 1970.2. Reprinted: 1973.3.

8   LANDESS, THOMAS H. "Unity of Action in The Velvet Horn."
     MissQ 23, no. 4 (Fall):349-61.
         The archetypal experience in The Velvet Horn "defines the
thematic terms in which the dramatic action must be understood."
The experience which Lytle explores is ultimately theological--
fall, suffering, redemption, and reintegration into the order of
things. This myth of Eden is the story of the family of man;
Lytle's version of the Eden myth begins in medias res. In the
juxtaposition of parts one and two he defines the essential
structure of the novel, "the relationship between the initiation
of Lucius and the Christ-like role of Jack Cropleigh." The
images of the velvet horn and tree are basic, while the tree is
the more dominant. Lytle emphasizes a special point of view to
reinforce the unity of action in Cropleigh's consciousness, "both
the eternal myth of the Garden . . . and the ritual of initiation . . . are perfectly contained." Part three underlines the
unity of all experience. "The Wake," the fourth section, is concerned with Lucius's introduction to the reality of death. The
fifth section is largely concerned with Lucius's newly won manhood. It is significant that the tree unifies the action, for
Lucius builds a house with the tree which destroyed Joe Cree.
See also 1970.2. Reprinted: 1973.3.

9   LANDMAN, SIDNEY J. "The Walls of Mortality." MissQ 23, no. 4
     (Fall):415-23.
         "Jericho, Jericho, Jericho" uses the third person limited
point of view to provide a portrait of a dying matriarch and in
this narration Lytle achieves "as successfully as any writer has
ever done" the tour de force of suggesting the throes of death.
Through detailed analysis the consciousness of Kate McCowan is
analyzed; parallels are drawn with other writers. Attention to
patterns of similes and the technical details which heighten Miss
Kate's mental state demonstrate Lytle's skill in suggesting
clarity and loss of consciousness. The story uses an ironic
reversal of its Biblical prototype to suggest the defeat of the
heroine. See also 1970.2. Reprinted: 1973.3.

10   POLK, NOEL. "Andrew Nelson Lytle: A Bibliography of His
     Writings." MissQ 23, no. 4 (Fall):435-91.
         Detailed bibliographical listing includes a careful descrip-
tion of Lytle's books, including textual history and variants.
Letters by Lytle are used to provide significant details about
composition. Periodical contributions, introductions, and
speeches are also listed. In addition, there is a listing of

unpublished materials including stories, plays, poetry, essays, and a journal. The secondary checklist includes all full-length essays and a representative sampling of reviews. (Much of this bibliographical material is omitted from "An Andrew Lytle Checklist" in Bradford's The Form Discovered.) See also 1970.2. Reprinted in part: 1973.3.

11   WEATHERBY, H.L. "The Quality of Richness: Observations on Andrew Lytle's The Long Night." MissQ 23, no. 4 (Fall): 383-90.
            Lytle's gift as a writer is "richness--diversity, fullness, plenitude." This is more than sharp detail, for in his world things, people, places stand out to emphasize their uniqueness. In "Jericho, Jericho, Jericho" there is little conveyed by abstract statement. In The Long Night the sequence of events which lead to Damon Harrison's death is a good example of Lytle's method; in details presented the inextricable connection of good and evil is stressed. Similarly, Pleasant McIvor's situation is presented in its particularity. The conflict "between the community and the exile," a persistent theme in all Lytle's fiction, is realized as a conflict between the "richness of actual being" and denial of that complexity. See also 1970.2. Reprinted: 1973.3.

12   WESTON, ROBERT. "Toward a Total Reading of Fiction: The Essays of Andrew Lytle." MissQ 23, no. 4 (Fall):425-33.
            E.D. Hirsch's argument that comprehension of meaning is the foundation for analysis is a method Lytle would endorse, for he has suggested that the "controlling image" provides a method for reading fiction. Similar to a Platonic ideal, such an image exists independently of any particular work, yet it is used as a device for holding a work together. This "concept, mood, voice, situation, or condition" is not the theme, for Lytle insists fiction is not "about," but rather it is an illusion of autonomous life. Once such a controlling image is identified, all other details fall into place. Action and point of view should be controlled by the artist, but not in terms of exact conceptual meaning; ultimately meaning results because of the working of the imagination. See also 1970.2.

1971

1   ANON. Review of Craft and Vision. Kirkus 39 (15 September): 1037.
            Characterizes The Sewanee Review as bulwark of conservatism, literary values, and excellence; considers this sampling does credit to the Review's particular vision, though notes stress is on craft.

2   ANON. Review of Craft and Vision: The Best Fiction From The
     Sewanee Review. PW 200 (6 September):42.
        Describes contents; calls it a first-rate collection.

3   COOK, MARTHA E., and YOUNG, THOMAS D. "Fugitive / Agrarian
     Materials at Vanderbilt University." RALS 1, no. 1 (Spring):
     113-20.
        Background is outlined about the Fugitive and Agrarian
     research materials at Vanderbilt Joint Universities Libraries.
     Among the eight significant manuscript collections are the papers
     of Lytle. Approximate indications of number of letters, manu-
     scripts, books, and miscellaneous materials including galley
     sheets and incoming letters for Lytle (and all of the other
     Fugitives and Agrarians represented in this collection) are
     provided.

4   FAIN, JOHN TYREE. "Segments of Southern Renaissance." SAB
     36, no. 3 (May):23-31.
        Provides a brief overview of Lytle's fictional production
     and reviews The Hero with the Private Parts, all of which are
     connected with Lytle's teaching. Theory and practice best seen
     in "The Working Novelist and the Mythmaking Process"; the title
     essay suggests that the most successful fiction is "cultural,
     institutional, archetypal" and that modern fiction is often weak-
     ened because the hero has only private parts to play. Objects to
     the omission of dates for the essays.

5   RODGERS, ELIZABETH H. "The Quest Theme in Three Novels by
     Andrew Lytle." Ph.D. dissertation, Emory University.
        Lytle's The Long Night, A Name for Evil, and The Velvet
     Horn have as a central theme man's search for wholeness. This
     archetypal action is dramatized in concrete terms in the novels.
     With each succeeding novel the imagery of the hunt, the cove, and
     the garden becomes more symbolic. The questing action becomes
     more complex and religious. The recurrence of the quest theme in
     these novels reveals the coherence of Lytle's vision, basically a
     religious one which grows out of his concern as Agrarian.

6   WARREN, R[OBERT] P[ENN]. "Robert Penn Warren on Andrew
     Lytle's The Long Night." In Rediscoveries. Edited by David
     Madden. New York: Crown Publishers, pp. 17-28.
        Reprint of 1971.7.

7   WARREN, ROBERT PENN. "Andrew Lytle's The Long Night: A Re-
     discovery." SoR 7, no. 1 (Winter):130-39.
        Provides background about the inception of the novel, which
     involves a tale told to Warren by Frank Owsley that went back to
     the late 1850s. Owsley, summoned by a kinsman, was told by this
     old man how he avenged the murder of his father by seeking out
     members of the gang responsible. Later Lytle was told the same
     story and it stirred his imagination; he then took this

"'twice-told'" tale, gave it a world, a human context for the
deeds of vengeance. The main change is in the nature of the
avenger; in the tale he ceases his role because he grows old; in
the novel the War falls across the action and provides the per-
fect cover for Pleasant's covert operations. While there are
some technical defects, the conception of the novel remains firm.
Reprinted: 1971.6.

1972

1   ANON. Review of Craft and Vision. AL 44 (May):348.
      Gives a partial listing of the authors included.

2   ANON. Review of Craft and Vision. Booklist 68 (1 March):550.
      Lists contents; assesses collection as valuable and draws
special attention to Lytle's observations on his own fiction.

3   ANON. Review of Craft and Vision. LJ 97 (15 February):672.
      A partial listing of the contents of the volume.

4   ANON. "The Best Fiction from the Sewanee Review." NewR 166
    (19 February):29.
      A brief favorable review of Craft and Vision. Describes
contents, cites Lytle's own "The Guide" as one of the better
tales. Approves of the editor's choices and intentions as stated
in the foreword.

5   BRADFORD, M.E. "Andrew Lytle." In Contemporary Novelists.
    Edited by James Vinson. New York: St. Martin's; London:
    St. James Press, pp. 792-94.
      Biographical sketch; listing of publications; listing of
manuscript collections; comment by Lytle about description of his
work; essay by Bradford: Lytle's art is in the tradition of
Flaubert, James, and Joyce. They are the product of one who has
thought carefully about the novel. The fiction renders "felt
life." Each of the major books is characterized in succinct insightful paragraphs.

6   BURGER, NASH K. Review of Craft and Vision: The Best Fiction
    from the Sewanee Review. NYTBR, 20 February, p. 35.
      Provides some background about The Sewanee Review in rela-
tion to Lytle's selection of stories; provides commentary on
several stories including Lytle's "The Guide"; and concludes that
the reader will see worked out in the collection "basic Agrarian
themes: man's need for harmony with other men in a meaningful,
ordered society."

7   CLARK, CHARLES CHESTER. "The Novels of Andrew Lytle: A
      Study in the Artistry of Fiction." Ph.D. dissertation,
      Louisiana State University and Agricultural and Mechanical
      College.
          "Old Scratch in the Valley" can be used as a base mark to
      gauge Lytle's development, for in that first published story he
      indicates his belief that the lost matriarchal society of the
      Southern family was its bulwark. His artistry is evident in each
      of the novels, and his historical consciousness is always cen-
      tral. Irony, symbolism, and increasingly complex structures
      allow Lytle to build archetypal experiences in agrarian settings.
      Lytle is no dealer in nostalgia, but rather a Christian artist
      concerned with changes in society.

8   COWAN, LOUISE. The Southern Critics. Dallas, Tex.:
      University of Dallas Press, pp. 71-73.
          Consideration of The Hero with the Private Parts; three
      features of Lytle's criticism are important: a sense of the mean-
      ing of history; patterns in fiction--especially myth; and an
      awareness of craft. The last of these characteristics makes
      Lytle's criticism "a virtual textbook for writers." In his hands
      technique is the instrument for revealing a total vision of life.

9   EDGIN, EDWARD CLARK. "A Critical Study of Andrew Lytle's The
      Long Night." Ph.D. dissertation, University of South Carolina.
          Examination of The Long Night as the center of Lytle's work
      both in terms of theme and artistry. The strong historical and
      moral consciousness provides the key to Lytle's thematic struc-
      ture. The folk ballad and frontier humor provide a traditional
      basis for the novel; also myth extends the implications of the
      story, an archetypal journey to experience. Close analysis,
      including analysis of influences upon Lytle, both personal and
      literary, is provided.

10   RUBIN, LOUIS D., Jr. "Fugitives as Agrarians: The Impulse
      Behind I'll Take My Stand." In A Catalogue of the Fugitive
      Poets. Edited by J. Howard Woolmer. Andes, N.Y.: J.H.
      Woolmer, pp. 9-26.
          Rubin's essay provides background about the Nashville
      Fugitive Poets, yet Lytle is only mentioned as someone "who
      played no part in their deliberations as a working group of
      poets." Emphasizes that while issues were formulated in I'll
      Take My Stand, it is in the mature fiction of men like Lytle
      "that the real search takes place."

11   _____. The Writer in the South. Athens: University of
      Georgia Press, pp. 87, 101.
          Mentions Lytle in connection with John Donald Wade's essay
      in I'll Take My Stand, and as an example of the "full literary
      flowering" of the Southern Renascence.

12   SULLIVAN, WALTER. "Southern Novelists and the Civil War."
      In Death by Melancholy: Essays on Modern Southern Fiction.
      Baton Rouge: Louisiana State University Press, pp. 72-75.
      The Long Night is a first novel written with skill and con-
structed with subtlety. While the book shifts directions when
the war episodes begin, the importance of family unifies its two
parts. As the plot develops the breach between private and public duty widens.

13   WESTON, ROBERT VERNON. "Andrew Lytle's Fiction: A Traditional
      View." Ph.D. dissertation, Stanford University.
      Lytle's fiction is examined as representative of a tradi-
tional, Christian point of view qualified by Southern experience.
Lytle works in the James-Flaubert tradition, and his sense of
myth is essentially Jungian. The fiction is examined in the
light of Lytle's own theories. Treatments of the fiction are
chronological; The Velvet Horn is examined as the culmination of
Lytle's concerns and abilities. Lytle's fiction is placed among
the best of contemporary fiction.

14   YU, FREDERICK YEH-WEI. "Andrew Lytle's A Name for Evil as a
      Redaction of The Turn of the Screw." MQR 11, no. 3 (Summer):
      186-90.
      Lytle used James for his own purpose, not simply to copy a
model. Suggests A Name for Evil is an analysis of failures of
the Agrarian movement; reads novel as allegorical to the situation of the Agrarians. Henry Brent grapples with the mystery of
a house for the same reasons Agrarians felt called to reaffirm
tradition(s) of the South. Detailed similarities and differences
from James support this thesis.

                                  1973

1   BENSON, ROBERT G. "The Progress of Hernando de Soto in
      Andrew Lytle's At the Moon's Inn." GaR 27, no. 2 (Summer):
      232-44.
      Through the actions of de Soto and his lieutenant Tovar,
Lytle shows how exploitation of the New World reenacted the
original disobedience of Lucifer and Adam, man's attempt to deify
himself. The novel presents the progressive rejection of God and
affirmation of a world campaign. Focuses on the three masses
celebrated at crucial points during the campaign to show the
protagonist's inevitable rejection of God. Considers the novel
a "significant work of historical fiction" whose lack of critical
notice stems from a failure to accept the reality of de Soto's
alternatives--good or Satan. See 1973.2.

2 _____. "Yankees of the Race: The Decline and Fall of
Hernando de Soto." In The Form Discovered. Edited by M.E.
Bradford. Jackson: University and College Press of
Mississippi, pp. 84-96.
   Essentially the same essay as 1973.1.

3 BRADFORD, M.E., ed. The Form Discovered: Essays on the
Achievement of Andrew Lytle. Jackson: University and College
Press of Mississippi, 124 pp.
   Reprints of 1970.4 (pp. 57-63), 5 (pp. 23-34), 6 (pp. 16-
23), 7 (pp. 42-56), 8 (pp. 3-15), 9 (pp. 64-72), 10 (as "An
Andrew Lytle Checklist," pp. 97-108), 11 (pp. 35-41). New
essays: M.E. Bradford, "That Other Eden in the West: A Preface
to Andrew Lytle," (pp. xi-xiv); Brewster Ghiselin, "Andrew
Lytle's Selva Oscura," (pp. 73-78); and Allen Tate, "The Local
Universality of Andrew Lytle," (pp. 79-83).

4 _____. "That Other Eden in the West: A Preface to Andrew
Lytle." In The Form Discovered. Jackson: University and
College Press of Mississippi, pp. xi-xiv.
   The title, A Wake for the Living, is especially significant
because all of Lytle's writing is an investigation of what it
means for western man to extend culture into the West. Lytle's
view that man is a social creature is crucial and his awareness
of a religious ground is important throughout his work. The
westward movement beginning with Columbus has been informed by a
dark spirit. For Lytle, identity derives from a sense of place,
kin, and friendship. A Wake, because it does suggest the unity
of the Tennessee of Lytle's fathers, should provide a gloss on
all of his work.

5 GHISELIN, B. "Andrew Lytle's Selva Oscura." In The Form
Discovered. Edited by M.E. Bradford. Jackson: University
and College Press of Mississippi, pp. 73-78.
   Lytle's thought can be grasped through penetration "to its
intuitive ground." The order attained is because of Lytle's
appreciation of "man concretely existent and active." His fiction examines the dark predicament of man in a secular time. An
illustration is seen in "Alchemy"; as the Spaniards sought their
desires, "'the dark thing'" stepped forward. Unlimited will,
unregulated liberty can only bring death. In The Long Night,
vengeance is diminished by a sense of community. In subsequent
fiction characters whose "abandonment of measure submits them to
compulsive process" come to the same alienation. The obverse,
to surrender to sensuality, or to seek to find Paradise, is
treated in At the Moon's Inn and The Velvet Horn.

6 KAZIN, ALFRED. Bright Book of Life: American Novelists and
Storytellers from Hemingway to Mailer. Boston and Toronto:
Atlantic, Little, Brown & Co., pp. 38, 65.

Lytle is listed as one of the Southern authors read with growing interest in the postwar years. William Alexander Percy, educated at Sewanee, shared with Lytle and the other Agrarian writers many of the same social views.

7   POLK, N.E. "An Andrew Lytle Checklist." In The Form Discovered. Edited by M.E. Bradford. Jackson: University and College Press of Mississippi, pp. 97-108.
     While the secondary materials listed here are more complete than the 1970 "Andrew Nelson Lytle: A Bibliography of his Writings" by Polk, in other respects, especially with regard to manuscript information and unpublished materials, deletions have been made. See 1970.10.

8   TATE, A. "The Local Universality of Andrew Lytle." In The Form Discovered. Edited by M.E. Bradford. Jackson: University and College Press of Mississippi, pp. 79-83.
     Lytle's fiction uses history to shape action. As critic he is an amateur in the sense defined by R.P. Blackmur, and his "passionate discourse" about literature is "creative" in a way similar to his own best fiction. The essays are "close translations" of works Lytle has read and reread, and a comparison of his essays with the prefaces of Henry James reveals many similarities. The most brilliant example of this formalistic historical criticism is "The Working Novelist and the Mythmaking Process." Lytle's sense of history conjoined with close reading of Tolstoy, Flaubert, and Faulkner allows him to produce "universal criticism" which takes its stance in particulars.

9   WATSON, STERLING. "Craft and Vision." FQ 5 (Spring):33-39.
     Lytle's collection reflects his consistent view as artist and as editor of The Sewanee Review. Through examination of "The Unattached Smile" by Harry Crews, Lytle's student, it is demonstrated how the artistic imagination is used to render, in Lytle's words "'the inward and complete nature of man.'" The collection consistently reflects the editor's commitment to issues of artistic craft, judgment, and place, and it also reflects Lytle's commitment to a magazine which reflects shared commitments among its writers. The artist uses imagination to find an entrance to the past: craftsmanship then renders that vision.

1974

1   BATAILLE, ROBERT. "The Esthetics and Ethics of Farming: The Southern Agrarian View." Iowa State Journal of Research 49, no. 2:189-93.
     While Lytle is only named in passing, this examination of the Agrarians in relation to ethics and esthetics of rural agrarian culture provides insight into positive aspects of the Southern

Agrarian position, a humane order opposed to contemporary urban, industrial existence. Ransom, Davidson, and Tate are examined in detail and the views of the Agrarians are ultimately to be understood as something more than "a naive ideology" or a tirade against modernity.

2   CLARK, CHARLES C. "The Fiction of Andrew Lytle: From Old
    Scratch's Cannibal World to Paradise." ORev 2:127-52.
        In tracing recurrent patterns in Lytle's fiction consistency in thematic representation is seen. The historical consciousness in Bedford Forrest and "Old Scratch in the Valley" exhibits the "seeds" of the mature fiction. Each of the major books is examined in relation to how heroes exhibit awareness of their loss of a proper sense of history. Related in all of Lytle's work is the decline of religion. In the fiction, man's proper attitude toward history and religion is reiterated through images; the actions of the major works are "blasphemous." Lytle's vision is archetypally rendered through anagogical vision wherein man must finally recognize the co-existence of good and evil. Lytle's artistry allows him to blend myth and Biblical allusions and to render a range of characters from the demoniac to the integrated.

3   FAIN, JOHN TYREE, and YOUNG, THOMAS DANIEL. The Literary
    Correspondence of Donald Davidson and Allen Tate. Athens:
    University of Georgia Press, 442 pp., passim.
        Lytle is mentioned in over twenty-five places. Information is especially provided about the role he played in interaction between, and among, the Agrarians during the period 1928-1932.

4   FOATA, ANNE. "Le fantastique au secours de l'allégorie: A
    Name for Evil de Andrew Lytle." RANAM 7:220-33.
        The first person narration of Henry Brent in A Name for Evil provides an avenue for introducing the fantastic because of the disjunction between the narrator and protagonist. Such separation between narrator and hero-victim is a classic process in the literature of the fantastic in the tradition of Henry James. When Brent speaks of what occurred, the Major seems real for him, but Lytle guides the reader in seeing the narrator himself as his own double. A frequent theme in the literature of the fantastic is the presentation of a deranged personality. Connections are drawn between the structure of A Name and Lytle's own critical insights about the relationship of the supernatural and nature. Also, because one of Lytle's main concerns has to do with the continuity of family, and thus society, the novella can be interpreted as an allegory of "a mad fancy," an impossible enterprise. Such a theme, the impossibility of creating an Eden, is a recurrent one in Lytle.

5   JOYNER, NANCY. "The Myth of the Matriarch in Andrew Lytle's
    Fiction." SLJ 7, no. 1 (Fall):67-77.
        A study of Lytle's critical remarks about man's attitude
    toward women and an examination of the heroines in "Jericho,
    Jericho, Jericho," "Mister MacGregor," and The Velvet Horn, re-
    veals a basic contradiction. The female protagonists do not
    "fare well"; Kate McCowan fails to keep the land; Mrs. MacGregor
    "fails to dominate her husband"; Julia fails "in preserving her
    marriage" and in keeping the "family line pure." These matri-
    archs, while perhaps idealized by men, are exceptions to the
    "mythic idea" of the Southern lady.

6   KINSMAN, CLARE D., and TENNENHOUSE, MARY ANN, eds. "Lytle,
    Andrew (Nelson)." In Contemporary Authors. 1st rev. ed.
    Vols. 9-12. Detroit: Gale, 548-49.
        A sketch with details of Lytle's career and writings, and
    quotations from the following: San Francisco Chronicle (1947.3),
    Saturday Review (1957.5), Critique (1968.9), Atlantic (1958.11),
    NYTBR (1958.9), WSCL (1967.4), Georgia Review (1968.2), and
    Mississippi Quarterly (1970.2) used for "sidelights."

7   O'BRIEN, MICHAEL, ed. "A Correspondence, 1923-1958: Edwin
    Mims and Donald Davidson." SoR 10, no. 4 (October):904-22.
        Lytle is mentioned in the introduction as an Agrarian, like
    Tate and Warren, who "loathed" Edwin Mims, the chairman of the
    English department at Vanderbilt. The letters do not mention
    Lytle.

                            1975

1   ANON. Review of A Wake for the Living. Booklist 72
    (15 September):102.
        Finds Lytle's account persuasive and engaging in its anec-
    dotal expertise.

2   ANON. Review of A Wake for the Living. Kirkus 43 (1 May):
    547.
        Anecdotal description of the contents of Wake; terms it a
    testy and condemning, but convivial, overview.

3   ANON. Review of A Wake for the Living. NY 51 (15 September):
    131.
        Short review of Wake recounts contents and places the book
    in the "great Southern storytelling tradition."

4   ANON. Review of A Wake for the Living. PW 207 (26 May):58.
        Brief description of Wake terms it engaging and entertain-
    ing; also illuminates Southern history.

5   BURGER, NASH K. Review of <u>A Wake for the Living</u>. <u>NYTBR</u>, 13 July, p. 14.

     A thoughtful consideration of <u>Wake</u>, which is a "spirited, conversational narrative in which large historical events are tumbled together with family legend, odd bits of local lore and gutsy anecdotes." Sees the value of Lytle's distinction between the public and private realms, and, most important, that between the family and the public realm. Lytle's <u>Wake</u> portrays no Eden, but "one wonders at last who are the living, who are the dead. Is this a wake for the past or the present?"

6   LANDESS, T.H. "The Uncompromised Agrarian." <u>NatR</u> 27 (26 September):1065-66.

     Review praises <u>A Wake for the Living</u> for its entertaining narration, and stresses its relevance to a modern America on the verge of twilight in which the Agrarians' prophecies regarding the debasement of the environment and the breakdown of communal civility have come to pass. Landess interprets the title to mean the past Americans are more alive than the present ones.

7   McMURTRY, LARRY. "An Anecdotal History of an American Family." <u>Book Week</u> (21 July), p. 4.

     In <u>A Wake for the Living</u> Lytle weaves anecdote and legend about individual members of his large family through many generations, but his stories are less vivid when they depend on material passed down to him. "The book is most successful when it is developing a picture of American rural and small town society in the 1920's and '30's." Lytle has a "finely balanced prose" and a sense of humor.

8   PHILLIPSON, JOHN S. Review of <u>A Wake for the Living</u>. <u>BS</u> 35 (August):128.

     Stressing Lytle's emphasis upon continuity, history, and family, <u>Wake</u> is described as a "truly humanitarian book." Lytle's tales reflect a time when people were responsible for their deeds, and contrasts with today when men live by abstractions.

9   ROCK, VIRGINIA J. "They Took Their Stand: The Emergence of the Southern Agrarians." <u>Prospects</u> 1:205-95.

     An extensive consideration of Agrarian Movement participants, with only cursory attention given to Lytle.

10   SIMPSON, LEWIS P. "The Southern Recovery of Memory and History." In <u>The Dispossessed Garden</u>. Athens: University of Georgia Press, pp. 72-73, and passim.

     Lytle's commentary on <u>Intruder in the Dust</u> is used as the authority to support the contention that "man's essential nature lies in his possession of the moral community of memory and history." This generalization provides insight into a substantial body of writing, the generation of the 1920s and 1930s, including Lytle.

11   SULLIVAN, WALTER. "Community." In <u>A Requiem for the Renas-</u>
     <u>cence</u>. Athens: University of Georgia Press, pp. 26-31, 37-38.
        <u>The Long Night</u> has not been given the attention it deserves,
     and, as in all Lytle's work, the family is central; yet here the
     demands of government conflict with the demands of family.
     Lytle's essay on Faulkner's <u>The Unvanquished</u> is called "brilliant"
     in the way it demonstrates Faulkner's use of imagery to suggest
     "the dissolution of the social fabric."

12   WRIGHT, SCOTT. Review of <u>A Wake for the Living</u>. <u>LJ</u> 100
     (15 June):1209.
        Brief review of <u>Wake</u>; terms the style impressionistic,
     sensitive, hard to follow; believes lack of clear organization
     limits appeal to those already familiar with Lytle's regional
     traditions.

13   YOUNG, THOMAS DANIEL. Review of <u>A Wake for the Living: A</u>
     <u>Family Chronicle</u>. <u>SR</u> 83, no. 4 (Fall):730-36.
        Review-essay on <u>A Wake for the Living</u>, Lewis Simpson's <u>The</u>
     <u>Dispossessed Garden</u>, and Allen Tate's <u>Memoirs and Opinions, 1926-</u>
     <u>1974</u>. Cites the "freshness and immediacy of the stories" and
     Lytle's ability to "select" the correct detail to evoke the de-
     sired response, as characteristic of Lytle, "one of our most dis-
     tinguished contemporary writers." Gives major themes of the book:
     the necessity of knowing origins; American history as not exempt
     from the consequences of the fall; the necessity of possession of
     land. Finds book deals ultimately with "the Southern myth," as
     is the concern of Tate and Simpson.

1976

1   FOATA, ANNE. "Aspects du récit dans <u>The Velvet Horn</u> d'Andrew
     Lytle." <u>RANAM</u> 9:165-81.
        <u>The Velvet Horn</u> is a classic <u>bildungsroman</u> and its plan of
     narrative reveals an archetypal experience. The information in
     the narrative is provided through a series of revelations super-
     imposed, which lead to the resolution of the mystery: who is the
     father of Lucius? Through analysis of the five sections of nar-
     rative from the points of view of the principal characters, it is
     demonstrated how Lytle builds the narrative so the reader can
     establish the order of events. In parts where Lucius remains in
     the foreground, there is drama about the development of his con-
     sciousness; allusions implicit in the first point of view, and
     explicit in the second, are clarified in the remaining narrative--
     that of Pete and Julia. All events in the novel support one
     another. A plural reading is necessary to appreciate this myth
     of eternal return and the idea of renewal as presented.

2   HARTLEY, LODWICK. Review of A Wake for the Living. SAQ 75
     (Spring):271.
         This short review of Wake describes it as a successful
     attempt to survey two centuries of his family as part of the
     American heritage, which does credit to Lytle's high reputation
     as biographer and novelist.

3   WEATHERBY, HAROLD L. "Not Beyond Recall." SoR 12, no. 3
     (Summer):673-77.
         Wake is powerful because of "the startling immediacy of the
     irrevocable past." Lytle's success as storyteller allows him to
     recover the Lytles and Nelsons who are dead, but who through art
     remain alive in a mysterious way. Lytle's ultimate concern is
     with substance, and the total order of existence with which mod-
     ern man has lost touch. The art of this book makes us submit to
     the past which "is." Skill in alternation between story and com-
     ment is important, for through the experience of these stories we
     perceive the mysterious union of flesh and spirit. Method allows
     the stories to unfold and then provide the proper amount of ex-
     plication. The compassionate treatment of Uncle Jack provides an
     excellent example of how Lytle works.

                              1977

1   CLARK, C.C. Review of A Wake for the Living. SHR 11, no. 4
     (Fall):411-12.
         Essentially an enthusiastic description of the book, and
     approval of how it has a style "that interweaves the erudite dic-
     tion" of its distinguished author and the vernacular of a Middle
     Tennessee countryman like Pleasant McIvor. Information is pre-
     sented of significance to Lytle's fiction. "Students of Southern
     Agrarianism should read the book carefully," for Lytle "inter-
     calates with his family history . . . serious observations on the
     human predicament."

2   GRAY, RICHARD. "The Nashville Agrarians." In The Literature
     of Memory: Modern Writers of the American South. Baltimore:
     Johns Hopkins University Press, pp. 47-48, 51-52.
         Lytle's "The Hind Tit" is discussed as essay in I'll Take
     My Stand, which is realized with "immediacy." The title illus-
     trates the strategy: Lytle identifies with the interests he
     chooses to defend.

3   ROCK, VIRGINIA. "Andrew Nelson Lytle (1902-)." In I'll Take
     My Stand by John Crowe Ransom et al. Baton Rouge: Louisiana
     State University Press, pp. 383-88.
         Concise biographical essay which surveys life and writings.
     The themes of the "redemptive power of Christian heritage and the
     family" as representative of the larger community are basic and
     also pervade A Wake for the Living. Lytle's commitment to his

Southern Agrarian heritage is "subsumed and shaped into his practice as artist" wherein he treats archetypal experience.

4   RUBIN, LOUIS D.   Introduction to I'll Take My Stand by John
     Crowe Ransom et al.   Baton Rouge: Louisiana State University
     Press, pp. xi-xxii.
        An analysis of the continued appeal of the book since its
reissue in 1962 and a qualification of earlier remarks printed as
introduction to the Harper edition about the metaphorical nature
of the book.   While that element of metaphor was important for
many of the contributors, including Lytle, we also need to note
the practical implications of what was written.   See 1962.3.

5   SARCONE, ELIZABETH FRANCINE.   "Andrew Lytle and the Mythmaking
     Process."   Ph.D. dissertation, Vanderbilt University.
        Lytle is one of the most valuable Southern writers of fic-
tion, and his neglect is due, in part, to narrow historical approaches.   The Velvet Horn can be analyzed in relation to the
earlier fiction.   Background from Jung, Erich Neumann, and interpretation of myth is provided.   Through close attention to patterns of "the search for the subject," symbols, and structure,
the organization of The Velvet Horn is examined.   The same symbolic patterns which have significance for Velvet Horn are also
apparent in relation to all Lytle's fiction.

1978

1   AHLPORT, DANIEL.   "The Redeeming Form: Tradition in Ransom,
     Davidson, Tate, Lytle, and Warren."   Ph.D. dissertation,
     University of North Carolina at Chapel Hill.
        The major members of the Fugitive-Agrarian group, including
Lytle, have been aware of ambiguities in modern man's awareness
of tradition.   While for some members of the group reunification
with tradition and the past seems impossible, for others there is
hope.   In the fiction of Lytle and Warren, restoration of the
connections between man, the past, and family can redeem him from
the destructive power of self-gratification and solipsism.

2   FOATA, ANNE.   "A propos d'un centenaire . . . (yeomen et
     gentlemen du vieux sud)."   RANAM 11:149-59.
        Presents an extensive examination of Andrew Lytle's Bedford
Forrest and his Critter Company, the centennial celebration of
Forrest's death, and the "yeoman" structure of the pre-Civil War
agrarian South.   It became Lytle's task to write about Forrest as
a yeoman, from the wilderness, who had become a cotton planter.
This characterization is the antithesis of the myth of the
Cavalier class "destroyed by yankee capitalism."
        Six months before the publication of Bedford Forrest and
his Critter Company, Lytle had collaborated with eleven other
Southerners in the publication of I'll Take My Stand: The South

and the Agrarian Tradition. Lytle advocated the "simple and independent life of the yeoman" upon which the Republic was founded. His characterization of Forrest was part of a larger reevaluation of the men who shaped the South. In Bedford Forrest, Lytle fastidiously details Forrest's campaigns.

In addition to Lytle's treatment of the agrarian South, several other works are considered--Howard Odum's work at the University of North Carolina at Chapel Hill, William Cash's The Mind of the South, William Taylor's Cavalier and Yankee: The Old South and the American National Character, and Frank Lawrence Owsley's Plain Folk of the Old South.

3   WESTON, ROBERT V. "Faulkner and Lytle: Two Modes of Southern
     Fiction." SoR 15, no. 4 (Winter):34-51.
        While Faulkner was a loner, Lytle must be seen in the con-
     text of an important literary tradition, and while Faulkner wrote
     much more, Lytle's fiction stands up well in terms of signifi-
     cance, quality, and value. For Lytle, history saves him from
     abstraction; in At the Moon's Inn imagination transforms raw
     fragments into a whole. Whereas in Faulkner the myth of the
     South is one where "the Curse" afflicts the South, in Lytle's
     myth the South is seen as "the last vestige of Christendom."
     While Faulkner's myth is clearly a fictional one, Lytle's be-
     liefs (perverse though they may sometimes seem) take on a more
     universal view of universal patterns. Also, while Faulkner
     ultimately must be compared with Balzac and Dickens, he produced
     relatively few complex characters and Lytle's Nuno Tovar, Henry
     Brent, and Jack Cropleigh are among the most complex in modern
     fiction. In matters of style, Faulkner's voice is always heard;
     Lytle's is less distinctive, yet this is because he is committed
     to a Jamesean sense of craft. Lytle's style produces a sensory
     appeal; The Velvet Horn has a lyrical richness as dense as
     Absalom, Absalom! or Agee's A Death in the Family. Unlike
     Faulkner, but resembling Agee, Lytle's style is descriptive and
     figurative. Velvet Horn can be interpreted as Lytle's answer to
     Faulkner's A Fable. He takes fiction into areas previously occu-
     pied by myth, but without sacrificing the human texture; the fic-
     tion is difficult, poetic, challenging but it is rewarding in a
     way different than the "turnpike velocities" of Faulkner. Con-
     templative, its destination is a beauty all its own.

1979

1   ALEXANDER, BENJAMIN BOATWRIGHT. "Andrew Lytle and the Total
     Sense of Family." Ph.D. dissertation, University of Dallas.
        Lytle's corpus, especially The Velvet Horn, has elicited
     interest, but no sustained study traces a unifying element in all
     Lytle's work. The family in its literal and symbolic dimensions
     occupies a central place in Lytle's fiction, literary criticism,
     and historical writing. Family in Lytle's writing is either

preserved or assaulted. Characteristics of the family are not
reserved just for the domestic family, however, and thus Lytle is
concerned with the familial nature of towns, communities, indeed
Christendom. Because of the loss of Christian values and the
rise of secular views too much emphasis is placed today on blood
kinship; then family's main properties--hierarchical structure,
identity, love, and memory--are perverted. Conflicts are traced
that occur throughout the fiction because of fundamental changes
in western society.

2   BINDING, PAUL. <u>Separate Country: A Literary Journey through
     the American South</u>. New York: Paddington Press, pp. 108-13.
         Recounts visit with Lytle at Monteagle; compares him to
other writers such as Madison Jones and Donald Davidson. Opin-
ions about Lytle's work not having the "universality of reference" found in some of the other Fugitives, such as Tate and
Warren, are expressed.

3   BRINKMEYER, BOB. "Return Visit: Andrew Lytle." <u>Southern
     Exposure</u> 7, no. 2 (Summer):150-51.
         Lytle concerned with the spiritual loss which has resulted
from disintegration of the traditional ideals of family, community and Christian morality. Brief attention given to biography,
criticism, and fiction. Lytle believes that modern liberal
philosophy has caused culture to cut itself off from Christian
heritage; while his fiction uses these ideas he "escapes any
taint of preachiness." Each of his four novels incorporates
criticism of the drift of western culture. Fiction and criticism
deserves to be read because it "makes us see"; Lytle's view warns
us of what can happen if value and traditions "give way to un-
checked technological progress." One of Lytle's most endearing
qualities is his sense of the "artist's moral responsibility to
his world."

4   BROWN, ASHLEY. "Andrew Lytle." In <u>Southern Writers: A
     Biographical Dictionary</u>. Edited by Robert Bain, Joseph M.
     Flora, and Louis D. Rubin, Jr. Baton Rouge and London:
     Louisiana State University Press, pp. 288-89.
         Basic information about Lytle's life, education, and teach-
ing career. Prominence of his family; his interest in theater;
and his identification with Tennessee are mentioned. While three
of his four novels are set in Tennessee, he is "keenly aware" of
the changes in European culture as a whole. Works are listed
through 1975.

5   SIMPSON, LEWIS P. "Southern Fiction." In <u>Harvard Guide to
     Contemporary American Writing</u>. Edited by Daniel Hoffman.
     Cambridge, Mass.: Harvard University Press, pp. 177-78.
         Lytle is cited with Caroline Gordon and Katherine Anne
Porter as a writer whose "quest for the absolute takes the form
of an emphasis on the Christian myth of the fall and redemption

of man." A Name for Evil (1947) and The Velvet Horn (1957) present the theme of the New World man's prideful attempt to acquire dominion over nature and self. In The Velvet Horn, Jack Cropleigh's sacrificial death occurs, not for humanistic or humanitarian reasons, but "to fulfill the Christian myth."

<u>1980</u>

1   BROOKS, CLEANTH. "The Crisis in Culture as Reflected in
     Southern Literature." In The American South, Portrait of a
     Culture. Edited by Louis D. Rubin. Baton Rouge: Louisiana
     State University Press, p. 189.
         Lytle is mentioned as one of a group of Southern writers
     who do "deal with the theme of the terrible division of the age."

2   COOK, MARTHA E. "The Artistry of I'll Take My Stand." MissQ
     33, no. 4 (Fall):425-32.
         John Donald Wade's and Andrew Lytle's essays present strong
     arguments for the rejection of industrialization. Their "tightly
     unified essays" are models of persuasive writing. Wade's essay
     is an organic presentation; Lytle's presents a concrete image of
     life in an agrarian setting. Lytle's style incorporates effec-
     tive aphorism; employs effective figures and anecdotes. Both
     essays stress that there remain models which the modern reader
     can use to fight progress.

3   CORE, GEORGE. "The Dominion of The Fugitives and Agrarians."
     In The American South: Portrait of a Culture. Edited by
     Louis D. Rubin. Baton Rouge: Louisiana State University
     Press, pp. 302-3.
         In an overview of the Fugitives and Agrarians major fig-
     ures are discussed and Lytle is mentioned as a significant fig-
     ure, yet one who never wrote "a novel of the first order" and
     whose "criticism is slighter than that of the others."

4   INGE, M. THOMAS. "The Continuing Relevance of I'll Take My
     Stand." MissQ 33, no. 4 (Fall):445-60.
         The book, never long out of print, is still read today
     both because of its style and the broad range of its topics. The
     essays continue to communicate because they define the grounds
     "on which culture can function"; Lytle is quoted to back up this
     assertion. Today there remain many reminders that the "twelve
     prophets of Nashville" saw clearly and still speak to contempo-
     rary problems.

5   KING, RICHARD H. A Southern Renaissance: The Cultural Awak-
     ening of the American South, 1930-1955. New York: Oxford
     University Press, pp. 57-58.
         A brief analysis of Bedford Forrest in relation to the
     Agrarian critique of the Regionalists in the 1930s. Lytle's

portrait of Forrest reveals his vision of the past which "white-washed" the earlier role of slave trader, and "excused" Forrest's lack of control over his troops, which led to the Fort Pillow massacre of black troops. King notes that Lytle ends the biography (rev. ed., 1960) "with a panegyric to the Ku Klux Klan."

6　MacKETHAN, LUCINDA HARDWICK. The Dream of Arcady, Place and Time in Southern Literature. Baton Rouge: Louisiana State University Press, pp. 142-43.
　　Within the chapter "Agrarian Quarrel, Agrarian Question," and in comparison to Ransom's essay in I'll Take My Stand, Lytle's is discussed as "more piquant and picturesque" since it portrayed an ideal Southern yeomanry. Lytle's contribution is not examined in any detail; however, this essay about the vitality of the "backward glance" of the Fugitive-Agrarians is insightful.

7　SULLIVAN, WALTER. "The Fading Memory of the Civil War." In The American South: Portrait of a Culture. Edited by Louis D. Rubin. Baton Rouge: Louisiana State University Press, p. 248.
　　Lytle's The Long Night is mentioned as one of the most interesting of all Civil War novels. Plot summary is provided; the war is seen as the beginning of "a new social and political dispensation."

8　WIMSATT, MARY ANN. "Political Recommendations of I'll Take My Stand." MissQ 33, no. 4 (Fall):433-43.
　　The insistence of the Agrarians "for humane traditions to govern economic theory and processes is still timely"; and it is within their understanding of "religious humanism" that the book's political implications developed. While America did not follow their suggestions, for a decade the Agrarians sought to convince readers that agricultural policies outlined in their manifesto would bring "economic salvation." Perhaps Ransom's argument for subsistence farming was built on Lytle's essay.

9　YOUNG, THOMAS D. "From Fugitives to Agrarians." MissQ 33, no. 4 (Fall):420-24.
　　An introduction to papers presented for the Society for the Study of Southern Literature at MLA, 1979. Young draws basic distinctions about the backgrounds of the two groups; about the publication of I'll Take My Stand; and about the major points emphasized, such as Lytle's concern that an effort be made "to preserve traditional folkways. . . ." He then suggests the continuing relevance of Agrarian themes for today's culture.

Master's Theses on Andrew Lytle

HOSKINS, JOHN S., III. "The Problems of Good and Evil in the Novels of Andrew Nelson Lytle." Vanderbilt University, 1947.

JUSTICE, DONALD R. "The Fugitive-Agrarian 'Myth.'" University of North Carolina, 1947.

SANTMYER, SUE PATRICK. "The 'Nashville Agrarians' as Critics of American Society." Vanderbilt University, 1951.

CROWELL, LLOYD TURNER, Jr. "The Agrarian Criticism of the New South." Vanderbilt University, 1953.

HARVEY, MARY A. "Andrew Nelson Lytle: A Critical Study of His Southern Novels and Short Stories." Vanderbilt University, 1960.

WALTZ, NELL F. "The Novels of Andrew Nelson Lytle." Vanderbilt University, 1960.

GLAZE, MYRTLE L. "Andrew Nelson Lytle: An Agrarian Writer." Birmingham-Southern College, 1963.

FAIR, HENRIETTA S. "The Technique of Andrew Nelson Lytle's The Velvet Horn." Vanderbilt University, 1964.

PEMBERTON, JAMES M. "Archetypal Symbolism in Andrew Nelson Lytle's The Velvet Horn." University of Tennessee, 1966.

FEARS, RUBEL G. "Agrarianism in the Works of Andrew Lytle." Mississippi State University, 1969.

STATHAM, RICHARD G. "Andrew Lytle's Southern Fiction: A Reappraisal." University of Georgia, 1971.

WOLF, MARILYN. "The Plutarchian Biographies of the Southern Agrarians." University of Dallas, 1971.

STRATTAN, LANE GODDARD. "The Velvet Horn by Andrew Lytle: A Study of Its Imagery." University of Florida, 1973.

SAINE, JAMES HAROLD. "Southern Agrarianism and the Civil War Biographies of Allen Tate, Andrew Nelson Lytle, and Robert Penn Warren." University of North Carolina, 1975.

WALKER, F.N. "A Retreat from Chaos: The Agrarianism of Andrew Nelson Lytle." University of Mississippi, 1975.

Walker Percy

Introduction

The wounded surgeon plies the steel
That questions the distempered part;
Beneath the bleeding hands we feel
The sharp compassion of the healer's art
Resolving the enigma of the fever chart.
                                    T.S. Eliot
                                    "East Coker"

Walker Percy was an intern in pathology when he was stricken with the tuberculosis that eventually led to his writing career. Now as a novelist and essayist, he is widely regarded as a diagnostician of the spirit, probing the death-in-life that assails twentieth-century man. Percy is especially concerned with the peculiarly American malaise, that feeling of alienation and meaninglessness seemingly incongruous with life in a land of great bounty and possibility.

Writing from a Catholic point of view, Percy demonstrates in his fiction and makes explicit in his essays that such a feeling of root-lessness defines the human condition. Man is a wayfarer, a creature not meant to feel at home in the world because his only true home is with God. Percy seems to say that the more an aware and sensitive person tries to live according to the dictates of secular society, and the more he succeeds in such an endeavor, the greater is the likelihood he will encounter a sense of estrangement. Such despair, Percy maintains, can actually be a sign of spiritual health if it leads to an ordeal of selfhood that eventually points one toward a transcendence of self, toward a wholeness in unity with God.

Percy's own catalytic ordeal emanated from a bout with tuberculosis that dramatically reoriented his life. After receiving his medical degree from Columbia University's College of Physicians and Surgeons, he interned for a time at Bellevue Hospital. While performing autopsies, quite often on the bodies of derelicts, he contracted tuberculosis and was forced into a regimen of bed rest and seclusion. During his convalescence, he began to read widely in existentialist literature: Dostoevsky, Sartre, Camus, Kierkegaard, Heidegger, Marcel. In these writers' themes of angst and alienation, he

61

recognized the same sensibility, a feeling of "outsidedness" he has called it, with which he himself had long struggled. (During his medical school training, he underwent psychoanalysis.) After his recovery from tuberculosis, he attempted to continue the practice of medicine by teaching at Columbia but soon suffered a relapse, for which he was again hospitalized. Following his second convalescence, he abandoned the formal practice of medicine although his scientific orientation and knowledge of physiology permeate his writing.

In place of the medical practice for which he had so long trained, he began a life of reflection and writing on some of the philosophical issues that concerned him during his years of conva- lescence. One result of the new direction that his life was taking was his conversion to Catholicism in 1947. Then began long years of writing essays and articles for scholarly and intellectual periodi- cals, writings that garnered him little public recognition. His most prevalent topic centered on language and its possible relationship to contemporary man's sense of estrangement. Then, as Robert Coles has observed, Percy's essay writing both widened to include a variety of topics such as psychiatry, the South, and national affairs, and nar- rowed for a closer scrutiny of the phenomenon of language, particu- larly in the field of semiotics.

Percy then turned to novel writing to make more concrete some of his philosophical and metaphysical concerns. He completed two novels before he succeeded in getting The Moviegoer published in 1961. Its publisher, Alfred A. Knopf, did not anticipate a wide audience for this novel; promotion was minimal and only close to five thousand copies were sold. Although generally favorable, reviews were scarce; and the book quickly was forgotten by critics and the reading public alike. It was forgotten, that is, until an unusual chain of circum- stances led to its nomination for, and later reception of, the National Book Award.

Because of its New Orleans setting, The Moviegoer attracted the attention of A.J. Liebling, husband of Jean Stafford, one of the judges for the award. Liebling read the book, liked it immensely, and recommended it to his wife. She too enjoyed the book and sub- mitted it for consideration to the National Book Award panel. The Moviegoer was named "best novel" of 1961, and thus a relatively unheard-of novel won one of the most coveted awards in literary circles. Knopf reportedly was quite displeased with the judges' choice and was heard to lament the declining standards of the awards committee. Today, The Moviegoer is often referred to as "a minor classic"; Percy's subsequent books have been published by Farrar, Straus & Giroux.

Interpretations of The Moviegoer, as revealed by reviews both upon its initial publication and upon its reissue resulting from the National Book Award, reflect how tardy reviewers were in discerning the religious implications of the novel. One reviewer, Stanley Edgar

Hyman (1962.4), actually chided Percy for attempting "to make Jack's search seem not neurotic but deeply spiritual." Even the judges for the National Book Award cited the book for being "an intimation . . . of mortality and the inevitability of that condition," seemingly missing the intimations of immortality that are the novel's true focus. In fact, Brainard Cheney (1961.5) was alone among reviewers in emphasizing that Binx's despair emanated from a spiritual rather than an "identity" crisis.

As would be expected by the surprising, albeit belated, success of The Moviegoer, the appearance of Percy's second novel, The Last Gentleman (1966), generated considerable critical attention. In a somewhat unusual fashion for a novel that follows a highly-touted first novel, The Last Gentleman generally was well received and was itself nominated for a National Book Award. Percy's subsequent novels, Love in the Ruins (1971), Lancelot (1977), and The Second Coming (1980), have all met with generally high acclaim. His collection of essays, The Message in the Bottle (1975), has been noted particularly for making recondite subject matter accessible and interesting to general readers as well as scholars.

Critical articles on Percy started appearing as early as 1964 with the publication of James Hoggard's "Death of the Vicarious" in Southwest Review (1964.1). Most of the critical material that appeared in the mid- and late-sixties either seriously misinterpreted or only partially explained Percy's first two novels. Anselm Atkins's article, "Walker Percy and Post-Christian Search" (1968.1), provides a corrective to the early criticism by discussing some of the misinterpretations and by demonstrating the spiritual nature of Binx's quest.

Substantive critical material did not appear until 1969 when two equally incisive pieces were published: Ellen Douglas's monograph, Walker Percy's 'The Last Gentleman': Introduction and Commentary (1969.3), and Lewis A. Lawson's article, "Walker Percy's Indirect Communications" (1969.5). Douglas provides biographical material on Percy, a perceptive explication of the novel, and a discussion of its major themes. She notes in particular the novel's Kierkegaardian framework and indicates Percy's concern that his readers recognize and confront their own despair. Similarly, Lawson, in writing about both The Moviegoer and The Last Gentleman, detected that not only was Percy dramatizing the Kierkegaardian progression of his characters but also was using the Danish philosopher's method of communicating theological concepts indirectly. Lawson has continued to write prolifically on Percy and has established himself as Percy's most perceptive critic. Among the numerous aspects of Percy's writing that Lawson has investigated have been the influence of William Alexander Percy upon his adopted son, Percy's special perspective as novelist cum physician, and the strains of Stoic philosophy and gnostic vision in the literature.

Critical, scholarly, and general reader interest continues to mount steadily for Percy. Interviews and commentaries appear in the popular press in addition to a steady stream of critical articles in scholarly journals. Numerous interviews of varying length and subject matter have followed the one conducted by Ashley Brown, which appeared in Shenandoah (1967.4). Thus far, the major thrust of Percy criticism has been devoted to analyzing his philosophical and linguistic essays as glosses to the novel, to exploring his Christian existentialism, and to attempting to place him in some conventional category of American literature, such as that of Southern writer, of Black Humorist, or of novelist of alienation. Percy has proved difficult to pigeonhole since he is not a Southern writer per se (as in the tradition of Faulkner or Welty) and, unlike other American writers, he has been influenced chiefly by European existentialists.

Areas of criticism that remain virtually unexplored are the American roots of Percy's novels (David L. Vanderwerken's article, "The Americanness of The Moviegoer" [1979.32], takes a sound step in that direction), and the influence of poets on Percy's writing (seemingly an obvious connection because of his fascination with language and metaphor and with his repeated allusions to Dante, Shakespeare, Hopkins, and Eliot). A compilation of Percy's interviews would also prove valuable as would a biography, especially one that would shed some light on Percy's early years with his parents. The specter of Percy's father, who committed suicide, looms in his novels like the ghost of Hamlet's father; but information about the elder Percy or his relationship to his oldest son is virtually nonexistent.

In 1972, Percy's works were the subject of a full-length study, The Sovereign Wayfarer by Martin Luschei (1972.13). This seminal work (which grew out of Luschei's doctoral dissertation [1970.4], the first devoted solely to Percy) provides a close examination of the first three novels and investigates the existential basis of Percy's thought. Three critical volumes were recently published within a two-year span: Robert Coles's Walker Percy: An American Search (1978.9) and two collections of critical essays, The Art of Walker Percy: Strategems for Being (1979.4), edited by Panthea Broughton, and Walker Percy: Art and Ethics (1980.55), edited by Jac Tharpe.

Percy continues to gain stature in American letters. One significant measure of his increasing recognition is indicated by the number of theses and dissertations concerned with his works. Specifically, he is discussed in over thirty doctoral dissertations, about half of which are devoted solely to his works. As a novelist, Percy garners that rare accolade in American literature, both critical and popular success. His latest novel, The Second Coming, climbed quickly to the best-seller charts and also generally found favor with critics. It received the first Los Angeles <u>Times</u> award for fiction, being named the best American novel of 1980. Still writing steadily at the age of sixty-five, Percy is currently at work on a book dealing with semiotics to be entitled <u>Novum Organum</u>.

C.D.

Writings by Walker Percy

The Moviegoer. New York: Alfred A. Knopf, 1961.

The Last Gentleman. New York: Farrar, Straus & Giroux, 1966.

Love in the Ruins: The Adventures of a Bad Catholic at a Time Near
   the End of the World. New York: Farrar, Straus & Giroux, 1971.

The Message in the Bottle: How Queer Man Is, How Queer Language Is,
   and What One Has to Do with the Other. New York: Farrar, Straus
   & Giroux, 1975.

Lancelot. New York: Farrar, Straus & Giroux, 1977.

The Second Coming. New York: Farrar, Straus & Giroux, 1980.

Writings about Walker Percy, 1961-1980

1961

1 ANON. "Briefly noted." Review of The Moviegoer. NY 37, no. 23 (22 July):78-79.
    "A parable of sorts . . . Mr. Percy, whose prose needs oil and a good check up, cannot let Bolling be."

2 ANON. Review of The Moviegoer. Booklist 57, no. 21 (1 July): 664.
    Brief review which outlines action. The glimpse at the end into the marriage and life together "end a finely etched, sensitive commentary" about rootlessness and fragmentation in contemporary life.

3 ANON. Review of The Moviegoer. Kirkus 29, no. 7 (1 April): 339.
    Brief review states novel begins at same point as Kierkegaard's "aesthetic mystique" yet closes "without reaching any finite revelation." The action is traced, and it is suggested that Binx's search will be found "curiously fascinating while elusive."

4 ANON. "Two True Sounds from Dixie." Time 77, no. 21 (19 May): 105.
    Percy's The Moviegoer is reviewed with Joan Williams's The Morning and the Evening and declared to be a success "clothed in originality, intelligence and a fierce regard for man's fate." His theme, that despair attacks in the inmost mind, is treated with exactly the correct blend of "seriousness and humor." Percy has a talent for making characters look and sound as though they are being seen and heard for the first time.

5   CHENEY, BRAINARD. "To Restore a Fragmented Image." <u>SR</u> 69,
     no. 4 (Autumn):691-700.
         Review of <u>The Moviegoer</u>. The concept of "modern man's
     fragmented image" was a popular theme with critics of the 1930s.
     While searching for the "complete man," many searchers have found
     that it is God's image, not "man's image of himself," that is
     fragmented. "The fragmentation came in their breaking off the
     human representation from His less formulable revelations of
     Himself to man." Both Dostoevsky, in <u>Notes from Underground</u>,
     and Camus, in <u>The Fall</u>, have explored this theme. In comparable
     form and illumination, Percy--"in the milieu of the post modern
     barbarians"--has reexamined this theme. Each novel revolves
     around a hero-narrator that reveals himself as "a damned man
     seeking salvation." The essence of humanism parallels the de-
     velopment of these novels. Dostoevsky "<u>exposed</u>" scientific hu-
     manism; Camus recognized it for what it was while clinging to it;
     and Percy abandoned it while stumbling "amid its shards and glim-
     mering confusion toward a clear but distant candle." Despite
     these similarities, <u>The Moviegoer</u> is more than exposition; the
     dramatic action is resolved "in terms of the plot and the hero's
     inner problem." Binx Bolling's real search, obstructed by his
     obsession with the movies, is for identity. It is not God that
     Binx is "<u>onto</u>" but himself. The irony that he ascribes to God
     is, instead, a "human emotion, evoked by man's disillusionment
     of his own sentimentality." The egotism that results in the
     "<u>underground man</u>" and the "<u>judge-penitent</u>" rejecting "the charity
     that would have saved them" is not present in <u>The Moviegoer</u>.
     Grace is afforded Binx and Kate by the very condition of their
     love. Kate's act of responsibility in the novel's closing scene
     is a symbolic step toward faith. Percy "has restored for us here
     the image of God that was fragmented by the humanists."

6   COOK, BRUCE A. Review of <u>The Moviegoer</u>. <u>Critic</u> 20
     (September):44.
         Binx Bolling's life has been devoted to the search, but he
     is doomed even though Percy seems unaware of this. While Percy
     indicates a happy ending, "it is extraneous to what has preceded
     it." The epilogue is tacked on. Style, not plot, is the virtue
     of this good novel.

7   CUMMINGS, ROBERT J. Review of <u>The Moviegoer</u>. <u>BS</u> 21
     (15 June):122.
         Essentially a plot summary of a "well-written" novel which
     possesses "a curiously unreal quality" because, while the setting
     is "beautifully evoked," the hero feels deep despair growing.

8   GARDINER, HAROLD C. Review of <u>The Moviegoer</u>. <u>America</u> 105
     (17 June):448.
         This brief review commends the novel for its "wonderful
     evocation of the spirit of time and place." Although Binx never

reaches any certitude regarding the outcome of his search, his
acceptance of responsibility toward the end of the novel portends
an optimistic future for him.

9   KENNEBECK, EDWIN. "The Search." Commonweal 74 (2 June):
     260-63.
         The Moviegoer presents Binx Bolling who "tries to find out
     why he is in the world," and gradually Percy leads us through
     "layers of soft dreams and crusty realities to discover in one
     man's soul the core of compassion." Percy's craft makes all the
     parts of this story create "one form" which illuminates all the
     scenes and characters.

10   McCLEARY, WILLIAM. Review of The Moviegoer. LJ 86, no. 10
     (15 May):1905.
         A first novel by a medical school graduate and writer of
     "numerous periodical essays of high quality." The main charac-
     ters are described: Binx and Kate, "both unhappy, look to each
     other for removal of a condition that once seemed . . . despair."
     "An interesting well written novel. . . ."

11   MASSIE, ROBERT. Review of The Moviegoer. NYTBR, 28 May,
     p. 30.
         Brief review which describes Binx as "the bewildered but
     amiable hero" of this "polished first novel." The action is out-
     lined, and it is asserted that Percy's interest in psychiatry "is
     evident in the way he probes at the mainsprings of his charac-
     ters." The "flavor . . . spirit . . . and dialogue" of New
     Orleans during Mardi Gras are suggested "with marvelous accuracy."

12   POORE, CHARLES. "Books of the Times." New York Times,
     27 May, p. 21.
         Generally favorable review that questions Binx's credibil-
     ity as a hero but praises the buoyancy and force with which the
     novel, "a searching study of tradition embattled with change," is
     presented.

13   SAXTON, MARK. "Shadows on a Screen, More Real than Life."
     Books 37, no. 52 (30 July):6.
         In part the story of Binx's case "for the unreality of
     . . . life," and an account of what occurs when "stratagems
     against unreality begin to fail." Very little occurs on the
     surface, but the climate changes as the "emotional expedients
     cease to work under pressure." This is a story often so
     "shrewdly witty, even outright funny" that one forgets it is
     about despair.

14   SEREBNICK, JUDITH. "First Novelists--Spring 1961." <u>LJ</u> 86,
       no. 3 (1 February):597.
         This review of <u>The Moviegoer</u> relies on Walker Percy's ex-
planation of his interest in philosophy, his choice of the novel
form, and his career as a doctor. Using "concrete life-situa-
tions," Percy attempts "'to portray the rebellion of two young
people against the shallowness and tastelessness of modern life.'"

1962

1   ANON. "The Moviegoer." In <u>Masterplots 1962 Annual</u>. Edited
       by Frank N. Magill. New York: Salem Press, pp. 212-15.
         This novel is provocative: Percy approaches the existen-
tialist themes of Camus obliquely. His hero, Binx, suffers from
despair, searches, and is finally drawn out of his spiritual
crisis. Finally Binx becomes aware of the need for "kindness"
and "compassion." Much more is implied than ever put into words
and one of Percy's strengths is his reserve. He allows his characters to move unobtrusively toward their moments of illumination.

2   ANON. "Story of a Novel: How it Won Prize." <u>New York Times</u>,
       15 March, p. 25.
         Brief article. Recounts the fortuitous chain of events
leading up to the National Book Award's being granted to <u>The
Moviegoer</u>.

3   DAVIS, DOUGLAS M. "A Southerner's <u>The Moviegoer</u> and His Per-
       plexing Prize." <u>National Observer</u>, 29 April, p. 21.
         Favorable review recounts <u>The Moviegoer</u>'s unenthusiastic
reception by readers and astonishing accolade by the National
Book Award Committee. The reviewer particularly cites Percy's
deft combination of serious subject matter with a light tone and
witty protagonist.

4   HYMAN, STANLEY EDGAR. "Moviegoing and Other Intimacies."
       <u>NL</u> 45 (30 April):23-24.
         When <u>The Moviegoer</u> received the National Book Award, "there
were howls of rage, as though the umpire had made a bum call
against the home team." The choice was defensible, however, because the novel deserves attention. Several characters, especially the main ones, are beautifully realized; and Percy deftly
handles language and symbolism. Outstanding is the novel's
"clear strong line of action," whereas chief among its faults is
an attempt "to make Jack's search seem not neurotic but deeply
spiritual."

1963

1   ANON. "Self-Sacrifice." TLS, 29 March, p. 221.
        Reviewed with Brian Moore's An Answer from Limbo, The
     Moviegoer is called a failure "by a narrow margin." Perhaps
     Percy is "too sophisticated," for while the subject of the novel
     is the "search" within the malaise, the promising theme of films
     is neglected. Percy writes "a little too glibly of despair."

2   ANON. "The Sustaining Stream." Time 81 (1 February):82-84.
        Percy is listed as part of a group of promising novelists
     whose first work had been published in the previous few years.
     The Moviegoer is cited for its irony and effective characteriza-
     tion, but faulted for its inconclusiveness: "If there is any-
     thing to say after the characters have acted out this demonstra-
     tion of emptiness, Percy does not say it."

3   BRADBURY, MALCOLM. "New Fiction." Punch (London) 244,
        no. 6397 (17 April):573-74.
        The Movie-Goer, "in a particularly American way," is a very
     good book. Percy owes a lot to prevailing tradition, but while
     the presentation of the hero is done in a way which offers ex-
     cuses for "delicious vignettes," the style succeeds. His hero's
     "wry self-presentation . . . creates comedy [in] a book well
     worth the reading."

4   DANIEL, JOHN. "Fatality and Futility." Spectator (London)
        210, no. 7036 (3 May):572-73.
        The novel traces Bolling's search as he rejects "ideals he
     no longer feels" and follows "the frail thread of genuine feeling
     as a lifeline." The novel is given force by the sanity of its
     hero who withdraws from a meaningless society. Percy has "postu-
     lated an intelligent audience, capable of thinking and caring and
     even smiling."

5   IGOE, W.J. "More than One America." Tablet 217 (11 May):
        513-14.
        Brings Camus's L'Etranger to mind; Percy's theme is "tax-
     ing," but this is "an uncommonly intelligent book" which observes
     much, not just about America but about western civilization.

6   TAUBMAN, ROBERT. "Feeling Better." New Statesman 65,
        no. 1674 (12 April):527.
        While the hero claims that his activities are confined "to
     working, money, movies, and women," it is not that sort of Ameri-
     can novel. Bolling is an original and engaging hero; this is "a
     good and unexpected novel," better in parts than in the whole,
     but with a "telling" style and tones which make it comparable to
     early Sartre or Nathanael West.

1964

1   HOGGARD, JAMES. "Death of the Vicarious." SWR 49 (Autumn):
    366-74.
         Binx Bolling, in The Moviegoer, recognizes the importance
    of the question of identity. With few exceptions, he finds that
    "most people are dead souls because they have no identity of
    their own." They deny this crisis by hiding behind traditions
    that they do not understand. In order to find meaning, individ-
    uals turn to the Romantic and the illusory, instead of to them-
    selves. The resulting lack of self-confidence makes people
    "afraid of contact with the unfamiliar" and of their own "per-
    sonal uniqueness." Binx neither accepts "the absurdity of ex-
    istence" nor denies God in realizing that he must employ "his own
    resources in finding meaning in life." By using a logical struc-
    ture of "repetition and development," Percy is able to explore
    "certain themes--doubt about the validity of society's attitudes
    toward marriage, religion, ambition, and work; and the ways to
    deal with the conflicts resulting from these attitudes." Choice
    is an important consideration for Percy, as is the humanist tra-
    dition, in attempting to give "both meaning and movement to life."
    Binx Bolling has accepted responsibility for himself; and in so
    doing, he makes the reader aware that in the "intimacy of direct
    personal involvement, rather than in vicarious experiences, is
    the basis for individual significance."

1965

1   KOSTELANETZ, RICHARD, ed. "The New American Fiction." In The
    New American Arts. New York: Horizon Press, pp. 194-236,
    esp. 224-25.
         This brief reference to Percy focuses solely on The Movie-
    goer, which is placed in a category of "novels of madness." As
    such, "the Christian framework seems . . . rather forced and ab-
    stract in contrast to the true feeling and terror of Bolling's
    neurosis."

2   TANNER, TONY. "Afterword: Wonder and Alienation--The Mystic
    and The Moviegoer." In The Reign of Wonder: Naivete and
    Reality in American Literature. Cambridge: Cambridge Univer-
    sity Press, pp. 349-56.
         The Moviegoer is discussed in terms of the development of
    the reign of wonder. Although Binx Bolling is the American
    counterpart to the French Outsider, his rebellion and alienation
    take a different course. He seeks "lodgement and anchorage in
    the world" without capitulating to its "false standards and dead
    values." Binx seeks ballast in order to "stave off the complete
    dissolution of his identity." The "American Moviegoer" and the
    "French Outsider" differ in their awareness of "'the possibility
    of a search.'" What Percy has in common with many of the writers

considered in this volume is an awareness of the "radical importance of a true way of seeing. . . ." For Binx Bolling, the
moviegoer, this means to "'listen to people, see how they stick
themselves into the world.'"

1966

1   ANON. "Guidebook for Lost Pilgrims." Time 87, no. 24
    (17 June):104.
        Views The Last Gentleman as Percy's conveyance for the
subtleties that exist between the North and the South. Percy's
use of wit, irony, and understatement give the novel more substance than The Moviegoer. The deceptive nature of this medita-
tion could obscure the real meaning--"a restless rustling of
faith, under the ironic humor and serenity a groping toward God."

2   ANON. "In the Southern Grain." NW 67 (20 June):106, 108.
        Suggests that The Last Gentleman fails to achieve "its
complex ambition." The problem lies in insufficient character
development. However, Percy has achieved success in sustaining
"a comic surface while his darker intentions gather below." Although the novel does not fully achieve its ambitions, there is
no doubt that Percy is "a writer of the first rank."

3   ANON. Review of The Last Gentleman. Booklist 63, no. 1
    (1 September):34.
        Sees The Last Gentleman as a vehicle through which Percy
can comment on "regional and individual attitudes on race,
religion, and social purpose" and relate his findings "with wry
mature humor but serious intent."

4   ANON. Review of The Last Gentleman. Choice 3, no. 7
    (September):22.
        Regards The Last Gentleman as a "thought-provoking" study
in contrasts between the "'New' South" and the North. This
reviewer sees Percy as "mellow, detached, acutely perceptive"
and regards his writing as "loose, polished, cool."

5   ANON. Review of The Last Gentleman. Kirkus 34 (15 April):
    444.
        The last gentleman, like the moviegoer, suffers from "a
kind of dislocation." The symptoms of his detachment include
"'fugue states'" and "moments of déjà vu." Percy achieves "a
harder satiric edge" than he achieved in The Moviegoer. His
style reflects the statement that he makes on contemporary life.
As a result, The Last Gentleman maintains consistent contrast
and sustained interest.

6   ANON. Review of The Moviegoer. Observer (London), 17 April,
      p. 22.
          Notes the paperback edition of The Moviegoer; suggests
      reading the novel "in conjunction with" Inside Daisy Clover by
      Gavin Lambert. Binx Bolling is characterized as a "compulsive
      cinemagoer who prefers his fantasies and the make-believe world
      on the screen to the reality of existence in New Orleans
      territory."

7   ANON. Review of The Last Gentleman. VQR 42, no. 4 (Autumn):
      cxxxiii, cxxxvi.
          The Last Gentleman is Walker Percy's original treatment of
      today's familiar hero--"that ineffectual soul in search of self
      and identity." Percy discards convention and structure for
      ambiguity and irresoluteness. The result is both disconcerting
      and delightful.

8   BRITTON, ANNE. Review of The Moviegoer. Books and Bookmen 11
      (March):79.
          Considers The Moviegoer a book worth rereading. Percy de-
      picts a character, Binx Bolling, in search of an appropriate
      search. Binx, an avowed movie addict, confronts reality with
      "dreamlike" responses appropriate to a John Wayne movie.

9   BUITENHUIS, PETER. "A Watcher, a Listener, a Wanderer."
      NYTBR, 26 June, p. 5.
          Discusses the merits of The Last Gentleman on a narrative
      level and "a level of implication." Questions of violence, race,
      love, and identity are important considerations in a novel that
      is more than a random series of coincidences. Percy has suc-
      ceeded in creating a novel that depicts "the contradictory nature
      of reality." Will Barrett meets the demands of both the plot and
      the civilization the plot imitates. Percy's use of irony com-
      bines "the Southern writer's sense of style and history with a
      razor-sharp perception of the technological, consumer-oriented
      civilization that the North has invented."

10   BUTCHER, FANNY. "Tale with a Picaresque Quality." Chicago
      Tribune Books Today, 24 July, p. 10.
          The promise of The Last Gentleman is lost in its overall
      confusion. The novel achieves a sense of movement and plot be-
      cause of its picaresque quality. Percy's attention to detail is
      extraordinary though often "extraneous." His most effective
      writing is in his depiction of the South. Although Percy's use
      of satire varies in its effectiveness, he is able to make occa-
      sional "illuminating" and "trenchant observations."

11   BYRD, SCOTT. "The Dreams of Walker Percy." Red Clay Reader,
      no. 3:70-73.
          The disquieting effect produced by The Moviegoer and The
      Last Gentleman requires the reader "to re-examine reality." In

both novels, Percy seeks "to extend the awareness of the reader until he can enjoy, as well as fear, the superimposition of illusion upon the literal world." In contrast to the comparison often made between Binx Bolling and the heroes of Camus, this essay focuses on Samuel Taylor Coleridge's definition of creative imagination in terms of "the mind which creates the world and the mind which is created by the world." Binx waits in the Gentilly suburb, "like the monks of the third century," hoping that "the world will create his mind." His problem is that he is alienated from the world. By contrast, the dominant women in the novel, Aunt Emily and Kate, try to create their worlds. The novel ends with a "fated sense of compromise." Although The Last Gentleman has a similar effect, the narrative focus is more complex. This time Percy's protagonist is more disoriented than alienated. Will Barrett tries to make contact with the world in spite of his bouts of amnesia. The Last Gentleman represents both search and conquest. It is important, in view of contemporary American culture, that Percy's hero "finds that he can minister as well as be ministered to." Percy's fiction has again provided his readers "discomforting delight."

12   CASEY, FLORENCE. "Coming in from the Cold." CSM, 23 June, p. 7.
     Regards Williston Bibb Barrett as "the last rural gentleman." His problems are based on his inability to grasp urban relationships, urban logic, or urban ambitions. By attaching himself to a "non-urban" Southern family, Barrett is able to gain a perspective on life. Walker Percy must continue to meet the intellectual demands of his audience in order to avoid becoming a victim of current literary trends.

13   CHRISTOPHER, MICHAEL. "The Last Gentleman, Authority, and Papa Hemingway." U.S. Catholic 32, no. 3 (July):47-48.
     The Last Gentleman described as an even better novel than The Moviegoer, and as a novel young people may like. Will Barrett's symptoms, which include déjà vu and fugue states, symbolize more than his sickness, and to read of him is to experience Barrett's dislocation. Percy's Catholicism never intrudes, yet clearly part of what Will and Sutter are looking for is God. Not a perfect book, it is a Christian one, which makes Percy "a name to be reckoned with."

14   CREWS, FREDERICK C. "The Hero as 'Case.'" Commentary 42, no. 3 (September):100-102.
     Regards the "absoluteness of death and the impossibility of genuine intimacy" as a key to understanding The Last Gentleman. The journey in the novel--from New York to Alabama to New Mexico --resembles the "steps of a philosophical proof." Percy allows his hero, Will Barrett, to discover that the only alternative to becoming immersed in role-playing is suicide. The total development of the novel is flawed by Percy's inability to see or to understand the inner conflicts of his main character.

15   DAVIS, DOUGLAS M. "From Mr. Percy, a Temptation Play for
      Folk-Rock Age." National Observer 5, no. 24 (13 June):22.
         The Last Gentleman establishes Walker Percy as "a novelist
of genuine purpose." Although the novel shares many similarities
with The Moviegoer, Percy's metaphysical concerns are more ambitious in the later work. Thematically, Percy's characters are
close to those of the Black Humorists. The novel's form, a synthesis of ideas and plot action, reflects the form of the medieval temptation plays. A practical response to the meaning of
life is never resolved.

16   DeMOTT, BENJAMIN. "The Good and the True." Book Week
      (12 June), pp. 2, 9.
         Bill Barrett, the hero of The Last Gentleman, does much to
generate the goodness that pervades the novel. This "tale of un-
ending human generosity" does not preclude ugliness, suffering,
or mental and spiritual anxiety. Told in "a genteel picaresque
mode," The Last Gentleman is a novel from another age although it
reflects the consciousness of the New South. Its weaknesses include obliqueness, patronizing language, and reflective irony.
Percy, however, has not given a tranquilizer to "the novel of
violence and despair" by "transforming the familiar American ter-
rors into comfortably endurable bothers." On the contrary, with
kindness and intelligence, he speaks to questions of goodness and
love.

17   DOLLEN, CHARLES. Review of The Last Gentleman. BS 26
      (1 July):133.
         Suggests the novel would be more interesting as a short
story. The major characters are merely representations of what
is wrong with American life. The story line's lack of depth
establishes Sutter Vaught as the novel's real hero. Walker Percy
betrays his talent in The Last Gentleman by "profound ignorance
of Catholic principles, religious orders, and civil rights work."

18   DONADIO, STEPHEN. "America, America." PR 33, no. 3 (Summer):
      448-52, esp. 451-52.
         The major theme of The Last Gentleman is the "opposition
between 'immanence' and 'transcendence.'" Because reconciliation
is not possible, the novel ends "in suspended animation, at precisely that point beyond which any further action is unthinkable."
This carefully conceived and executed novel falls short in three
episodes--the white reporter as "'pseudo-Negro,'" the Negro student entering an all-white Southern university, and Barrett's
raft trip across the river to his aunts' house--each of which
occurs when Percy tries to go beyond his "fictional world."

19   GOODMAN, WALTER. "An Elegant Quest for Ordinariness." Life
      60, no. 25 (24 June):20.
         Considers Walker Percy talented, insightful, and eloquent.
However, The Last Gentleman is not the vehicle that proclaims

Percy's "estimable resources." The novel is weak in both story
and character development. Although minor characters have dimension, major characters sacrifice dimensionality for "ideas." The
tangents that the story takes ensure repetition--rather than
"true development."

20   GRUMBACH, DORIS. "Book Reviews." America 114, no. 25 (Whole
      no. 2972) (18 June):858.
          The strength of The Last Gentleman is its simplicity. The
      novel transcends classification as a Southern novel; the reader
      is persuaded of the universality of Barrett's "modern disease."
      Walker Percy's "unadorned, straightforward" fiction of the inner-
      self deserves consideration.

21   HICKS, GRANVILLE. "One of the Roaming Kind." SatR 49
      (18 June):29-30.
          Compares The Last Gentleman to Percy's first novel, The
      Moviegoer. Although The Moviegoer is more tightly constructed,
      each novel employs "the same kind of wit and the same power to
      shake the reader out of his assumptions." Percy's leading char-
      acters, Jack Bolling and Bill Barrett, are both spokesmen for
      Percy's "own sardonic view of the human comedy."

22   JOHNSON, LUCY. "Percy and Amis." Progressive 30 (October):
      49-50.
          The Last Gentleman reviewed with The Anti-Death League by
      Kingsley Amis; Percy's book is eccentric, but successful. While
      not a realistic novel, it is entirely believable that Will
      Barrett is liked by everyone with whom he comes into contact;
      even more important is Percy's ability to suggest the complexity
      of an America not monolithic and far beyond the "old honorable"
      times of gentlemen.

23   KEITH, DON L. "Walker Percy Talks of Many Things." Delta
      Review 3, no. 3 (May-June):38-39.
          Interview conducted just before the appearance of The Last
      Gentleman. Percy comments on his interest in storytelling, re-
      vision of The Moviegoer, habits of composition, his concept of
      fiction as telling "someone something about himself he already
      knows," and his fiction as a vehicle for incarnating ideas (as
      did Sartre and Marcel).

24   KITCHING, JESSIE. Review of The Last Gentleman. PW 189,
      no. 19 (9 May):76.
          Views The Last Gentleman as a "modern fantasy." Humor,
      satire, and "odd, chance-met ingredients" pervade the novel.

25   KNIPP, THOMAS. Review of The Last Gentleman. Sign 46, no. 1
      (August):59-60.
      Brief consideration of the novel and Barrett's "only par-
tially successful attempt to cope" with the persons and qualities
of soul which make his relationships inadequate. A good novel,
but its quiet tone and obliqueness may earn it fewer readers than
it deserves.

26   McNASPY, C.J. "Books: Critics' Choices for Christmas."
      Commonweal 85, no. 9 (2 December):268-69.
      The Last Gentleman is a wider and more encompassing por-
trayal of experience and life than The Moviegoer. The "burden
of history" that Will Barrett symbolizes is neither a "textbook
case" nor a dimension of Faulkner's Yoknapatawpha characterizations. It is both more personal and more complex.

27   MORGAN, BERRY. Review of The Last Gentleman. Delta Review 3,
      no. 3 (May-June):39.
      Plato's "Apology" states that poets, while they say many
fine things, do not understand their meaning. The central character of this novel "is a little like that poet." Percy's "masterful style," wit, and insight provide access to the mind and
heart of his subjects; this novel will be not just entertaining,
but "consoling and healing" for persons like Billy Barrett caught
in the false world.

28   MORSE, J. MITCHELL. "Fiction Chronicle." HudR 19, no. 3
      (Autumn):507-14.
      This review of The Last Gentleman is preceded by a brief
analysis of contemporary novelists and criticism: the skill of
many writers is overshadowed by the technical prowess of less
capable craftsmen. Fortunately, Percy has something to say, and
he says it well. Percy's insight and skill are maintained until
the close of the novel. At that point, The Last Gentleman "falls
to pieces in every way--artistically, intellectually, and mor-
ally." Because in spite of Percy's skill at characterization,
Williston Bibb Barrett is destined to have another fugue.

29   OATES, JOYCE CAROL. "Gentleman Without a Past." Nat 203,
      no. 4 (8 August):129-30.
      Considers Percy's power to be in his "reaction against the
naturalistic, the half-comic half-horrified reflection of the
naturalistic through a whimsical temperament." The hypnotic
spell that Percy casts with words is lost in the meaning of the
larger units of the paragraph and the chapter. Although there
are many inconsistencies in the novel, "this novel is one no
critic should want to snipe at, for it is rare to encounter a
work engaging in nearly every line."

30 PHILLIPS, ROBERT. "Southern Chronicle." North American
     Review, n.s. 3, no. 4 (July):37-38.
          Barrett's story, "a fugue on the theme of déjà vu," in-
     cludes repetition which is intentional, yet the book "rambles"
     and the reader is unsure of its direction. Nevertheless, Percy
     gives us several "fascinating characters," "some of the best
     dialogue of the decade," and much to think about. It "will not
     be easily dismissed."

31 PINE, JOHN C. Review of The Last Gentleman. LJ 91, no. 11
     (1 June):2877.
          Considers The Last Gentleman as a portrait of the "modern
     South" in the manner portrayed by Truman Capote in In Cold Blood.

32 POORE, CHARLES. "A Candide in a Brooks Brothers Shirt." New
     York Times, 16 June, p. 45.
          Walker Percy's second novel, The Last Gentleman, is another
     view of the "reality" of the modern world. His ironic wit creates
     a landscape somewhere "between the worlds of F. Scott Fitzgerald
     and William Faulkner." The reality for Percy is not that God is
     dead--but can modern man survive? Is it too late? Is modern man
     dead?

33 ROSENTHAL, RAYMOND. "The Ceremony of Innocence." NL 49,
     no. 13 (20 June):22-23.
          Considers The Last Gentleman as "a spiritual voyage of dis-
     covery." The novel incurs problems because of its ambitious de-
     sign. Although Percy presents thoughts, images, and landscapes
     with precision, the larger patterns and issues of the novel are
     unformed and blurred. The themes of "loneliness, wonder, and
     innocence" are complicated by Percy's introduction of ideas. In
     spite of the novel's shortcomings, Walker Percy is able to cap-
     ture the inner meaning of the landscape of America and his region.

34 SHEED, WILFRID. "Ravening Particles of Anxiety." Critic 25
     (October/November):92-93.
          Considers The Last Gentleman "one of the best-written books
     in recent memory." The dexterity with which Percy writes is
     often encountered negatively. An "accordion" effect occurs in
     The Last Gentleman because Percy is able to combine a parody of
     an "on-the-road novel" with "a mysterious-gothic-family novel,"
     a "novel of galloping-disaster," and "a deathbed baptism."
     Percy's decision to substitute an important character with the
     philosophical musings of his casebook seems to be a mistake. His
     humor, language, and religious intent are too complex to succumb
     to paraphrase or formula; The Last Gentleman is a novel to be re-
     read. Reprinted: 1968.8.

35   TRACHTENBERG, STANLEY. "Beyond Initiation: Some Recent
      Novels." YR 56, no. 1 (Autumn):131-38, esp. 137-38.
           In his search for identity, Barrett progresses beyond
      initiation because he uses his initiation as preparation for the
      possibility of "'giving measure and form to time itself.'"

36   TRACY, HONOR. "Humidification Engineer." NewR 154 (18 June):
      27-28.
           This review of The Last Gentleman praises Percy's use of
      detail but questions his ability to probe consciousness. Al-
      though parts of the novel are "excellent," the whole appears un-
      focused and rambling. Several questions are raised: Why is Will
      Barrett "the last gentleman"? How does Percy use irony and
      humor? What does the quotation from Kierkegaard mean? How does
      Percy deal with characterization?

37   WAIN, JOHN. "The Insulted and Injured." NYRB 7, no. 1
      (28 July):22-24.
           The Last Gentleman is reviewed with The Gates of the Forest
      by Elie Wiesel and The Night Visitor and Other Stories by B.
      Traven. Percy's novel is as "complex and ambitious" as the other
      novels reviewed. The Last Gentleman is considered "a novel about
      the South" because of the central character's birthright. Will
      Barrett's journey represents "the journey of the modern South
      back to self-recognition." Percy's narrative method--"prismatic,
      discrete, a matter of half-conveyed hints"--requires the reader
      to work out many enigmas. In the process, the reader confronts
      irony and satire. The novel's only well-defined character,
      Sutter Vaught, is "a kind of holy lecher," who believes that
      pornography is "a moral positive because it recognizes Christian
      values in order to subvert them." Percy's use of a "notebook" to
      interject philosophical thoughts is an overused device.

38   WILKIE, BRIAN. Review of The Last Gentleman. Commonweal 84,
      no. 19 (19 August):537-39.
           Considers The Last Gentleman a complex and moving explora-
      tion of "the plight of modern man, post-modern sensibility, the
      spiritual crisis of our time, the decline of the west, and so
      forth." The seemingly arbitrary and episodic nature of the novel
      should not obscure the intricacy, understatement, irony, and
      satire that Percy uses to question "the whole machinery of one's
      sensibility."

                              1967

1   ANON. "Fiction: The American Game of Happy Families." TLS,
      21 December, p. 1233.
           Bill Barrett's journey in The Last Gentleman is a search to
      find out "what is everyone really thinking and feeling?" Percy
      is at once abstract and analytical. Barrett's confusion is a

symbol for "the suicidal confusion of the South" which is, in
turn, analogous to the selfishness and violence of the Great
Society. The real discovery is in recognizing the need "for new
authority and new resources."

2   BLOUIN, MICHAEL T. "The Novels of Walker Percy: An Attempt
     at Synthesis." Xavier University Studies 6 (February):29-42.
     The Moviegoer and The Last Gentleman should be considered
in relation to the Southern historical past under which they were
conceived. The questions of birthright and vocation became--"How
to live and how to die? and What do bravery and courtesy mean?"
As code and challenge, these questions, "one of being and one of
doing," complicate the role of the individual Southerner. The
first reflects the matriarchal world; the second, the patriarchal.
Both loom in "fiction and fact" as the "creators and destroyers"
of the young, male inheritors of the New South. The resulting
characters are figures of "irony and pathos." For many, negation
takes the form of avoidance or non-commitment. Resolution and
synthesis can be accomplished, in Percy's terms, by a "moderate,
socio-moral, intersubjective affirmation of the sacramental unity
of marriage as a metaphor for all relationships engaged in by
homo viator." For Percy, the family becomes the "symbol for
society-at-large and a matrix for drama, truth and redemption in
the career of the individual." Actions, redemptive and non-
redemptive, are worked out in relation to Percy's themes of "love
and death, tyranny and despair"--as presented within the confines
of the communal family.

3   BRAYBROOKE, NEVILLE. "The Cruel Time." Spectator (London),
     no. 7235 (24 February):228.
     Brief mention of The Last Gentleman: the opening scenes
are very carefully done, but the brilliant clarity of the first
statement of theme becomes subsequently lost as the hero moves
beyond New York, and his wanderings take on a Don Quixote-like
quality.

4   BROWN, ASHLEY. "An Interview with Walker Percy." Shenandoah
     18, no. 3 (Spring):3-10.
     Percy talks about his background, his writing, and The Last
Gentleman. His early life was centered around science. Also,
after contracting pulmonary tuberculosis, Percy was hospitalized
in the Adirondacks for two years. His interest in existentialism
developed as he read Dostoevsky's Notes from Underground,
Kierkegaard, Heidegger, Gabriel Marcel, Sartre, and Camus.
Although Percy became aware of some of the shortcomings of
science, his devotion to it--based on "its elegance and pre-
cision"--has not diminished.
     In trying to understand "what it is to be a man and to live
and to die," Percy no longer approaches the question as a scientist but as a novelist. In the process, he has learned to tell
stories. His stories are closer to the stories of Bellow,

Malamud, and Heller than to those of other Southerners. Percy
most admires the modern French novel for "its absolute seriousness in its investigation of human reality."

As novelist, he feels that his training in psychiatry "is
only indirectly useful." His concern with "the dislocation of
man in the modern age" is concern for the individual--not the
type; the individual in The Last Gentleman is Will Barrett.
Percy acknowledges Barrett's kinship to Dostoevsky's Prince
Myshkin. Barrett's potential rests in his ability to "see things
afresh, both the Northern and Southern culture." Binx Bolling,
the hero of The Moviegoer, is the model for Barrett's character.
Barrett, however, is much sicker than Binx. While Binx "enjoys
his alienation," Barrett becomes a passionate pilgrim in search
of a father-figure. Percy allows the reader to view Barrett "as
a sick man among healthy business men or as a sane pilgrim in a
mad world." The Last Gentleman can be considered a satire. For
some readers and reviewers, too much was satirized. Percy will
continue to write although for him "it is the conception which is
painful and the delivery which is easy."

5   CHENEY, BRAINARD. "Secular Society as Deadly Farce." SR 75,
    no. 2 (Spring):345-50.
        Although The Last Gentleman is another chapter in Walker
    Percy's "prognosis on an ailing secular society," it is not a
    "repetition" of The Moviegoer. Percy uses "the flexibility and
    tone" inherent in the farcical form in his attempt "to motivate
    a hero whose problem is a lack of motivation." The title itself
    suggests farce. Williston Bibb Barrett, "a hollow man left with
    only his good manners," eventually must confront his mental ill-
    ness and his identity crisis. The novel's closing passage re-
    flects hope--"hope that underpins all faith."

6   FLEISCHER, LEONORE. "Paperbacks: Fiction." PW 192, no. 16
    (16 October):59.
        This brief sketch of The Moviegoer introduces the paperback
    edition.

7   GUERARD, ALBERT J. "Saul Bellow and the Activists: On The
    Adventures of Augie March." SoR, n.s. 3, no. 3 (Summer):
    582-96, esp. 585.
        Walker Percy is mentioned along with Roth, Gold, Monroe
    Engel, Malamud, and James Baldwin as an activist, a designation
    provided by David Stevenson in an article for Daedalus in 1963.
    An activist is defined as one who believes in "energy, vitality,
    sheer activity as moral goods." The Adventures of Augie March
    marked a new development in the modern American novel. Its im-
    pact can be measured by the number of novelists espousing "activ-
    ist attitudes, picaresque plot and looser, more adventurous
    prose." In taking risks, new heroes were created; the real and
    fictional worlds combined to make a statement about "social con-
    ditions and feelings following World War II." The activist

attitude itself is older than Whitman. The most crucial risk
Bellow took was in rescuing the novel from a "crisis in language."

8   HAYES, RICHARD. "Books: Critics' Choice for Christmas."
     Commonweal 87, no. 9 (1 December):308.
          This brief mention of *The Last Gentleman* quotes Stark Young
     in an attempt to describe the novel's pervasive encounter with
     "Southern grace under pressure"--"a dim, sweet echo of bright
     lances broken, if you like foolishly, in some tragic combination
     of chivalry and exhaustion.'"

9   HOFFMAN, FREDERICK J. "Varieties of Fantasy." In *The Art of
     Southern Fiction: A Study of Some Modern Novelists*. Carbon-
     dale and Edwardsville: Southern Illinois University Press;
     London and Amsterdam: Feffer & Simon, pp. 129-37, 186n.
          The Moviegoer and *The Last Gentleman* depend upon fantasy
     and circumstance. In *The Moviegoer*, fantasy is equated with Binx
     Bolling's preoccupation with movies and movie stars. The cine-
     matic world gives Binx the security that he is unable to find in
     the real world. His problem is an inability to bring the seg-
     mented parts of his suspended consciousness into focus. *The
     Moviegoer* can be characterized as a "refurbished Baudelairean
     portrayal of *ennui*, *despair*, and the abyss."
          The Last Gentleman can be characterized as "a picaresque
     novel concerning the adventures of a subtly sincere person who is
     trying to get into exact focus with present circumstance." Will
     Barrett, a "twentieth-century *Candide*," must face many disturbing
     questions: "'Do you believe in God? Do you think God entered
     history? How do you define a gentleman?'" Both of Percy's
     heroes are disturbed by the "chaos and villainy" of the world.
     Each must finally relinquish his fantasy--"good guy" movies or
     old clichés--in order to adjust to the "real" world.

10   KLEIN, MARCUS. "Melted into Air." *Reporter* 36, no. 3
     (9 February):61-62.
          The myth of "the Southern myth" has been important to the
     literary development of the region. Although the loss of this
     myth has been more important than its actuality, the tradition
     has served Southern writers from William Byrd (1674-1744) to
     Ellen Glasgow and Faulkner. Walker Percy appears to be one of
     the last recipients of the Southern myth; however, he is "un-
     guarded and wears the aspect of a man fingering a threadbare myth
     while he looks the other way." In both *The Moviegoer* and *The
     Last Gentleman*, Percy's heroes seek to escape from "the malaise."
     Their search is neither Platonic nor Existential. In both cases,
     the real search is always evaded. God and Reality are talked
     about, but Percy does not strenuously deal with either. *The Last
     Gentleman* is "almost the same novel" as *The Moviegoer*. The de-
     tours of the narrative have caused Bill Barrett to lose defini-
     tion.

11   LEHAN, RICHARD. "The American Novel: A Survey of 1966."
<u>Wisconsin Studies in Contemporary Literature</u> 8 (Summer):
437-49, esp. 439-40.
     Within this review-essay the fact is stressed that often
heroes obtain truth too late to act, and <u>The Last Gentleman</u> is a
case in point. Barrett's situation is the result of a series of
displacements. He is as passive as Malamud's Yakov in <u>The Fixer</u>,
not because he is afraid, but because he is bewildered. The
novel is a "moving study of modern displacement," yet marred by
Percy's unconvincing solution to Barrett's problem.

12   MAXWELL, ROBERT. "Walker Percy's Fancy." <u>Minnesota Review</u> 7,
no. 4:231-37.
     Walker Percy is considered "a true Renaissance Man in this
age of the Electronic Village." A brief biographical sketch reviews Percy's career in medicine and criticism. Maxwell includes
comments on "Symbol as Hermeneutic in Existentialism" (1956),
"Three Existentialist Modes" (1956), "Semiotic and a Theory of
Knowledge" (1957), "Symbol, Consciousness and Intersubjectivity"
(1958), "The Message in the Bottle" (1959), and "Naming and Being" (1960). Percy's cross-over into fiction marked by <u>The
Moviegoer</u> and <u>The Last Gentleman</u> is a sign of "the Renaissance
Man." Kierkegaard's influence sets the tone for both novels.
Yet Percy does more than illustrate "a pantheon of philosophical
distinctions with fictional mobility." He is a gifted novelist
and narrator; his prose style is "fluid, idiomatic, many-leveled,
always personal." His characters are "people who create their
own arguments, their own metaphors, their own interior rhythms,
who may stun and engage us despite ourselves."

13   PENDLETON, DENNIS. "<u>The Last Gentleman</u>." In <u>Masterplots 1967
Annual</u>. Edited by Frank N. Magill. New York: Salem Press,
pp. 184-85.
     Percy's novel seems to end in a way different from the
novel he set out to write, and along the way he provides many
perceptive things to say about the South and what it means to be
a Southerner, but it is finally a book about "the plight of modern man." Percy writes "with élan and with a richness and pre-
cision of language." The main character, Will, is on a search,
but finally the book seems to "slide off into ambiguity." It is
the Vaught family that seems to save Will, but somewhere along
the way the family seems to take over and Percy does not seem
able to intervene. Nevertheless the book is a "compellingly
readable" one.

14   PRICE, R.G.G. "New Novels." <u>Punch</u> (London) 252, no. 6596
(8 February):210.
     Although <u>The Last Gentleman</u> has "some kind of intellectual
structure," the novel's strength is its landscape. What is said
is surpassed by what is seen.

15   SHEED, WILFRID. "Additions to the Galaxy." <u>National Catholic</u>
      <u>Reporter</u> 3 (8 February):7.
         Brief review of <u>The Last Gentleman</u>; Percy must be "very
      nearly our premier prose stylist." With J.F. Powers he shares a
      power of observation "which misses nothing but condemns nothing."

                              <u>1968</u>

1   ATKINS, ANSELM. "Walker Percy and Post-Christian Search."
     <u>Centennial Review</u> 12, no. 1 (Winter):73-95.
        Explores Binx Bolling's search in <u>The Moviegoer</u> by "indi-
     cating the philosophical and theological framework within which
     Binx's search is conceived, and by showing how his search, thus
     understood, explains his actions and attitudes." Atkins attempts
     "to ascertain the nature and mechanics of Binx's search." Each
     search must begin with an "awakening to strangeness." For Binx,
     the initial search began in a Korean ditch. Alienation, "the
     prevalent human condition," is expressed by images of "'malaise,'"
     "'everydayness,'" "'precarious existence,'" and "'anyone any-
     where.'" Each condition represents an obstacle to the search.
     Alienation, according to Percy, can be overcome by "intersub-
     jective communication with another," by "rotation," or by "repe-
     tition." Repetition can be aesthetic, "a vicarious experience
     achieved through identification with a character in a book or
     movie," or existential, "a moment in the personal, passionate,
     serious search." Binx moves through each of these stages before
     arriving at his existential repetition, "the <u>true way out of</u>
     <u>despair</u>." His search, like all searches, is a quest. Percy's
     philosophical essays and Binx's description of himself as amne-
     siac, exile, pilgrim, and castaway work together to define "the
     search." "Traditional values have caved in, leaving chasms of
     meaninglessness in Binx's world, and he refuses to fill them with
     fakes. He is the complete post-Christian." Tracing the progress
     of the archetypal quest in western culture, Atkins proceeds by
     defining the "post-Christian" search. Presupposing nothing, the
     post-Christian search "is content to wait. . . ." There are no
     signs, only "signlessness." "Invincible <u>apathy</u> (or unbelief) is
     the 'only possible starting point' for the post-Christian search."
     Binx Bolling's search is more than a search for identity; he is
     "the beachcomber of <u>The Message in the Bottle</u>." See also 1971.11.

2   CREMEENS, CARLTON. "Walker Percy, the Man and the Novelist:
     An Interview." <u>SoR</u>, n.s. 4, no. 2 (Spring):271-90.
        In creating a portrait of Percy, this interview also con-
     siders "the state of Southern fiction and the state of the lit-
     erary vocation in the South." Percy speaks directly to questions
     concerning his role as a writer. Although he finds any medium--
     novel, article, interview--appropriate for expressing his views
     on "the social issues or the race issue in the South," Percy
     recognizes the need for balance in order that art not "be

overwhelmed by his own predilections." In addition, modern
writers must avoid "the temptation to understand the issues of
the times in terms of sociology, in terms of abstractions." The
question of discrimination is one that Percy hopes will be solved
in the South. His role as a novelist "is to transmit universal
truths . . . so that in the action of communication he experiences a recognition, a feeling that he has been there before, a
shock of recognition." Percy considers his medical training and
knowledge of science essential in a culture "saturated by the
whole scientific ethic." Fiction becomes another means of exploring reality. Percy's exploration of reality was influenced
by Dostoevsky, Sartre, Camus, and Marcel. They share similar
concerns: an interest in the novel's form, the "union of philosophy and literature," and the nature of reality. Therefore, the
short story is not an appropriate form for Percy. His apprentice-
ship in becoming a writer included two unpublished novels. Like
Franz Kafka, Percy believes "All you have to do is wait." And
yet "if you can get the first sentence right, the whole rest of
the book follows that first sentence."

3   DICKEY, JAMES. "The Revolving Bookstand . . . Recommended
     Summer Reading." American Scholar 37, no. 3 (Summer):524.
          This review of The Last Gentleman is also a commentary
     about Walker Percy and his use of language. Percy's power is in
     his creativity, his originality, and his ability to "reflect the
     mysterious quality of amazement that is characteristic of the
     poetic view of the world."

4   FLEISCHER, LEONORE. "Paperbacks: Fiction." PW 193, no. 5
     (29 January):100.
          This notice of the paperback edition of The Last Gentleman
     describes the novel as one young man's journey to find out what
     life is about.

5   HENISEY, SARAH. "Intersubjectivity in Symbolization."
     Renascence 20, no. 4 (Summer):208-14.
          One must understand Percy's "theory of symbolization" in
     order to appreciate what is happening in The Moviegoer. For
     Percy, symbolization is "how one communicates or fails to commu-
     nicate with others." Intersubjectivity can become a cure for
     alienation by providing "one with another unformulable person
     with whom he may hold communion." In The Moviegoer, Jack Bolling
     and Kate Cutrer exemplify this bond of intersubjectivity and the
     themes of alienation and symbolization. Jack, however, recog-
     nizes his problem and his unsuccessful attempts to find a cure.
     By recognizing that "it is a person that he needs, not a thing,"
     Jack realizes that there are no "formulae" in resolving the
     world's absurdity. Together, Jack and Kate make a step toward
     "beginning to be integrated with the world."

6   LEHAN, RICHARD. "The Way Back: Redemption in the Novels of
     Walker Percy." SoR, n.s. 4, no. 2 (Spring):306-19.
        Like those of Faulkner, Percy's novels present an existen-
     tial view--"the confused mind struggling unsuccessfully for final
     answers in an absurd and chaotic situation." Unlike Faulkner,
     Percy is concerned with the problems of everydayness. He endows
     his narrator, or central character, with "a reflective conscious-
     ness"--with this "double consciousness" comes irony, paradox, and
     contradiction. In both the novels and the philosophical essays,
     Percy's alienated characters can achieve peace "through social
     communion." The search, for each of Percy's characters, is a
     search for love in order to return "to the prolapsed world from
     which he escaped with the new-found hope that he can begin to put
     the pieces together." "The 'return' in Percy's novels is always
     for two, never one. . . ." Although Percy achieves a sense of
     alienation and a sense of dislocation appropriate to "'rotation'"
     in The Moviegoer and The Last Gentleman, he does not achieve a
     convincing "'return.'" Perhaps this is because "Percy raises
     problems more complex than his solutions. . . ."

7   PETERSEN, CLARENCE. "Paperbacks: Out of the Draft." BW,
     10 March, p. 11.
        This review of The Last Gentleman views the protagonist as
     a drop-out who drops in. In the process, he begins to learn
     about life.

8   SHEED, WILFRID. "Walker Percy: The Last Gentleman." In The
     Morning After: Selected Essays and Reviews. New York:
     Farrar, Straus & Giroux, pp. 18-21.
        Reprint of 1966.34.

9   THALE, JEROME. "Alienation on the American Plan." Forum H
     (Houston) 6, no. 3 (Summer):36-40.
        In The Moviegoer, Walker Percy is concerned with the expe-
     rience, not the literature, of alienation. His treatment of this
     theme requires a "maximum of fidelity, employing understatement
     rather than intensification." Percy's use of understatement re-
     flects his understanding of the terms of alienation for an Ameri-
     can. The controlling metaphor, "that a man's life can become so
     thin and unreal that the movies provide a more substantial and
     satisfying reality," is presented with little distortion--"moral
     or dramatic." On a superficial level, the novel can be read for
     the sheer delight of Percy's accuracy and fidelity. The despair
     of the characters in The Moviegoer is a reflection of Binx
     Bolling's despair. In that despair, Binx attempts a search "to
     find himself and become engaged with the world around him." His
     relationship with Kate is a positive step. Percy's weaknesses
     are few; his virtues are crucial "because ultimately what he is
     saying is so familiar and fundamental that its success and value
     must lie in the saying."

10   THALE, MARY. "The Moviegoer of the 1950's." <u>Twentieth Cen-</u>
     <u>tury Literature</u> 14, no. 2 (July):84-89.
          This essay compares the impact of Nathanael West's <u>Miss</u>
     <u>Lonelyhearts</u> with Walker Percy's <u>The Moviegoer</u>. Each can be con-
     sidered "a small success, steadily loaned, slightly sold, largely
     ignored in the big pictures of American fiction." Each is an
     important American novel. The parallels that exist include nar-
     rative and thematic considerations. The protagonists of each
     novel are in search of "something which will charge with signifi-
     cance this short life we lead . . . something as meaningful as
     Christ." Percy's theme, "survival in a world paralyzed in
     clichés," is realized because of his use of irony. Binx Bolling's
     life itself is lived in "conscious irony." However, his tone is
     not always ironic. Percy endows Binx with insight and a variety
     of voices that range "from mysticism to clichés to plainest prose
     without producing any incongruity."

11   WHITTINGTON, MARY JAYNE GARRARD. "From the Delta. . . ."
     <u>Delta Review</u> 5, no. 2 (February):30.
          A glimpse of William Alexander Percy's background is pre-
     sented in this piece on Trail Lake Plantation, the model for the
     sharecropping system presented in <u>Lanterns On The Levee</u>. Al-
     though the methods used by Percy and his father have been re-
     placed by "industry, diversification, mechanization--and time,"
     this Plantation represents "a continuity that spans the years and
     the changes." Walker Percy is mentioned, along with his brothers
     Phinizy and LeRoy, as one of William Alexander Percy's adopted
     sons to whom Trail Lake was left.

12   WOLFE, PETER. "Knowing the Noumenon." <u>Prairie Schooner</u> 42,
     no. 2 (Summer):181-85.
          Walker Percy's investigations into "the atoms of human ex-
     perience" in <u>The Moviegoer</u> and <u>The Last Gentleman</u> "place him in
     the French novelistic tradition." Both of Percy's heroes, Binx
     Bolling and Will Barrett, "stand apart from modern social creeds."
     Each seeks to answer questions of self through "complex physical
     and emotional journeys." Percy's use of language can be compared
     to that of Jonson, Swift, and Joyce; his "agile poised style" re-
     inforces his theme.

                                   <u>1969</u>

1   BRADBURY, JOHN M. "Absurd Insurrection: The Barth-Percy
     Affair." <u>SAQ</u> 68, no. 3 (Summer):319-29.
          Because the modern South is "no longer a cultural entity"
     and history now is viewed as little more than a imaginative con-
     struct (particularly in <u>The Sotweed Factor</u>), the characters of
     Barth and Percy inhabit a world which "offers nothing to want and
     they have lost the means of wanting." Equally disaffected are
     the women with whom the protagonists interact. As cures for such

existential despair, psychoanalysis and sex provide momentary
relief only. Despite these thematic similarities, differences
exist in the novelists' works, particularly with regard to
moral orientation. "It is patently futile, even impertinent,
to seek answers or cures in Barth's work. He is essentially a
fabulist. . . ." Although Percy's novels end indeterminately,
they nonetheless contain suggestions of a religious solution to
the modern anomie; and "the cumulative effect suggests the
Catholic existentialism of, say, Gabriel Marcel." Barth and
Percy both depart from their literary progenitors in that their
"new Southern world is a tragicomic absurdity."

2   DABBS, JAMES McBRIDE. "Walker Percy." In Civil Rights in
    Recent Southern Fiction. Atlanta, Ga.: Southern Regional
    Council, pp. 65-73.
       The Moviegoer and The Last Gentleman are examined for their
    commentary on the civil rights movement. Although Percy does not
    make race relations a central issue, his insights about life in
    the South demonstrate the deleterious effects of segregation.
    The protagonists' recognition of role-playing, or knowing one's
    place, leads to understanding about both the South's emphasis on
    physical place and the spiritual abyss which such emphasis
    obscures.

3   DOUGLAS, ELLEN. Walker Percy's "The Last Gentleman": Intro-
    duction and Commentary. Religious Dimensions in Literature,
    Seabury Reading Program. New York: Seabury Press, pp. 5-28.
       Presented are a short biographical sketch of Percy, an
    analytical summary of the novel, and a discussion of its major
    themes. The gentlemanly coda, of which Will Barrett is the last
    personification, is delineated in depth in William Alexander
    Percy's Lanterns on the Levee. Percy's ancestry and his debili-
    tating bout with tuberculosis suggest parallels between the lives
    of the author and his protagonist. The book itself primarily de-
    tails Will's meeting with the Vaught family and his subsequent
    "lunatic adventures and encounters with the denizens of the mod-
    ern wilderness." Will's return to the South reveals to him "that
    his father's world is dead." With that realization he attaches
    himself to Sutter, who indicates that neither the transcendence
    of science nor the immanence of sexual union provides viable
    modes of being in the world. Sutter himself fails to see that
    Will is above all, "a good man . . . in [whom] manners are truly
    morals." The improbability of Will's love for the insubstantial
    Kitty mars the book. The major themes of the novel are framed as
    philosophical questions, such as that of transcendence versus
    immanence, alienation, and Kierkegaardian stages of existence.
    Percy's method is to provide no answers, but rather to force the
    reader "to hold the mirror up to his face, and confront his own
    desolation and despair, and perhaps thereafter begin to look for
    some new answers."

4   LAWSON, LEWIS A. "Kierkegaard and the Modern American Novel."
    In Essays in Memory of Christine Burleson. Edited by Thomas
    G. Burton. Johnson City: Research Advisory Council, East
    Tennessee State University, pp. 111-25, esp. 124-25.
        Noted are the existential progressions of Binx Bolling and
    Will Barrett as examples of Percy's use of "the strategies of
    Kierkegaard."

5   _____. "Walker Percy's Indirect Communications." Texas
    Studies in Literature and Language 11, no. 1 (Spring):867-900.
        Percy employs two fictional strategies derived from
    Kierkegaard: that of portraying his characters as progressing in
    existential modes and that of communicating theological concepts
    indirectly. The novels, in fact, can be read as Percy's own in-
    direct communication of concepts made explicit in his essays.
    For example, "a very helpful introduction" to The Moviegoer is
    his essay "The Coming Crisis in Psychiatry." There Percy ex-
    presses his concern that psychiatry has failed either to realize
    that anxiety may issue from the state of modern culture rather
    than from the individual or to address man's need for transcen-
    dence. Illustrative is Binx's malaise, which deepens as he be-
    comes increasingly successful in worldly pursuits. Binx's search
    for transcendent values begins to fructify when he rejects the
    salve of rotation afforded by the movies and accepts "repetition,
    the quest returning to the past," thus exemplifying concepts
    developed in "The Man on the Train." Percy further personifies
    these interior states in his characterization of Will Barrett.
    Will's friendship with the Vaught family precipitates a return
    to the South, an opportunity for a type of repetition that will
    shed light on his condition. "The only trouble is that in his
    new objective empirical paradise, his anxiety, amnesia, and dis-
    location become increasingly worse." In his despair, he turns
    to Sutter, who had indirectly communicated to Will the need for
    authentic selfhood.

                                1970

1   BERGEN, DANIEL P. "In Fear of Abstraction: The Southern
    Response to the North in Twentieth-Century Fiction and Non-
    Fiction." Ph.D. dissertation, University of Minnesota.
        Organized around the idea that the "concrete" view of
    reality which prevails in the South, as contrasted to the ab-
    stract view of the North, is evident in the Southern response to
    the North. The Southerner, in both fiction and non-fictional
    autobiographies, who receives the world concretely, is dislocated
    when he encounters the human and physical environment of the
    North. This study of ten writers of fiction and nine writers of
    nonfiction, documents a definite fear of abstraction. In fic-
    tion, such as Percy's, the outcome of the Southern encounter with
    the North is dislocation epistemologically.

2   LAWSON, LEWIS A., ed. Introduction to <u>Kierkegaard's Presence</u>
    <u>in Contemporary American Life: Essays from Various Disci-</u>
    <u>plines</u>. Metuchen, N.J.: Scarecrow Press, p. xvi.
        <u>The Moviegoer</u> and <u>The Last Gentleman</u> are mentioned in the
    introduction as being among "the most recent novels to display a
    use of Kierkegaard."

3   LAWSON, LEWIS A. "Walker Percy's Southern Stoic." <u>SLJ</u> 3,
    no. 1 (Fall):5-31.
        The classical stoicism which molded the thought and fash-
    ioned the life of William Alexander Percy resounds in both his
    poetry and his autobiography, <u>Lanterns on the Levee</u>. Central to
    his vision is "the Aurelian conviction that the self is the only
    kingdom known to human existence which has the possiblity of both
    freedom and control." Walker Percy acknowledges the virtues of
    the Stoic view but rejects it for the greater optimism of
    Christianity. This dichotomous attitude of admiration for, but
    renunciation of, stoicism is manifested also in the relationships
    of Percy's protagonists to their father figures. In <u>The Movie-</u>
    <u>goer</u> tension exists between Aunt Emily and Binx because he cannot
    accept her ethical but fatalistic world view. Will Barrett re-
    creates through memory the stoic adjuration of his suicidal
    father and realizes the futility of such pessimism. As alterna-
    tives, the characters choose the Kierkegaardian modes of rotation
    and repetition as strategies for finding a spiritual solution to
    their sense of alienation.

4   LUSCHEI, MARTIN LOUIS. "The Sovereign Wayfarer: Walker
    Percy's Diagnosis of the Malaise." Ph.D. dissertation,
    University of New Mexico.
        Percy's novels illustrate a dialectic between four forms of
    confinement--everydayness, inauthenticity, abstraction, and a
    condition as wayfarer--and four forms of recovery--ordeal, rota-
    tion, repetition, and intersubjectivity. From this dialectic
    evolves Percy's synthesis in which man becomes "a sovereign
    wayfarer, a co-celebrant of being." Percy has gleaned his
    philosophical perspective from reading the works of Kierkegaard
    and Marcel. See also 1972.13.

5   VAN CLEAVE, JIM. "Versions of Percy." <u>SoR</u> 6, no. 3 (Summer-
    Autumn):990-1010.
        In the "Southern idealism" represented by Aunt Emily and,
    indirectly, in Binx's existential response to such idealism, <u>The</u>
    <u>Moviegoer</u> bears a strong relation to William Alexander Percy's
    <u>Lanterns on the Levee</u>. In his book Will Percy viewed his life
    as a pilgrimage directed toward a specific ideal: going to col-
    lege, enjoying a <u>Wanderjahr</u>, and serving in wartime were phases
    in becoming a Southern aristocrat like his ancestors. For Binx
    such experiences only serve to increase his sense of wonder about
    his unique selfhood. Binx is well able to assume roles but only
    with the added consciousness that, in doing so, he is

impersonating a self. His heightened consciousness contributes to the lack of communication between Emily and himself, and "the real test of impersonation in The Moviegoer is always communication." Therefore, Binx's consciousness is "ultimately a more potent ordering force even than Emily's willed idealism" because it makes possible the empathy which Binx extends towards Kate.

6   WATKINS, FLOYD C. "The White." In The Death of Art: Black and White in the Recent Southern Novel. Mercer University Lamar Memorial Lectures, no. 13. Athens: University of Georgia Press, pp. 28, 37-38, 47, 58-59.

In The Last Gentleman, as in several other novels considered, there are "no bad Negroes." Percy's problem with the race question is that he makes too many generalizations. His contention that Southern white men do not know Negroes as well as they believe parallels his own lack of knowledge of the Southern mind.

7   WEINBERG, HELEN A. "Minor Novelists in the Activist Mode." In The New Novel in America: The Kafkan Mode in Contemporary Fiction. Ithaca: Cornell University Press, pp. x, 182-83.

Binx Bolling exemplifies the hero as "spiritual activist" in search of a transcendent self, "but he never moves beyond the brink of despair. . . ."

1971

1   ANDERSON, DAVID C. "Mr. Percy's Positive Statement." Wall Street Journal, 17 May, p. 12.

Percy's "attempts at satire sometimes look crude," but he has nonetheless examined the nation's anomie with his usual "insight and compassion."

2   ANON. "Lapsed from Grace." TLS (1 October), p. 1165.

Though the writing, particularly in the descriptive passages, is powerful, Love in the Ruins is of interest more for its omissions than for its satirical targets. Percy fails to investigate the etiology of man's psychic distress or to discover the realities behind American political upheaval.

3   ANON. "1971: A Selection of Noteworthy Titles." NYTBR, 5 December, p. 83.

Review of Love in the Ruins: "Love is a stay against anarchy in this ironic novel set in the future . . . which disconcertingly resembles Now."

4   ANON. Review of Love in the Ruins. American Libraries 2 (July):762.

This note designates the novel as "a tragicomic view of life in the 1980's."

5   ANON. Review of <u>Love in the Ruins</u>. <u>AR</u> 31 (Summer):283.
     This brief review assesses the novel as "a marvelously
funny and satirical science fiction Christian allegory."

6   ANON. Review of <u>Love in the Ruins</u>. <u>Booklist</u> 67 (1 July):895.
     ". . . A satire on pseudoprofound novels and a sardonic
commentary on the bogging down of religion, culture, and inter-
racial, intergroup, and interpersonal relationships in the not-
too-distant future." Mentions <u>The Last Gentleman</u> as "more
straightforward."

7   ANON. Review of <u>Love in the Ruins</u>. <u>Choice</u> 8 (October):1018.
     This commentary finds <u>Love in the Ruins</u> to be a "beauti-
fully comic and humane work" in which "Percy's style shows mastery of language." The reviewer also remarks that the publication of this work establishes Percy as "an incisive critic of our
age."

8   ANON. Review of <u>Love in the Ruins</u>. <u>Kirkus</u> 39 (15 March):319.
     This brief review assesses the novel as "a fanciful, sug-
gestible, strafingly comic view of man. . . ."

9   ANON. Review of <u>Love in the Ruins</u>. <u>PW</u> 199 (29 March):44.
     <u>Love in the Ruins</u> "is both a high comedy in which all the
ridiculous tensions of our current way of life are brilliantly
satirized, and a joyful shout of praise for man's ability to
survive against all odds."

10 ANON. Review of <u>Love in the Ruins</u>. <u>VQR</u> 47, no. 3 (Summer):
     R96.
     Brief, favorable review.

11 ATKINS, GEORGE TYNG ANSELM, Jr. "Freedom, Fate, Myth, and
     Other Theological Issues in Some Contemporary Literature."
     Ph.D. dissertation, Emory University.
     Consists of five separate essays and a methodological in-
troduction. Religion is a dimension in western literature, often
as profound as the theologian's tradition. The "situation,
horizon, or subjective stance" of an interpreter, however, is
significant. Northrop Frye, Paul Ricoeur, Saul Bellow, Camus,
and Percy are studied. <u>The Moviegoer</u> must be analyzed in the
light of Kierkegaardian and Heideggerian concepts; Binx's moviegoing is not an escape, but one of the ways he conducts his
"'horizontal search.'" See also 1968.1.

12 AVANT, JOHN ALFRED. Review of <u>Love in the Ruins</u>. LJ 96
     (15 May):1728.
     This short critique finds that "at first Percy's style
seems as beautifully controlled as ever, musical and poetic and
delicately nuanced; but the whimsical content ultimately over-
whelms the writing, which inevitably falls apart."

13   BROYARD, ANATOLE. "Apocalypses and Other Ills." New York
      Times, 15 May, p. 29.
      Avoiding the futuristic novelist's trap of turning a char-
acter into a walking billboard of ideas, Walker Percy makes Tom
More "almost redundantly human," with the result that More "is a
charming fellow, an appealing tragicomedian. . . ." Although its
distopian plot is rather shopworn, the novel is "far less preachy
than 1984 or Brave New World [and] much funnier too." The underlying message of the novel seems to be that democracy has gone
awry because of "a knuckling under to soulless pragmatism, a belief that everything is measurable--and manipulable."

14   BRYANT, JERRY H. The Open Decision: The Contemporary
      American Novel and Its Background. New York: Free Press,
      pp. 273-77.
      The Moviegoer, like numerous other contemporary American
novels, deals with the existential issues of freedom and consciousness. The novel's protagonist, Binx Bolling, experiences
the exile but also the freedom of one who escapes "everydayness"
into a search for heightened consciousness. Among "the instru-
ments of consciousness" available to Binx are movies, which focus
one's attention upon the unique inherent within the everyday.
Binx never fully explores his search, but instead effects a compromise by abandoning his exile for the community he finds in
responsibilities toward others.

15   BUNTING, CHARLES T. "An Afternoon with Walker Percy." NMW 4,
      no. 2 (Fall):43-61.
      In a wide-ranging interview, Percy responds to questions
about his philosophical viewpoints, themes, characters, and approaches to novel writing. He acknowledges that the "deeper
themes of [his] novels are religious" and that the principal
difficulty in conveying religious concepts lies in the language
of faith being overworked and, therefore, rendered banal. He
agrees with Flannery O'Connor's view that the religious novelist
has to convey his message obliquely. He acknowledges the importance of Sartre's influence on his thinking and writing, but
feels that ultimately Sartre's "own vocation contradicts his
philosophy." Percy agrees that it was difficult to make credible
the point of view of his disturbed protagonists. Additionally,
he remarks that he deliberately placed Love in the Ruins in the
Western tradition through allusions to Faust and Don Giovanni "as
a counter-attack against certain Orientalizing and other influences." He replies to a question about the "spiritual odysseys"
of his protagonists by indicating that his novels satirize a
quest for self qua self. Percy agrees with Kierkegaard that the
only legitimate quest is the one for God, citing an observation
of Kierkegaard's to the effect that "the only way the self can
become self is by becoming itself transparently before God."
Percy places his novel-writing in the European rather than American tradition, adding that "I guess the only American novelist
who influenced me would be Mark Twain--Huckleberry Finn."

16   CARR, JOHN. "An Interview with Walker Percy." <u>GaR</u> 25, no. 3
     (Fall):317-32.
        Percy reflects on his philosophy and on his writing. He
     contrasts the "rather dark view which is based on stoicism,
     Greco-Roman Stoicism" of William Alexander Percy with his own
     Catholic view. He sketches the steps that he took in his con-
     version to Catholicism, including his disillusionment with the
     behavioristic model of psychology and mechanistic approach to
     medicine stressed in his student days. Percy also registers his
     disapproval of thesis novels, indicating that his approach is to
     "put a man in a certain situation and see what happens." In dis-
     cussing his status as a Roman Catholic novelist, he says: "I
     think my writings reflect a certain basic orientation toward,
     although they're not really controlled by, Catholic dogma." Re-
     garding his first two protagonists, Percy mentions that they both
     go to the desert as part of their search. He also acknowledges
     the Kierkegaardian dimensions of his first two novels, revealing
     that Binx leaps from the aesthetic mode in which he was existing
     to the religious, bypassing the ethical entirely; whereas Will
     Barrett had dismissed a religious solution to his dilemma and
     missed the implications of Jamie's baptism. Percy admits that,
     despite his intention, most readers do not see Binx's religious
     conversion in <u>The Moviegoer</u>. On the absence of explicit sexual
     description in his novels, Percy responds that he finds it un-
     necessary to include it in his novels, preferring to indicate
     that sex "is a symbol of failure on the existential level." On
     the subject of Southern writing per se, Percy observes, "I think
     that the day of regional Southern writing is all gone." He ad-
     mits, though, that the South is still sufficiently differentiated
     from other national regions by its religious fundamentalism and
     its experience with the Negro. Finally, he indicates that his
     novels lack strong women characters because he writes "about
     women from the exclusive point of view of the hero or anti-hero.
     As such, the view of women or anyone else may be limited by the
     narrowness of the vision." Reprinted: 1972.5.

17   CARTER, PHILIP D. "Oh, You Know Uncle Walker." <u>WP</u>, 17 June,
     pp. C1, C4.
        Discussed are Percy's relationship to the community of
     Covington, Louisiana, where he resides, and his family background
     and literary roots in Greenville, Mississippi. Included are some
     observations on Percy's philosophy and personality and some com-
     ments made by Percy during an interview.

18   CASS, MICHAEL McCONNELL. "Stages on the South's Way: Walker
     Percy's <u>The Moviegoer</u> and <u>The Last Gentleman</u>." Ph.D. disser-
     tation, Emory University.
        The forces of Southern tradition resist but do not amelio-
     rate the societal changes breeding the anxiety of Percy's pro-
     tagonists. Indeed, such tradition both complicates and exacer-
     bates the heroes' existential despair. In place of Southern

tradition and its popular alternative, secular humanism, Percy proffers the salve of Christian hope and love.

19   CATINELLA, JOSEPH. Review of Love in the Ruins. SatR 54 (15 May):42-43.
         The reviewer assesses the novel as "a beauty--a stunning satire conceived with mock-heroic intensity, peopled by absurd but recognizable human beings, and written with a gusto that makes most doomsday books look like effete comic strips."

20   COOK, BRUCE. "To Walker Percy, Man's Prognosis Is Funny." National Observer, 24 May, p. 17.
         In addition to a review of the novel, this article contains commentary about Percy's background and personality and also remarks made by Percy during an interview. The writer assesses Love in the Ruins as "one of those novels with something to offend everybody" and "Percy's finest work to date." Percy indicates that he views his approach to writing as "diagnostic and therapeutic" and attributes "the strong moralistic strain in [his] writing" to his medical training.

21   CORMIER, ROBERT. Review of Love in the Ruins. Sign 51, no. 2 (September):48-49.
         The novel is "exhilarating and widely comic," and while it deals with, among other things, factions in the Catholic Church, it is not a "Catholic novel." It is instead about the condition of man, and Percy's protagonist is, while flawed, concerned with repairing his fellow man.

22   DAVENPORT, GUY. "Mr. Percy's Look at Chaos, 1983." Life 70 (21 May):16.
         The reviewer assesses Love in the Ruins as being at once "a very funny book because it wets down so much solemnity and lets the gas out of so much arrogance [and] a very sad book: its prophecy is constructed of our worst fears."

23   DEUTSCH, ALFRED. Review of Love in the Ruins. Sisters Today 43 (August-September):57-58.
         Suggests that Love in the Ruins could be approached as "a fictional explication" of Yeats's "The Second Coming." The novel suggests that "the center did not hold." Possibly Thomas More represents the "best" who "'lack all conviction.'" A strong feature of the novel is Percy's resistance "to rush into apocalyptic frenzy," but the pace is such that if Percy is frightened, he frightens no one else.

24   DUFFY, MARTHA. "Lapsometer Legend." Time 97 (17 May):94.
         This two-part article contains a review of Percy's third novel followed by a brief biographical sketch. The review finds Love in the Ruins to be "a rather abrupt departure from the past [novels]" and a satire with "something to offend just about

everyone." But it is shored by "a rueful equanimity and a lin-
gering hope." The brief biography gives glimpses of Percy's up-
bringing, personality, and unusual publication history. Particularly noted is Percy's observation that "for the first time in
150 years, the South is back in the Union and can help to save
it."

25   FIELDING, GABRIEL. Review of Love in the Ruins. Critic 30,
     no. 1 (September/October):69-72.
         The action is too cumbersome "for the good of Mr. Percy's
     plot or comic art" and there is a "plethora of in jokes and
     alliterative cracks at the Faith as she is instituted." In
     essence, Love in the Ruins is "the film [Binx Bolling of The
     Moviegoer] was watching: a composite glued together from frag-
     ments swept from the cutting room floors of heyday Hollywood."

26   HILL, WILLIAM B., S.J. Review of Love in the Ruins. America
     124 (22 May):548.
         This note finds the book "has practically none of the
     faults that are usually found in novels about the future."

27   HORNER, ANTONY. Review of Love in the Ruins. Books and
     Bookmen 17 (November):45.
         Commends "the skilful turn of phrase that Mr. Percy brings
     to his story [and] the mordant humour with which the work is
     liberally spiced."

28   JANEWAY, ELIZABETH. "The End of the World Is Coming."
     Atlantic 228 (August):87-90.
         Although apocalyptic and utopian writing has long been
     generic to the Western mind, the anti-Utopian novel with its
     message that the long-awaited Messiah either loses or falsifies
     is "more specifically a product of our time." Love in the Ruins
     falls within the latter genre as do two other novels published
     around the same time, Marge Piercy's Dance the Eagle to Sleep and
     Doris Lessing's Briefing for a Descent into Hell. Of the three,
     Love in the Ruins is the best, "largely because it breaks many of
     the new rules [of the genre] and holds to some of the old. . . .
     Unlike most anti-Utopias, this is a charming and funny book.
     Present blurs into future, the familiar into revolutionary but
     plausible change. Percy's fantasy is disciplined, and when he
     deals in horror, he eschews it entirely. The horror in More's
     life is convincing because it is familiar."

29   KAZIN, ALFRED. "The Pilgrimage of Percy Walker." Harper's
     242 (June):81-86.
         The Moviegoer marks a departure from the influence of
     Faulkner on Southern fiction because it demonstrates that "the
     South at last had its own worldliness to satirize." Although
     Southerners used to consider themselves outside the mainstream
     of American life, "Binx shows, in every passage of his involve-
     ment with the sophisticated upper middle class of New Orleans,

it is the South itself that today makes outsiders of its people,
breeds a despair that will never know it is despair." Additionally, strong similarities are apparent between the novelist,
"a seeker who after being ejected from the expected and conventional order of things has come to himself as a stranger in the
world" and each protagonist of the first three novels. Ultimately, the contrast "of the 'regular' American world that can
never understand the panic it breeds and [of] the self training
itself to face despair, to become a microscopist of salvation,
[is what] gives The Moviegoer its special wry charm." See
1973.16.

30   KILEY, JOHN. "Something Else." Triumph 6 (December):32-35.
        The style of Love in the Ruins is successful, but its view
of a world so fragmented seems out of touch with reality. The
book is both a "Catholic novel" and also "something else on the
metaphysical level" because it is so concerned, as is its Dr.
More, with abstraction. The novel itself spends too much time
with "lapsometer-foolishness" when things within it bid the hero
go higher. Nevertheless, the book succeeds in its "inspired
inventiveness."

31   McGUANE, THOMAS. Review of Love in the Ruins. NYTBR, 23 May,
        pp. 7, 37.
        Thoughtful commentary on Percy's earlier books and Love in
the Ruins. Percy has provided a fictional vision of the culture's
"potential fragmentation." Percy's most interesting accomplishment "is his delineation of a comedy of love against a field of
anarchy." While he "seems unwilling to stray from certain ortho-
dox principles," he exhibits a "considerable eloquence."

32   McPHERSON, WILLIAM. "The Greening and the Crumbling." WP,
        17 June, pp. C1, C6.
        Deems the "third novel by the Dostoyevsky of the bayou" as
"important" and not to be missed.

33   MARSH, PAMELA. "Tomorrow the World Ends." CSM, 3 June, p. 10.
        This review of Love in the Ruins finds a "chilling" scien-
tific detachment in Percy's treatment of his characters and deems
it difficult "to care whether or not [Tom More] and the suburban
community of Paradise survive the crack-up of civilization their
author threatens them with." Much of the review consists of
Percy's own commentary on the novel, made during a press confer-
ence in New York.

34   MORSE, J. MITCHELL. "Fiction Chronicle." HudR 24 (Fall):
        526-40, esp. 531-33.
        The form of Love in the Ruins "doesn't work"; the Caucasian
and Catholic chauvinism is untenable, and the "quality of Percy's
prose has suffered."

35   MURRAY, ALBERT. <u>South to a Very Old Place</u>. New York:
      McGraw-Hill, pp. 197-209.
          A black author relates his personal reactions to meeting
      Percy. The latter's genial hospitality is typical of the good
      manners of the "reconstructed southerner" in contrast to the con-
      descension of "the all too sympathetic northern do-gooder." Al-
      though following in the literary tradition of William Alexander
      Percy, "a paternalistic old delta plantation racist to the end
      of his days," the younger Percy reveals an enlightened attitude
      toward blacks. Additionally, the "mutual acknowledgment of a
      downhome angle of vision and sensibility" which Percy shares with
      the writer is genuine and unforced. In their discussion of
      southern fiction both authors agree on the necessity of not being
      "overwhelmed by [Faulkner]," but rather "to profit from his
      achievement. . . ."

36   MURRAY, MICHELE. "Bad Catholic Stars in Crazy Plot."
      <u>National Catholic Reporter</u> 7 (27 August):7.
          Percy's "mature, skeptical, Catholic" landscape of mind
      fits together to shape a unified comic vision; his heroes search
      not for absolutes, but for a part of reality in which they can
      live. Dr. Tom More of <u>Love in the Ruins</u> is on such a quest, but
      his problem is acute. Finally Percy seems to imply that the
      price of being human is to struggle. The novel is successful,
      not because of its limited and sane picture of man, but because
      it is a work of art created by a man who cares for the imperfect.

37   PERCY, WALKER. "Authors That Bloom in the Spring: Excerpts
      from Press Conference." <u>PW</u> 199 (22 March):23-24.
          Recorded are some of Percy's remarks in reference to his
      forthcoming novel, <u>Love in the Ruins</u>. Noting that the violence
      in America, a pervasive concern of the book, had abated somewhat,
      he observes ". . . my book could be described as entertainment
      for Americans who are thinking things over in a period of eerie
      tranquility."

38   PETTINGELL, PHOEBE. "Walker Percy's Sci-Fi Detour." <u>NL</u> 54,
      no. 10 (17 May):11-12.
          <u>Love in the Ruins</u> contains themes and characters familiar
      to readers of Percy's fiction, but they are presented with less
      force and control than in the previous works. The science fic-
      tion form and the comedy are further detractions.

39   PRESCOTT, PETER S. Review of <u>Love in the Ruins</u>. <u>NW</u> 77
      (17 May):106-7.
          Percy is described as "an amiable prophet, an evenhanded
      satirist and a charming writer," whose third novel is marked by
      "an elegant wit, a delicate refusal of solemnity, [and] a disci-
      plined guilelessness that inhibits him from winding issues to
      the sticking point."

40   _____. "The Year in Books: A Personal Report." <u>NW</u> 78
        (27 December):60.
            Citing <u>Love in the Ruins</u> as one of the year's notable
        books, the reviewer observes that "as always, Percy writes about
        neurosis and existential terror in an amiably satirical tone."

41   PRITCHETT, V.S. "Clowns." <u>NYRB</u> 16 (1 July):15.
            This critique on <u>Love in the Ruins</u> is coupled with one on
        Jerzy Kosinski's <u>Being There</u>. Tom More is seen as a clown, a
        wise fool who perceives the madness inherent in the seemingly
        sane world. Although Percy is "a spirited and inventive writer
        [who has] a charred hell-fire edge to his observations," ulti-
        mately one wonders what "as a novelist, [he] wants us to do."

42   RULE, PHILIP C. Review of <u>Love in the Ruins</u>. <u>America</u> 124
        (12 June):617.
            Though crediting the novel with "some very funny moments,"
        the reviewer finds that "there is no plot and the futuristic
        setting adds little."

43   SHEED, WILFRID. "The Good Word: <u>Walker Percy Redivivus</u>."
        <u>NYTBR</u>, 4 July, p. 2.
            While approving of <u>Love in the Ruins</u>, Sheed suggests that
        Percy's satire treads the line which Muggeridge, Waugh, and
        Huxley found difficult when affirmation is made. As Catholic and
        Southerner, Percy labors under two stereotypes, "impossible odds,"
        but he nevertheless has written a novel which handles its symbols
        well. The hero's Catholicism is "pagan, carnal, incarnate," and
        as a reflection of current Catholicism "in its current dither,"
        More's characterization is a success. Percy's portrayal of
        Southerness through his picture of the Bantus is rather more
        complex. Reprinted: 1978.26. See also 1972.18.

44   SHEPHERD, ALLEN. "Percy's <u>The Moviegoer</u> and Warren's <u>All the
        King's Men</u>." <u>NMW</u> 4, no. 1 (Spring):2-14.
            Both Walker Percy's <u>The Moviegoer</u> and Robert Penn Warren's
        <u>All the King's Men</u> "offer brilliant and deeply felt analyses of
        two men poised on the brink of the abyss." But despite similari-
        ties to Percy's novel, <u>All the King's Men</u> is the more substantive
        work. It is structured in "a solid and various base in the po-
        litical operations of Governor Stark," whereas <u>The Moviegoer</u> is
        marred by repetitive scenes and vignettes. Percy, on the other
        hand, is more skillful in handling the "split or double conscious-
        ness," which both protagonists possess.

45   SISSMAN, L.E. "Inventions." <u>NY</u> (11 September):121-24.
            Though written by "a distinguished novelist with a sense of
        humor and a sense of style," <u>Love in the Ruins</u> is seriously
        flawed. Tom More is unconvincing as a first-person narrator;
        for, despite his grave instability, the tone of the book is "con-
        trolled, sardonic, flat, flip, smartass, and totally incongruent

to the character. . . ." Also, as a novel of the futuristic, or
anti-Utopian, genre Love in the Ruins "fails . . . to bring the
immediate future to life. . . . But the most serious fault in
Love in the Ruins is that it does not take its own characters
seriously enough." In all, the book conveys a "suspicious sour-
ness" which suggests perhaps that "Walker Percy has given up on
man as a fit subject for rehabilitation [and instead is] baiting
and mocking man, in an affirmation of faith, to the greater glory
of God."

46   SMITH, JULIAN. "Elegant Paranoia." CC 88 (7 July):835.
          A short critique which deems Love in the Ruins "very funny,
terrifying, and ultimately a symbol for our times." Additionally,
the reviewer designates Tom More as "probably the most significant Catholic hero since Waugh's Guy Crouchback--and just as
tired, middle-aged, wifeless, childless, conservative, and de-
serving of a happy ending."

47   TANNER, TONY. "Interior Spaciousness--Car, Bell Jar, Tunnel
          and House." In City of Words: American Fiction, 1950-1970.
          New York: Harper & Row, pp. 260-62.
          Will Barrett's need to create for himself an "interior
spaciousness," a sense of "being in the world without being of
it," reflects a mindset both of contemporary American novelists
and of their protagonists. Percy's particular delineation "of
the classic dilemma of the American hero in his relations to
society" is to suggest "indirectly that a man may exist between
transcendence and immanence as a 'wayfarer'. . . ."

48   TAYLOR, MARK. Review of Love in the Ruins. Commonweal 95
          (29 October):118-19.
          While the reviewer registers "petty complaints" that the
novel's satire sometimes degenerates into lampoon and that More's
girlfriends are scarcely distinguishable in their characterizations, he mainly lauds Love in the Ruins as "a remarkable anatomy
of our times," in which Percy reveals human behavior "with the
vigor and delight of the accomplished satirist."

49   THEROUX, PAUL. "Christian Science-Fiction." BW, 16 May, p. 4.
          Mixed review deems the observations of the novel as per-
ceptive but weighted down by overdrawn characterizations and a
contrived plot.

50   VAN BRUNT, H.L. "The Headiest, Happiest Holiday Gifts:
          Books." SatR 54 (27 November):46.
          Included in a compilation of good gift selections, Love in
the Ruins is characterized as "a guided tour through the chaos of
a future United States where everything comes together and falls
apart--by one of the better Virgils around."

51   VAUTHIER, SIMONE. "Le temps et la mort dans The Moviegoer."
     RANAM 4, no. 4:98-115.
        Presents a careful examination of the role of "time" and
     "death" in The Moviegoer. The novel itself is framed by time and
     death; it opens with Binx Bolling's recollection of his older
     brother's death and closes with the imminent death of his younger
     half-brother. In between, Binx is subconsciously consumed by the
     death of his father. Contrasting life and death and the past
     with the present, Percy creates a portrait of modern man's
     alienation. From theme to specific images, there is the constant
     juxtaposition of contrasting elements. As a result, Binx is in
     a state of despair. In his effort to manipulate time, by "rota-
     tion" and "repetition," Binx hopes to find the right questions to
     ask. His marriage to Kate is by no means a solution nor the end
     of his search. By confronting the reality of death, a theme
     often considered "'un-American,'" Percy has created "the most
     modern and the most American" of heroes.

52   YARDLEY, JONATHAN. "Stethoscope of the Spirit." NewR 164
     (22 May):25-26.
        Percy's third novel confirms that "there is not a better
     comic writer around" and indicates an "orderly progression" in
     theme and character. His protagonists are of a type: "out of
     sorts with modernity, wry traditionalists flailing against tech-
     nocratic society. . . . In all three is an ultimate accommoda-
     tion, an acceptance of pain in its various modern forms balanced,
     or made possible, by a discovery of love." Yet though similar,
     each novel is distinctive. "Love in the Ruins is his most im-
     mediately political novel, and indeed can be read purely as po-
     litical satire." The novel is not "fashionable," and its final
     note of affirmation may even be viewed as "sentimental." Its
     view is that of a "conservative," in the sense of one "who per-
     ceives society's assets and possibilities, wants them preserved
     and developed, but values the past and offers no easy or rigid
     answers."

                              1972

1   ANON. Review of Love in the Ruins. PW 201 (27 March):80.
        "Half-funny, half-doomsday, and might even be interpreted
     by some as a kind of blue-sky love story."

*2   BROBERG, JAN. "Walker Percy--En udda amerikan." Studiekam-
     raten 54:119-20.
        Source: 1973 MLA International Bibliography, entry 10580.

3   BUCKLEY, WILLIAM F., Jr. Firing Line: The Southern Imagina-
     tion. Columbia, S.C.: Southern Educational Communications
     Association, 13 pp.
        A transcript of the Firing Line program originally telecast
     on PBC, 24 December 1972. To a query about what advantages

living in the South offers a writer, Percy responds that one
advantage is "of a perspective so that you are in a subculture
in one sense, and in another sense you are able to look at the
main culture from outside." Further clarifying the distinction
of the South from the rest of the country, Percy remarks that
"perhaps it is still possible to characterize the South as having
a tradition which is more oriented toward history, toward the
family, . . . toward storytelling, and toward tragedy." Percy
explains that around 1920 Northern and Southern culture began to
merge. As a consequence, the literature of the South stopped
being primarily romantic or defensive and became more universal
so that the region "made itself understood to people from other
parts of the country." He further indicates that "the two cul-
tures have merged so that the South is more or less like the rest
of the country." In response to a question about why writers
remained in the South when racial segregation was de jure, both
Percy and Welty indicate that they are concerned with analyzing
the complexities of the human condition rather than publishing
social tracts. On the dangers of the cultural merging of diverse
regions, Percy cites one in particular, homogenization, and
states that "the task of a novelist . . . is somehow to humanize
the new American culture." He says that one of the most positive
effects of the American cultural fusion is "the South is no
longer defensive [about racism]." To a remark about the South's
loss of the Civil War as a sort of fortunate fall, Percy responds
that in Love in the Ruins he hoped to show "that the reconciliation [of the nation] would take place in the South and extend to
the black-white reconciliation, liberal-conservative. This was
a hope and it would certainly be poetic justice if this would
happen." Additionally, he differentiates his approach to novel-
writing from that of Welty, saying that he thinks and writes as
a scientist. Reprinted: 1973.9.

4   BYRD, SCOTT. "Mysteries and Movies: Walker Percy's College
     Articles and The Moviegoer." MissQ 25, no. 2 (Spring):165-81.
          Percy's college articles in Carolina Magazine reveal his
youthful attitudes toward art and popular culture, attitudes
which are developed more fully in The Moviegoer. An essay entitled "The Willard Huntington Wright Murder Case" chronicles
Wright's rebirth, after a nervous breakdown, as the mystery
writer S.S. Van Dine. Although Percy credits Van Dine with im-
proving the genre of detective fiction, he also accuses the author
of undermining his artistic talent by abandoning his more serious
writing. Through the associations of mystery novel reading with
Binx's father and Kate, Percy indicates his concern that the
genre can increase one's sense of alienation, an idea he expands
in "The Man on the Train." "The Movie Magazine: A Low Slick,"
Percy's second long article, "offers a clear presentation of
movie stars as images, rather than actors, and also an assertion
of the generally low cultural level of movie fans, both of which
anticipate the treatment of such matters in The Moviegoer."

5   CARR, JOHN, ed. "Rotation and Repetition." In <u>Kite-Flying</u>
     <u>and Other Irrational Acts: Conversations with Twelve Southern</u>
     <u>Writers</u>. Baton Rouge: Louisiana State University Press,
     pp. 34-58.
         Reprint of 1971.16.

6   COLES, ROBERT. Review of <u>Love in the Ruins</u>. <u>American Scholar</u>
     41 (Summer):480.
         In this compilation of "favorite books," Walker Percy's
     first three novels are recommended. "Percy has a wonderful sense
     of humor, a sharp eye, an alert ear; and he is a storyteller who
     at the same time explores with great subtlety man's psychological
     and spiritual life."

7   DOWIE, WILLIAM, S.J. "Walker Percy: Sensualist-Thinker."
     <u>Novel</u> 6:52-65.
         Unlike most American novelists, Percy injects the felt life
     of experience into the realm of ideas and values. In both theme
     and content, Percy's novels "celebrate the activity of the senses
     [and reveal] the mind of the philosopher as well." His protago-
     nists use the awarenesses afforded by their senses and their ex-
     periences as important clues in their search into the mystery of
     existence. "Only by . . . confronting the reality of objects can
     the lost hero find his way." Thus, for the protagonists, "immer-
     sion in immediate experience is one response to the spirit of
     abstraction" that impedes their self-discovery. Conversely,
     "some kind of intellectual search is the only vital response to
     the malaise that settles in the midst of otherwise happy expe-
     riences." For example, while Binx Bolling will not allow his
     life to be abstracted according to his Aunt Emily's code and
     instead pursues sensual experiences, he "always preserves an
     underlying sense of the insufficiency of the good life." <u>The</u>
     <u>Last Gentleman</u> is less thematically complete than <u>The Moviegoer</u>
     or <u>Love in the Ruins</u>, although the basic preoccupations remain
     the same. Barrett searches for a way to unite experience and
     thought while Sutter settles into an uneasy dichotomy which
     threatens his desire to live. The novel ends unsatisfactorily
     with Will Barrett merely going "back to his old searching ways."
     Like Percy's first two protagonists, Tom More is also a quester.
     Of the protagonists, More most fully resolves the experience
     versus thought conflict in his sexual union with Ellen in mar-
     riage and in his spiritual union with God in the Eucharist.
     Through his fiction, Percy evidences his belief "that to survive
     one needs to resist complete absorption in either pole of sensa-
     tion or thought, that one must hold the tension somehow."

8   GASTON, PAUL L. "The Revelation of Walker Percy." <u>Colorado</u>
     <u>Quarterly</u> 20, no. 4 (Spring):459-70.
         The protagonists of Walker Percy's first two novels, Binx
     Bolling of <u>The Moviegoer</u> and Will Barrett of <u>The Last Gentleman</u>,
     both feel so unsettled in the modern world that they embark upon

searches to find themselves. While Binx's is a search within
himself, Will's is more of a picaresque journey. Yet both these
searches reveal serious ailments within society; by way of their
journeys, therefore, the protagonists also become "sick doctors
intent on discovering the nature of our illnesses." Both heroes
are fully realized characters; they are not just authorial masks
of the clinician cum author, Dr. Percy. Not so with the character of Tom More, who "directly and dramatically fulfills in the
novel the role of diagnostician that Percy has taken upon himself." Therefore, Tom More loses much of his particular identity
as his voice is that of the prophet of apocalypse. Fittingly
then, Percy's third novel does not contain the fiction dis-
claimers found at the beginning of the first two novels. Percy
has set his novel of apocalypse right in his own home town of
Covington, Louisiana; precisely because it is a comfortable,
nondescript place, Percy is in effect warning his readers likewise to look in their own back yards for signs of decay and im-
pending destruction.

9   GOODWIN, STEPHEN. "After the Faulkner." Shenandoah 23, no. 2
    (Winter):70-77, esp. 75-77.
        Although this review of Love in the Ruins deems Percy's
    satire as "delicate and deft and marvelously comic," it also
    decries the novel as "gimmicky," noting that "the deep perturba-
    tions of the soul don't seem deep at all but as tinny as the gad-
    get which measures them."

10 HYNES, JOSEPH. "Percy's Reliques." Cross Currents 22
    (Winter):117-20, 128.
        Love in the Ruins shares thematic preoccupations not only
    with Percy's previous two novels but also with the works of lit-
    erary predecessors, notably those of Evelyn Waugh. Each of
    Percy's novels is centrally concerned with "diagnosing and cur-
    ing the human condition." In favoring "gradual evolution" as a
    corrective to society's excesses, Percy resembles Waugh. Addi-
    tionally, both authors share similar approaches to "psychology,
    religious convictions, and muted gladness after long
    voyages. . . ."

11 LAWSON, LEWIS A. "Walker Percy: The Physician as Novelist."
    SAB 37, no. 2 (May):58-63.
        Even though Walker Percy abandoned the practice of medicine
    in favor of writing, he has sustained an abiding interest in the
    medical field. Yet despite his distinctive point of view as
    physician cum novelist, his troubled characters scarcely put much
    faith in scientific solutions to their problems. For example,
    Kate of The Moviegoer and Will Barrett of The Last Gentleman both
    undergo psychotherapy, but use their extensive lay knowledge to
    outwit their therapists. Binx though, with his increased aware-
    ness at the end of the novel, does choose medicine although he
    had earlier rejected the career of his dead father. Also, a

significant physician does appear in The Last Gentleman in the
figure of Dr. Sutter Vaught. Seemingly a disgrace to the profession, Sutter acknowledges through his actions and observations
two principles important to another physician-existentialist,
Karl Jaspers: "Sutter knows that the body is more than flesh,
but that the physician is not the appropriate profession to deal
with that transcendent, 'more than' quality." Thus, Sutter
attracts Will Barrett, an engineer for whom science also lacked
answers to existential dilemmas. Barrett is particularly im-
pressed when Sutter defers to the powers of the priest as Jamie
is dying. Thus, Percy seemingly is pursuing a new direction in
his thinking. "Whereas when he gave up medicine he felt that it
was blind to spiritual, existential matters, he now must believe
that there is at least a minority, perhaps growing, scientific
view that encompasses the transempirical within its ken." Therefore, it is likely that in a future novel, "Dr. Percy will devote
his full attention to the physician who recognizes his own illness and admits that he cannot alone heal himself." Lawson remarks in his end notes that such a character, Tom More, did indeed appear in Percy's subsequent novel, Love in the Ruins.

12   LeCLAIR, THOMAS EDMUND. "Final Words: Death and Comedy in
      the Fiction of Donleavy, Hawkes, Barth, Vonnegut, and Percy."
      Ph.D. dissertation, Duke University.
         Death is central to the body of fiction produced by these
five novelists, and determines the ways characters in this fiction embrace selfhood. This also contributes both to the black-
ness and comic modes employed. In Percy's three novels death is
immanent, but also a transcendent event through which the onto-
logical and spiritual visions of his heroes are tested.

13   LUSCHEI, MARTIN. The Sovereign Wayfarer: Walker Percy's
      Diagnosis of the Malaise. Baton Rouge: Louisiana State
      University Press, 269 pp.
         This first full-length study of Percy explicates his first
three novels, and also includes biographical material and an
analysis of Percy's development as a novelist. The first section
chronicles Percy's transformation from physician to writer, citing the catalytic effect of his confinement with tuberculosis and
concomitant exploration of existentialist thought. The second
section examines focal concepts which Percy gleaned from such
existentialist thinkers as Kierkegaard, Marcel, Sartre, and
Heidegger and indicates the way in which Percy synthesized these
concepts to shape his own philosophy. The remaining sections
investigate the fictional treatment of Percy's philosophy within
the novels.
         In The Moviegoer, Binx Bolling synthesizes the traditional
values emphasized by Aunt Emily and the insight gained during his
self-imposed exile in Gentilly to create for himself an authentic
union with Kate, a union which includes "a religious awareness
born of his despair." In the second novel, Will Barrett's

existential search takes the form of a pilgrimage across the
country. His sojourn leads him out of his exile in New York to
his Southern homeland and then to the desert of New Mexico, where
he finally is "jarred out of pure possibility" by the dramatic
circumstances attending Jamie's death. At the novel's end, Will
shows "some sign of shouldering the burden of his existence,"
indicating the possibility that "the grace of inwardness will now
enter his life. . . ."
     Love in the Ruins, "Percy's most comprehensive diagnosis of
the malaise," maps "the land that lies in twilight under an
Eclipse, plagued by the modern Black Death of the spirit." Particularly threatening to civilization is the miasma of consensus
anthropology that attempts to synthesize a mechanistic scientific
model with Judeo-Christian values. Tom More, who epitomizes the
riven self, recovers himself through ordeal; and the novel tri-
umphantly "ends on a note of . . . authentic affirmation." In
naming the malaise in his novels, Percy achieves a reversal of
alienation and points the way "toward a recovery of being." See
also 1970.4.

14   SIMPSON, LEWIS P., ed. "Introduction: The South and the
     Poetry of Community." In The Poetry of Community: Essays on
     the Southern Sensibility of History and Literature. Spectrum
     Monograph Series, Vol. 2. Atlanta: Georgia State University
     School of Arts and Sciences, pp. xi-xii.
        Percy's apocalyptic vision in Love in the Ruins is cited
     for its ironic contrast to the utopian vision which informed the
     founding of America.

15   SPIVEY, TED R. "Religion and the Reintegration of Man in
     Flannery O'Connor and Walker Percy." Spectrum Monograph
     Series, Vol. 2. Atlanta: Georgia State University School of
     Arts and Sciences, pp. 67-79.
        Both Flannery O'Connor and Walker Percy frame their fiction
     within a religious context, presenting their protagonists as
     spiritual seekers on a pilgrimage toward God. In their depiction
     of these quests, O'Connor and Percy demonstrate their deep under-
     standing of myth and ritual. Their characters face death and
     destruction and arrive at a "moment of integrating vision that
     . . . invokes the sacred . . . who is the one integrating
     Spirit." Binx Bolling of The Moviegoer undertakes a spiritual
     quest, but he "is not passionate enough in his need to continue
     the quest. . . . Except that he is married, the end of the book
     finds him in much the same condition as the beginning. . . ."
     The Last Gentleman's Will Barret, on the other hand, experiences
     "the action of mercy" at the very beginning of the novel through
     "the miracle of his encounter with a young woman whom he comes to
     love." Barrett's quest culminates with his taking responsibility
     for Jamie's baptism and receiving in turn "that gift of love that
     makes possible not the final victory over the forces of destruc-
     tion inside himself and Sutter, but an initial victory on the
     path of pilgrimage."

16   SULLIVAN, WALTER. "Southern Novelists and the Civil War."
      In Death by Melancholy: Essays on Modern Southern Fiction.
      Baton Rouge: Louisiana State University Press, pp. 66-67.
          This brief reference to Percy maintains that he and other
      contemporary Southern writers ignore the Civil War and ventures
      that they "would be better novelists if they had been born and
      begun to writer sooner, and I suspect all of them would have
      searched for their imagery in the Civil War."

17   TAYLOR, LEWIS JEROME, Jr. "The Becoming of the Self in the
      Writings of Walker Percy: A Kierkegaardian Analysis." Ph.D.
      dissertation, Duke University.
          The existential solution to despair discovered by Percy's
      protagonists illustrates Kierkegaardian concepts of the progres-
      sive stages in the self's becoming.

18   WILLS, GARRY. "Catholic Faith and Fiction." NYTBR,
      16 January, pp. 1-2.
          Writing in reply to Wilfrid Sheed's assertion, in his review
      of Love in the Ruins (1971.43), that "Catholicism in its current
      dither strikes even some of its own members as a harmless aberra-
      tion," Wills argues that contemporary interest in Catholicism by
      novelists is important. For Percy, able "to appropriate . . .
      Catholic subculture, to feel it as a dying thing . . . represents
      a new honesty." Through escape from pretended beliefs, Catholic
      writers (such as Wilfrid Sheed, Thomas Kenally, Elizabeth
      Cullinan and Percy) have gained room to maneuver, and thus these
      new writers "have more sides" than just the Catholic.

                                    1973

1   ABÁDI-NAGY, ZOLTÁN. "A Talk with Walker Percy." SLJ 6, no. 1
      (Fall):3-19.
          Percy describes the philosophical nature of his novels,
      citing his use of "the particular in order to get at the general
      issues." He notes Binx Bolling as a young man "in an existen-
      tialist predicament," alienated from two conflicting modes of
      being, Southern stoicism and Christian Catholic. He differen-
      tiates his main characters from participants in American counter-
      culture groups: while the latter engage in general revolt against
      the existent culture, Percy's protagonists "are much more con-
      sciously embarked on some sort of search . . . a much more serious
      search for meaning." He concurs with the interviewer that his
      approach to existentialism is akin to that of the French Catholic
      Gabriel Marcel and that Love in the Ruins dramatizes the philo-
      sophical dilemma posited by Marcel. He acknowledges that he
      deals more deliberately with social and political issues in Love
      in the Ruins than in the previous two novels and emphasizes that
      the novel ends with "a suggestion of a new community, new recon-
      ciliation." In attempting an explanation of the American

writer's ability "to couple the grim seriousness with hilarious
humor," Percy cites the Kierkegaardian view of the leap into
faith as humorous and also the importance of Mark Twain's
Huckleberry Finn in having "established the tradition of this
very broad and satirical humor. . . . In this country we call it
black humor, a disproportion between the gravity of the character's predicament and the hilarity of the humor with which it is
treated." When asked if this comedic approach results in "the
absurd creation of the American Sisyphus" as opposed to the
serious defiance of Camus's King, Percy demurs, indicating the
difference, for example, between Binx Bolling and "the Camus and
Sartrean heroes of the absurd. . . . Camus would probably say the
hero has to create his own values whether absurd or not, whereas
Binx does not accept that the world is absurd." He then elabo-
rates on the relationship between the comedic mode and the
writer's sense of communicating alienation. He acknowledges the
tendency of American writers, like Philip Roth, to use "black
comedy" and then adds: "I think I owe a good deal of the kind of
humor that I use to Jewish humor, which is a very wry, self-
critical sort of humor." He notes his kinship with Heinrich
Böll, a German Roman Catholic who "uses the most devastating
satirical humor, often extremely anti-clerical. . . . I find it
perfectly natural for a Catholic writer to fall into this harsh,
satirical comic technique." In response to a query about the
"absence of practical religion from the novels," Percy refers to
his preference for an indirect approach. In commenting on "a
theme I use in all my novels: the recovery of the real through
ordeal," he contrasts such ordeal with rotation and repetition,
which offer "simply aesthetic relief, therefore temporary."
Percy agrees that Will Barrett was depicted as much sicker than
Binx Bolling, adding that "a good deal" of the second novel "was
satire directed to events happening in the South." Finally,
Percy assesses the current status of the South.

2   ANON. Review of Love in the Ruins. Catholic Library World
     44, no. 7 (February):425.
         The annotator adds his own kudos to "a great chorus of
critical approval. . . ."

3   BERRIGAN, J.R. "An Explosion of Utopias." Moreana 10, no. 38
     (June):21-26.
         In wishing to create a utopia, Tom More resembles his
sainted ancestor. The utopia of the latter-day More would be a
technological paradise in which personality dysfunctions are displaced through diagnosis and treatment by the lapsometer. More's
solution to society's ills exists within "a tissue of conflicting
utopias, all of them flawed, all of them, sooner or later, failures." Other utopian solutions are represented in the escapism
sought by More's first wife, in the revolution of the Bantus, in
the "primitivism" of the swamp denizens, in the sexual freedom of
the Love Clinic, and in the wealth of Lola and other Paradise

111

Estates residents. In short, Percy "has woven into his novel almost all of the aberrant solutions to the human dilemma that our generation has produced."

*4   BORGMAN, PAUL. "The Symbolic City and Christian Existential-
      ism in Fiction by Flannery O'Connor, Walker Percy, and John
      Updike." Ph.D. dissertation, University of Chicago.
         Source: Weixlmann and Gann (1980.58), p. 155.

5   BOYD, G.N., and BOYD, L.A. Religion in Contemporary Fiction:
     Criticism from 1945 to the Present. San Antonio, Tex.:
     Trinity University Press, pp. i-99, esp. 44.
         Brief essay. Articles cited include Anselm Atkins
     (1968.1); Sarah Henisey (1968.5); Alfred Kazin (1971.29);
     Lewis A. Lawson (1969.5; 1970.3); Richard Lehan (1968.6); and
     Robert Maxwell (1967.12).

6   BRADFORD, MELVIN E. "Dr. Percy's Paradise Lost: Diagnostics
     in Louisiana." SR 81 (Autumn):839-44.
         Tom More is a "tenuous being," living in "theologically
     weighted memories and daydreams." Rather than being "soberly
     satiric," the novel "is a mere caricature of the present shape
     of things" and serves as a vehicle for progression to Kierke-
     gaardian modes of being. Further, Percy's satirical emphasis
     upon More's Cartesian mind/body schism erroneously shifts too
     much focus upon the self. The time sequence within the book
     does help to give it some cohesive form but not enough to order
     the novel sufficiently. More positively, Percy's ·"high comedy
     . . . marks a progression in his thinking," reflecting "his
     clear-headed and Christian observation of the current intellec-
     tual 'scene.'" See also 1974.3.

7   BRADLEY, JARED W. "Walker Percy and the Search for Wisdom."
     LaS 12, no. 4 (Winter):579-90.
         In essays and novels, Percy's search for wisdom focuses on
     language, particularly in its function as "a symbol of our com-
     prehension of our life around us." Of chief influence in the
     formation of Percy's philosophical view is the writing of Gabriel
     Marcel and of Henri Bergson, and to a lesser extent, that of José
     Ortega y Gasset. Despite these European influences, Percy's
     "writing is in the style and tradition of 'The Fugitive Group'
     which developed around John Crowe Ransom in the years between
     the two world wars. . . . Percy's work is like the Fugitives
     in his reaffirmation that the spiritual values of the Western
     cultural tradition are still the means by which man may grasp
     reality in the modern world." Percy's philosophy coincides with
     that of Marcel in that "a major feature of Gabriel Marcel's
     thinking is the concept of man's life as a 'pilgrim in an abid-
     ingly mysterious land.'" Percy's view, however, is more bla-
     tantly Christian than that of Marcel. "Walker Percy is un-
     abashedly Christian in the Western tradition carved out by Henri
     Bergson."

8   BROOKS, CLEANTH. "The Current State of American Literature."
     SoR, n.s. 9, no. 1 (Spring):273-87, esp. 285-87.
          Remarks made at the University of Mississippi, summer of
     1972, writers' conference. In assessing the present state of
     American literature, Brooks bases his response on his considera-
     tion and interpretation of the assessments of William Jovanovich
     (PW, 10 April 1972), Alan Pryce-Jones (TLS, 19 May 1972), and
     A. Alvarez (Under Pressure, 1965). There seems to be a consensus
     that readers are turning away from fiction to history, biography,
     and autobiography. Confessional literature, the writer's ex-
     ploration of inner consciousness, is also popular.
          Brooks disagrees with Pryce-Jones's theory that the popu-
     larity of confessional literature is "the American writer's
     failure to cope with his situation and his consequent sense of
     bitter frustration." The real problem, as Brooks sees it, is
     that American writers are affected by "the crisis in culture."
     The American tradition of individualism and dissent provides the
     foundation for current explorations of the inner self. The role
     of the writer becomes that of "diagnostician"; he tells us "that
     something is wrong, and he may be able to define the malady."
     In the role of "diagnostician," the author is neither surgeon nor
     political prophet.
          For the Southern writer, as for "urban blacks and Jews of
     New York City," community has not dissolved. There is "a real
     cultural base." This should not limit the Southern writer to
     writing about the South. Walker Percy uses the South in The
     Moviegoer and The Last Gentleman; the theme in both novels is
     alienation. Yet, each protagonist "comes to find in his native
     region a challenge and a resource."

9   BUCKLEY, WILLIAM F., Jr. "The Southern Imagination: An
     Interview with Eudora Welty and Walker Percy." MissQ 26,
     no. 4 (Fall):493-516.
          Transcript of television program. Reprint of 1972.3.

10   BYRD, SCOTT, and ZEUGNER, JOHN F. "Walker Percy: A Check-
     list." BB 30, no. 1 (January-March):16-17, 44.
          This initial bibliography of primary material chronologi-
     cally lists articles, essays, reviews, and books by Percy and
     interviews with him. The checklist begins with a list of Percy's
     college articles and concludes with an interview entry dated
     Fall, 1971.

11   CHESNICK, EUGENE. "Novel's Ending and World's End: The Fic-
     tion of Walker Percy." Hollins Critic 10, no. 5 (October):
     1-11.
          Percy differs from many contemporary novelists in that he
     still believes in the necessity of strong personal relationships
     as a solution to the alienation of vacuous present-day existence.
     His theory of intersubjectivity, an "interpenetration of lives
     and knowledge," appears in both his essays and novels. But

particularly as his novels grow increasingly fantastic and
apocalyptic, Percy's faith in intersubjectivity mars his fiction.
In a "fantastic world all things are made incredible," including
the possibility of satisfying personal relationships. Further-
more, in his endings Percy ultimately leaps over "the ethical
mode into the religious," just as his characters do, thereby
abandoning "a set of literary-ethical values."

12   COOK, BRUCE. "The Search for an American Catholic Novel."
     American Libraries 4, no. 9 (October):547-49, esp. 549.
        Within a general discussion of "the Catholic novel" as con-
     ceived and taught in the nineteen-fifties, changes of the sixties
     are considered. J.F. Powers, Wilfrid Sheed, and Percy are dis-
     cussed, and Love in the Ruins is described as a "funny, compli-
     cated" novel which satirizes modern America and aspects of
     Catholicism.

13   GALLO, LOUIS JACOB. "From Malaisian to Saint: A Study of
     Walker Percy." Ph.D. dissertation, University of Missouri,
     Columbia.
        Percy synthesizes Southern, Christian, and existential per-
     spectives to formulate an answer to the contemporary anomie. He
     has delineated his views in a series of nonfiction essays which
     investigate such philosophical concepts as intersubjectivity,
     alienation, and symbolization. The characters of his first three
     novels illustrate these concepts in their progression "from
     alienated malaisians to Christian saints."

14   HENDIN, JOSEPHINE. Review of The Sovereign Wayfarer: Walker
     Percy's Diagnosis of the Malaise. MFS 19, no. 4 (Winter):
     603-5.
        This review includes commentary on both The Sovereign Way-
     farer and Miles Orwell's Invisible Parade: The Fiction of
     Flannery O'Connor. Percy and O'Connor are viewed as "mavericks,"
     as "novelists of the demythologized South." In particular,
     Luschei's work is lauded as "an absorbing, successful attempt to
     provide a conceptual base for Walker Percy's fiction." Espe-
     cially "invaluable" is material Luschei has culled from Percy's
     essays, which he links to such existentialist influences as
     Marcel and Kierkegaard, thereby providing "a biography of Percy's
     mind." What Luschei's critical commentary lacks, however, is "a
     consideration of Percy's style, imagery, and special
     effects. . . ."

15   HOLMAN, C. HUGH. Review of The Sovereign Wayfarer: Walker
     Percy's Diagnosis of the Malaise. AL 45, no. 3 (November):
     476-77.
        Mixed review that ultimately recommends the book as "an
     indispensable work for all serious students of Percy's
     novels. . . ."

16   KAZIN, ALFRED. "The Secret of the South: Faulkner to Percy."
      In Bright Book of Life: American Novelists and Storytellers
      from Hemingway to Mailer. Boston: Little, Brown & Co.,
      pp. 37-38, 46, 60-67.
            Essentially the same as 1971.29.

17   LEHAN, RICHARD. "Into the Ruins: Saul Bellow and Walker
      Percy." In A Dangerous Crossing: French Literary Existen-
      tialism and the Modern American Novel. Carbondale: Southern
      Illinois University Press, pp. 107-45, esp. 133-45.
            To the usual existential concerns of alienation and a sense
      of absurdity, Percy adds "two states of narrative consciousness,
      one of perception and the other of reflection, and also a sense
      of the grotesque." The anxiety of his characters is ameliorated
      when they find someone else to share or understand their sense of
      dread. Authentic life, for Percy, is a search for just such a
      sense of shared consciousness. The modes of rotation and repe-
      tition are used to effect such a search. Both The Moviegoer and
      The Last Gentleman illustrate these concepts; but Love in the
      Ruins, while likewise delineating absurdity, "is a very different
      kind of novel for Percy."

18   PRESLEY, DELMA E. "Walker Percy's 'Larroes.'" NConL 3,
      no. 1:5-6.
            The apparently Southern expression "Larroes catch medloes"
      used by Sharon in The Moviegoer is perhaps a corruption of
      "'Layovers to catch meddlers'--a rebuke elders give inquisitive
      children, meaning 'something to make children (or fools) ask
      questions.'"

19   STELZMANN, RAINULF A. "Adam in Extremis: Die Romane Walker
      Percys." Stimmen der Zeit (Freiburg) 191:206-10.
            While there are few American novelists with a Catholic
      worldview, Percy must now be placed with J.F. Powers and Flannery
      O'Connor. A writer of essays which examine the alienation of
      modern man and the possibilities of healing, Percy examines the
      danger posed to individualism in each of his three novels. Four
      basic motifs are incorporated. First, heroes seek happiness in
      erotic sexuality, yet this is unrewarding; ultimately they are
      led to marriage. Secondly, while science has considerable sig-
      nificance for Percy, he has basic reservations about its en-
      croachment upon the spiritual life and its ability to heal.
      Thirdly, it is difficult for man to pursue his search for a mean-
      ingful life because all life's phenomena are turned upside down;
      existence suffers from a radical perversion. Finally, these
      troubles make religious belief difficult for Percy's heroes, but
      steps toward belief are made in each novel. Percy's world is one
      determined almost entirely by European existentialism, a literary
      world of crisis one cannot read but with "fear and trembling."

20   SULLIVAN, WALTER. "Southerners in the City: Flannery
      O'Connor and Walker Percy." In The Comic Imagination in
      American Literature. Edited by Louis D. Rubin, Jr. New
      Brunswick, N.J.: Rutgers University Press, pp. 339-48.
          Besides sharing a common region and religion, O'Connor and
      Percy both focus on "the alienation of contemporary man." The
      Moviegoer is typical of Percy's work in that "it is about a young
      man's effort to grasp reality and thereby to overcome his exis-
      tential malaise." Binx effects his recovery partially through
      his moviegoing whereby he discerns "the authentic within the
      make-believe," a perceptive facility shared only by his fatally
      ill half-brother Lonnie. The death of Lonnie gives the novel a
      Christian perspective as Binx reconciles his alienation into a
      commitment to God and to his fellow wayfarers.

21   WEBER, BROM. "The Mode of 'Black Humor.'" In The Comic
      Imagination in American Literature. Edited by Louis D.
      Rubin, Jr. New Brunswick, N.J.: Rutgers University Press,
      pp. 361-71.
          Percy is listed among "established black humorists [who]
      seem unable to create in any other mode of vision." Love in the
      Ruins is cited as being "in the great black humor tradition of
      Hawthorne, Melville, Faulkner."

*22   WESTENDORP, T.A. "Recent Southern Fiction: Percy, Price and
      Dickey." In Handelingen van het XXIXe Vlaams Filologencongres
      Antwerpen [16-18 April]. Edited by J. Van Haver. Zellik,
      Belgium, pp. 188-98.
          Source: 1974 MLA International Bibliography, entry 11459
      and F43.
          Available from the Secretariaat van de Vlaamse Filologen-
      congressen, Sint-Bavolaan 7, 1730 Zellik, Belgium.

23   WILLIAMS, MINA GWEN. "The Sense of Place in Southern Fic-
      tion." Ph.D. dissertation, Louisiana State University and
      Agricultural and Mechanical College.
          Study of the evolving sense of place in Southern fiction,
      especially in relation to the Southern novel. Three chapters
      consider major nineteenth-century writers, major twentieth-
      century writers, and the art of Eudora Welty. Modern Southern
      novelists, such as Robert Penn Warren and Percy, write of the
      South as place affected by a sense of displacement.

24   YARDLEY, JONATHAN. "The New Old Southern Novel." PR 40
      (Spring):286-93.
          The works of fifteen Southern writers, including those of
      Percy, are analyzed primarily for their departure from tradi-
      tional Southern fiction. In his first three novels, Percy "has
      provided the definitive portrayal of the ticky-tacky new South,
      a portrayal drawn with clarity, humor, and gentlemanly outrage."
      But by also emphasizing enduring human values, especially in the

epilogue of <u>Love in the Ruins</u>, "Walker Percy takes us back to where we started [in the tradition of Southern fiction]: closeness to the land, neighborliness, humility before the lessons of history." See also in Peter Taylor <u>Guide</u> (1973.12).

<u>1974</u>

1   ALTERMAN, PETER STEVEN. "A Study of Four Science Fiction Themes and Their Function in Two Contemporary Novels." Ph.D. dissertation, University of Denver.

   Study of ways the science fiction novel is becoming assimilated into the larger genre of contemporary fiction. William Golding's <u>The Inheritors</u> and <u>Love in the Ruins</u> are examined because they incorporate science fiction into their structures. Four themes--the alien being; the mad scientist; the doomsday machine; and the extrapolated future--are examined. These themes, important for Percy, are a useful way of examining a new kind of speculative fiction which incorporates science fiction.

2   ANON. "Walker Percy." In <u>Contemporary Literary Criticism</u>. Vol. 2. Edited by Carolyn Riley and Barbara Harte. Detroit: Gale Research Company, pp. 332-35.

   Percy is introduced as "a National Book Award-winning stylist and satirist . . . best known for his novels <u>The Moviegoer</u> and <u>Love Among</u> [sic] <u>the Ruins</u>." Excerpts from the following: Wilfrid Sheed (1968.8), Richard Lehan (1968.6), Peter Wolfe (1968.12), Jerry Bryant (1971.14), Martha Duffy (1971.24), Alfred Kazin (1971.29), and Stephen Goodwin (1972.9).

3   CHENEY, BRAINARD. "Correspondence." <u>SR</u> 82, no. 1 (Winter): 194-96.

   In a letter to the editor, the author takes to task Melvin E. Bradford's review of <u>Love in the Ruins</u>, which appeared in Autumn, 1973. He chides Bradford's use of the perjorative term "tenuous being" in connection with Tom More, contending that such a characterization is consistent with the "sick world" that Percy portrays. Additionally, Cheney refutes Bradford's contention that the book is not a novel in the traditional sense, citing Tom More's confession near the end of the novel as a reversal from pride to contrition which portends his ultimate salvation. See 1973.6.

4   DEWEY, BRADLEY. "Walker Percy Talks about Kierkegaard: An Annotated Interview." <u>Journal of Religion</u> 54 (July):273-98.

   Acknowledging Kierkegaard "as the man to whom I owe the greatest debt," Percy relates his initial difficulty in understanding the Danish philosopher. He indicates that he "had almost given up" until he read <u>Concluding Unscientific Postscript</u> with ease and then was able to grasp some of the more abstruse works such as <u>Sickness unto Death</u>. When asked about the role of

Kierkegaard's writings in his spiritual development, Percy
acknowledges the powerful influence of the essay "The Difference
between a Genius and an Apostle": "If I had to single out one
piece of writing which was more responsible than anything else
for my becoming a Catholic, it would be that essay of Kierkegaard's." The interviewer concludes that "Kierkegaard provided
Percy with much of his underlying view of man, with much of the
larger conceptual framework for the novels."

5   DUFFEY, BERNARD. Review of The Sovereign Wayfarer: Walker
    Percy's Diagnosis of the Malaise, by Martin Luschei. SAQ 73,
    no. 2 (Spring):275.
        Luschei's study "is readable and thorough and will be of
major assistance in understanding [Percy]."

6   GASTON, PAUL L. Review of The Sovereign Wayfarer: Walker
    Percy's Diagnosis of the Malaise, by Martin Luschei. GaR 28,
    no. 3 (Fall):540-43.
        This "earnest and largely constructive" study is commenda-
ble as an introduction to Percy, but "mechanical plot summary and
exposition" are emphasized at the expense of more valuable information, such as Percy's relationship to other existentialist
thinkers.

7   GODSHALK, WILLIAM L. "Walker Percy's Christian Vision." LaS
    13, no. 2:130-41.
        Although Walker Percy's novels are often analyzed for their
existentialist vision, his perspective is essentially Christian.
Particularly in Love in the Ruins, he examines the pitfalls of
"spiritual pride," manifested so graphically in the central
character, Thomas More. Consumed by an overwhelming hubris, in
himself and his lapsometer, "More plans to correct the maladjust-
ments of the Western mind and to lead the world to a new era of
peace." Neither the new Christ he conceives himself to be nor
the Faustus that he resembles, More is closer to "a modern Everyman." He bounds from one extreme to another--angelism, bestialism; psychiatrist, mental patient; depression, exaltation. "More
partakes of all sides: he is Everyman, who is tempted, falls
(into the Inferno-like Pit), and finally recovers when he gains
knowledge of his true role in the Christian universe." One of
his temptations lies in his inability to choose only one of the
three women that he rescues. Each of them symbolizes conflicting
values: Moira, unrestrained eroticism; Lola, total immersion in
music; and Ellen, the Protestant work ethic. In his state of
unabashed pride, he feels that he can co-exist with all three
women and, by extension, their respective values. "God may be
able to accept all three, but More is finite and cannot." He is
abetted in his hubristic delusion by the Lucifer-like Art
Immelmann. The turning point in the novel occurs when More
banishes Immelmann by "a long and venerable tradition in

religion," prayer. The Coda of the novel emphasizes More's reliance on work, marital love, and grace through the sacraments.

8 KING, BARBARA. "Walker Percy Prevails." Southern Voices 1 (May-June):19-23.
    In this wide-ranging interview, Percy talks first about the influences on his thinking and writing, e.g., his Catholicism: "I don't think my writings are meant to preach Catholicism, but the novel can't help but be informed by a certain point of view--and this happens to be a Catholic point of view." Acknowledging his similarity to European novelists of ideas, he admits to being "a polemicist and a moralist. I mean moralist in a large sense, of saying this is the way the world ought to be and not the way it is." Reminiscing about his "Uncle" Will, he reveals that "a great deal of The Moviegoer and The Last Gentleman have to do with the differences between me and my uncle." On the subject of writing ("a solitary, private, miserable business"), he reveals that "the whole secret [to it] is that you have to get excited about something, either for or against it." Psychiatrists figure in his novels, he says, "mainly for satirical purposes . . . [because] there's a tendency in this culture to treat psychiatry as a religion. . . ." He claims never to have been interested in Southern writing in the Faulknerian tradition: "I was concerned with what happens to an alienated young man who in fact was fed up with the whole Southern scene." He observes that "the function of writers and novelists and poets is probably the highest in the culture, because their job is to make people understand themselves."

9 LAUDER, ROBERT E. "The Catholic Novel and the 'Insider God.'" Commonweal 101 (25 October):78 81.
    The differences in the novels of Catholic writers, Graham Greene and Walker Percy, mirror differences in pre- and post-Vatican II theology. In the older Catholic view, God's relation to man was extrinsic rather than intrinsic. Accordingly, "Greene's vision of Catholicism is vertical while Percy's is horizontal. . . . The paradigm of all Greene's Catholic novels is that God is the outsider, though the loving outsider, pursuing sinners who eventually become saints. It is precisely the 'outsider-God' image that allows for Greene's frequent use of theological paradox." In contrast, "the controlling insight in Percy's vision is not one of theological paradox but of God's presence in all of human life and the Catholic's awareness of that presence." Indeed, the leitmotif of Percy's first three novels is that of the spiritually bereft wayfarer seeking the transcendent. Even despite its heavy satire, Percy's "best book," Love in the Ruins, "a kind of a Catholic 1984, . . . is still an affirmation of the everydayness of religious faith and God's presence in the everyday." Though "radically different," the Catholic perspectives of Greene and Percy "fit into the same tradition. . . . However, to the extent that Vatican II theology

forms the Catholic community, Percy's type of novel will become
more and more significant."

10   LeCLAIR, THOMAS. "The Eschatological Vision of Walker Percy."
      Renascence 26, no. 3 (Spring):115-22.
          The implications of eschatology--whether immanent, tran-
      scendent, or (in Love in the Ruins) cultural--provide a test for
      Percy's heroes which awakens them to the possibility of a life
      filled with authenticity and grace. In each of Percy's first
      three novels, the death of a child is instrumental in the hero's
      existential and spiritual recovery. Binx's acceptance of
      Lonnie's death earns him "the possibility of advancement up
      Percy's spiritual ladder to the acceptance of God." Only after
      Jamie's death is Will able to "ask Sutter the proper questions,"
      questions pertinent to salvation. Thomas More initially misses
      the spiritual implications of his daughter's death; but his own
      failed suicide attempt "clears his vision." He is then able to
      confront and foil the "cultural eschatology or apocalypse" facing
      his society.

11   TAYLOR, LEWIS JEROME, Jr. "Walker Percy and the Self."
      Commonweal 100 (10 May):233-36.
          An existentialist thinker and writer in the mold of
      Kierkegaard, Percy goes beyond mere analysis of contemporary
      despair to ask "the vital question how. How can one make the
      necessary movements that can take him from inauthentic to authen-
      tic existence?" For each of his protagonists such movement be-
      gins with "an initial decisive break" with the past, a break
      which allows the hero to see his essential life position as a
      wayfarer. The ensuing search for "authentic selfhood" entails
      "struggle, resignation and suffering" and leads to a "final
      movement to self-recovery. . . ."

12   _____. "Walker Percy's Knights of the Hidden Inwardness."
      Anglican Theological Review 56, no. 1 (January):125-51.
          Will Barrett and Tom More exemplify Kierkegaard's knights
      of faith. These "protagonists make the essential movements that
      Kierkegaard describes as leading from the aesthetic into the
      religious mode." This progression is precipitated by the ordeal
      of suffering which they undergo, the type of catalyst Kierkegaard
      saw as necessary for an awakening to one's essential selfhood.
      Both men deliberately choose exile from their society, an exis-
      tentialist act which the Danish philosopher called the "movement
      of infinite resignation," and thereby each becomes a "knight of
      the hidden inwardness." Each endures the suffering such isola-
      tion imposes; their resignation propels them into "the second
      and decisive leap of the religious mode, namely the 'movement of
      faith.'" For Will Barrett, this decisive movement occurs during
      his confrontation with Sutter after Jamie's baptism. Tom More
      regains his lapsed faith when, in his confrontation with Art
      Immelmann, he prays for the divine intercession of St. Thomas
      More.

1975

1 ANON. Review of The Message in the Bottle. Booklist 72,
    no. 1 (1 September):14.
        A brief notice: "mysterious processes of language have
    prompted Percy's laborious but elegant rhetorical exercise."
    While he claims to be an amateur, "unversed readers" may be left
    bobbing in Percy's "considerable intellectual wake."

2 ANON. Review of Message in the Bottle. Choice 12, no. 10
    (December):1304.
        Entertaining and pleasant to read: the main point is that
    there is a correlation between the "meanings of linguistic expres-
    sions and the spiritual and intellectual preparation needed for
    understanding."

3 ANON. Review of The Message in the Bottle. Kirkus 43, no. 8
    (15 April):497.
        "A deadly serious work" about theoretical linguistics.
    Percy promises a great deal, yet that "final diagram of the
    triadic structure . . . seems almost recondite."

4 ANON. Review of The Message in the Bottle. NYTBR, 7 Decem-
    ber, p. 70.
        A brief comment: "difficult essays." "Nearly half are
    intended for specialists, but intelligible to curious lay
    readers."

5 ANON. Review of The Message in the Bottle. PW 207 (28 April):
    42.
        This short review contends that "Percy never does provide a
    definitive answer" to the provocative question which opens the
    book--"Why does Man feel so sad in the Twentieth Century?"--but
    nevertheless "gives the reader . . . a number of mind-stretching
    clues."

6 ANON. "Walker Percy." In Contemporary Literary Criticism.
    Vol. 3. Edited by Carolyn Riley. Detroit: Gale Research Co.,
    pp. 378-81.
        Percy depicts "in his extraordinary novels the morally
    frustrating attempts of his sharply limned characters to deal
    with the 'waste land' of contemporary society in which they must
    live and love. For Percy, the bayou country around New Orleans
    is synecdochic for modern America." Excerpts are from the fol-
    lowing: Mark Taylor (1971.48), Jonathan Yardley (1973.24), and
    Melvin E. Bradford (1973.6).

7   BISCHOFF, JOAN. "With Manic Laughter: The Secular Apocalypse
     in American Novels of the 1960's." Ph.D. dissertation, Lehigh
     University.
          The term "apocalypse" is used to build upon its religious
     origins. Five 1960s novels by Heller, Mailer, Hawkes, Pynchon,
     and Percy are examined. Percy's Love in the Ruins shares images
     with Revelation. While the images in novels by these five writ-
     ers resemble Revelation, the tone differs. These apocalyptic
     novels are full of laughter.

8   BOATWRIGHT, JAMES. Review of The Message in the Bottle. NewR
     173 (19 July):28-29.
          "Without question [the collection of essays] demonstrates
     that for seriousness and keenness of mind, Walker Percy has few
     rivals in American letters." The reviewer particularly commends
     "the book's richness, its intellectual power, its coherence." He
     notes that "the first half of the book is the part most readers
     will learn most from: the essays in the second half . . . are
     pretty tough."

9   CIARDI, JOHN. "Why Is 20th Century Man So Sad?" Chicago
     Tribune Book World, 29 June, p. 6.
          The Message in the Bottle is not an easy book. The ques
     tions the author asks are worthwhile, but, as Percy admits, he is
     an amateur linguist who must arouse speculative interest without
     giving definitive answers. Percy's ideas are disjointed, and
     there is no overall shape to the book, or even an attempt to
     answer the question posed on the first page: "Why does man feel
     so sad in the 20th Century?" The style fails to give meaningful
     structure to the material.

10   CRAIN, JANE LARKIN. Review of The Message in the Bottle.
     SatR 2 (28 June):24.
          Although "Percy is an especially congenial and lively
     stylist," ultimately "he does not come to terms with the very
     area of concern that he needs to illuminate--modern man's sense
     of radical alienation from that which exists and from that which
     matters."

11   CUFFE, EDWIN D. "Chickens Have No Myths." America 133, no. 4
     (16 August):76-77.
          Review of The Message in the Bottle. These essays about
     language make the reader hope that Percy will go back to his
     novels--"not that this book is a failure . . . it is hard going."
     If we could understand the mystery of language better, we could
     also understand the strange behavior of man, "a wanderer, a
     castaway." Connections are established between Percy's Love in
     the Ruins and the essays; he continues to return to the enigma
     of "the symbol making of man the wayfarer."

12   FREISINGER, RANDALL ROY. "'To Move Wild Laughter in the
      Throat of Death': An Anatomy of Black Humor." Ph.D. disser-
      tation, University of Missouri.
          Extended definition of the literary genre labelled "Black
      Humor." Draws upon the work of approximately fourteen novelists
      including John Barth, Stanley Elkin, Bruce Jay Friedman, Joseph
      Heller, Ken Kesey, Thomas Pynchon, Kurt Vonnegut, and Percy,
      within an informing structure of Kenneth Burke's "pentad" of key
      terms: act, agent, scene, agency, and purpose. The views of
      the Black Humorist range from the affirmative gestures of Heller
      and Kesey to the muted hopefulness of Barth and Pynchon.

13   FULLER, EDMUND. Review of The Message in the Bottle. Wall
      Street Journal, 14 July, p. 8.
          The essays reveal Percy to be "a reflective, probing
      Christian humanist, one of whose most characteristic abilities
      is to pile question upon question, for page upon page, any one
      of which is grist for a week's thought."

14   GARVEY, JOHN. "Fantastic Stories." Commonweal 102
      (1 August):315.
          It has recently again been suggested that storytelling can
      be a vehicle for religious thought; "fantastic stories" such as
      those of Tolkien and Lewis in myth and science fiction provide
      "alternative presents, or pictures of the future." Perhaps this
      is why Percy in Love in the Ruins uses a future setting for such
      a setting can be "prophetic" as warning, not as prediction.

15   HARDY, JOHN EDWARD. "Percy, Walker." In Encyclopedia of
      World Literature in the Twentieth Century. Vol. 4. Edited by
      Frederick Ungar and Lina Mainiero. New York: Ungar, pp. 278,
      281.
          Short overview about Percy's three novels "of spiritual
      quest." The three heroes have so much in common that they seem
      to be "studies of the same man" in different "'phases.'" Percy's
      writing has an urbanity lacking in other Southern writers; his
      talent is rich and original and his place in "America letters
      seems already assured."

16   JOHNSON, MARK. "The Search for Place in Walker Percy's
      Novels." SLJ 8, no. 1 (Fall):55-81.
          The pilgrimages of Walker Percy's protagonists may be
      viewed in one sense "as a search for a place in the world, a mode
      of existence. . . ." Such a perspective "illuminates one of
      Percy's major themes while at the same time revealing his devel-
      oping sense of place in his novels. . . . Places are used in
      Percy's novels in three ways: as vehicles of his philosophy,
      particularly of some specific points drawn from Kierkegaard; as
      illustrations of artificial as opposed to authentic environments,
      with a heavy emphasis on the former; and finally, in each of the
      novels one of the structures emerges as a representative metaphor

for the mode of existence of the protagonist and the condition
of his society. These distinctions overlap, but there is generally an observable shift in the successive novels away from the
illustration of philosophical concepts toward an integration of
place into the dramatics of the novels themselves, communicating
as well as underlining characterization, themes and ironies."
For example, Binx Bolling and Will Barrett both occupy basements,
illustrating the Kierkegaardian metaphor that living in the
aesthetic stage corresponds to dwelling in the cellar of existence. In The Last Gentleman, Rita's New York apartment reveals
her inauthenticity as it changes in ambience from a "Barbados
cottage" to an "Indian hogan" as easily as she changes costumes.
In Love in the Ruins, Percy uses place to reveal theme and character more skillfully than in the previous two novels.

17   KENNER, HUGH. "On Man the Sad Talker." NatR 27, no. 35
      (12 September):1000-1002.
         Review of Message in the Bottle. Because Percy has focused
      so intently on man's singular capacity for language and linked
      that facility with man's sense of alienation, "he has probably
      made a breakthrough" of such import that this book "may one day
      rank with De Revolutionibus Orbium Coelestium. . . ." Percy
      resembles Copernicus in having "the main essential correct."
      Just as Copernicus insisted on the sun's centricity in the uni-
      verse, Percy has asserted "the Naming Faculty" as central to
      man's uniqueness.

18   KING, RICHARD H. Review of The Message in the Bottle. NL 58
      (13 October):18-19.
         The reviewer particularly cites "The Man on the Train" as
      "nothing less than an esthetic for the alienated consciousness."
      Of the essays as a whole, it is noted that "Percy's entire argu-
      ment can be read as a secular version of the 'Word become
      flesh. . . .'"

19   KISSEL, SUSAN STEVES. "For a 'Hostile Audience': A Study of
      the Fiction of Flannery O'Connor, Walker Percy, and J.F.
      Powers." Ph.D. dissertation, University of Cincinnati.
         Examination of how O'Connor, Percy, and Powers use struc-
      ture to anticipate their unwilling audience. In all three
      writers' work major characters begin with secular views; then
      through comic patterns a process of correction is introduced.
      These writers often provide a change in character awareness at
      the end; they succeed in communicating Catholic values because
      their presentation is made in complex, sometimes ironic or
      ambiguous ways.

20   LeCLAIR, THOMAS. "Death and Black Humor." Crit 17, no. 1:6,
      21-22.
         The centricity of death in Percy's novels, his comic inver-
      sion, and "his malice toward conventional religious, social, and

scientific pieties" place Percy within the tradition of Black
Humor.

21   _____. Review of The Message in the Bottle. NYTBR, 8 June,
      p. 6.
      Percy's "learning, precision, and passion for concepts" are
matched in contemporary novelists only by Gass and Bellow. His
essays focus on the "singularity of language" and demonstrate
that man is "qualitatively different from other animals." Message
is "ambitious, dense, and difficult," and while many of the
essays are primarily for specialists in language, the book can
be read by all who wonder why men speak, yet remain sad. Despite
repetition and unity of focus Percy's probes remain discrete,
what Percy calls "'the terra incognita of language use.'"

22   McMURTRY, LARRY. "What Language Reveals--And What It Con-
      ceals." BW, 19 May, p. B6.
      Favorable review of The Message in the Bottle that finds
the essays generally "a pleasure to read," despite Percy's being
"as formidably technical as Noam Chomsky or Levi-Strauss."

23   McNASPY, C.J. "'Why Does Man Feel So Sad?'" National
      Catholic Reporter 11 (29 August):7.
      Percy's learned Message in the Bottle, obviously the work
of a major writer and no "mere linguist," has passages which read
like fiction. His questions about language will prove of benefit
for nonlinguists since he provides "hundreds" of paragraphs as
probing as Pascal's Pensées.

24   MICHAELS, WALTER. Review of The Message in the Bottle. GaR
      29, no. 4 (Winter):972-75.
      As a collection, the essays pose problems because of the
variety of their scope and purpose, and because of the perplexity
of Percy's "peculiar synthesis of views derived from European
phenomenology and American empiricism." Another major flaw
exists in Percy's tackling the wrong opponents: in structuralism,
Bloomfield rather than Saussure; in modern semiotics, Tarski instead of Barthes. But "perhaps the major weakness of this book
turns out to be its limited sense of its own audience."

25   MURRAY, JOHN J. Review of The Message in the Bottle. BS 35
      (August):126.
      Odd review of Message wherein objections, agreements,
omissions are listed, but in such an obscure way that the review
is useless.

26   NAGEL, THOMAS. Review of The Message in the Bottle. NYRB 23,
      no. 14 (18 September):54-56.
      Percy's examination of problems about language is worth
study despite the fact that he does not provide documentation of
sources and is "unaware of much of the work pertinent to their

solution." The general questions of the nature of meaning which
interest Percy have been a topic of the philosophy of language
for decades, and Percy's suggestion of the need for an alternative to the scientific ideal of observation is "not radical
enough." The concluding essay which calls for a "physical basis
of meaning" seems to suggest Percy can get no further than to
invent a mythical physiology; what is, however, required is a
view of language as used by those within a community of speakers,
"not a spiritualizing" of the subject.

27   PINDELL, RICHARD. "Basking in the Eye of the Storm: The
      Esthetics of Loss in Walker Percy's The Moviegoer." Boundary 2
      4:219-30.
          Binx commingles two metaphysical extremes in the course of
The Moviegoer: he seriously searches for the meaning of his life
while he also relishes his existential angst. He juggles these
paradoxical modes by another, more deliberately paradoxical approach to life: "a simultaneous assumption and disavowal of the
world." Further, Binx's strong sense of irony gives him an aesthetic and emotional distance "that makes the commonplace beautiful." Finally, it is in his style, best exemplified in his description of evening in Gentilly, that Binx locates a place for
himself.

28   RIEHL, ROBERT ELLISON. "The Ordeal of Naming: Walker Percy's
      Philosophy of Language and His Novels." Ph.D. dissertation,
      University of Texas at Austin.
          In his fiction Percy indicates that contemporary debasement
of language issues from society's exaltation of the scientific
method. Additionally, he implies that man can reverse this de-
generative process through the conscious ordeal of naming anew
his experience.

29   RUBIN, LOUIS D., Jr. et al. "Twentieth-Century Southern Lit-
      erature." In Southern Literary Study: Problems and Possi-
      bilities. Edited by Louis D. Rubin, Jr., and C. Hugh Holman.
      Chapel Hill: University of North Carolina Press, pp. 133-64,
      esp. 138-41.
          Transcript from a panel discussion conducted by scholars of
southern literature. Cited is Percy's view that the stoic,
rather than the religious, tradition of the South has declined.
Will Barrett is mentioned as a personification of the southerner
so estranged from the traditional code that he fails to understand it. One panelist maintains that he knows "of no contemporary author who has given better testimony [than Percy] to the
indelible character of southern culture as it still exists."
Another panel member asserts that Percy's religious view, though
Roman Catholic, is rooted in his southern background.

30   TORRENS, J. "Walker Percy's Bicentennial Message." <u>America</u>
      133 (25 October):256-58.
           Eschewing the nationalistic hyperbole that characterizes
      bicentennial observations, Percy advances a realistic look at the
      state of the nation. His essays can be read as glosses to his
      novels: in particular, "The Man on the Train" to elucidate <u>The</u>
      <u>Moviegoer</u>; "The Delta Factor" as philosophical background on <u>The</u>
      <u>Last Gentleman</u>; and "Notes for a Novel about the End of the
      World" as a preface to <u>Love in the Ruins</u>. In fact, the progres-
      sion of the essays, as well as that of the novels, seems to have
      led inexorably to the eschatological theme of <u>Love in the Ruins</u>.
      Despite his condemnation of the nation within the novel, "the
      final paradox about [Percy], the laconic crier of urgent news, as
      Percy admits, is that he makes use of all the facilities which
      America offers in order to scold it."

31   TYLER, ANNE. "The Topic is Language--With Love and Skill."
      <u>National Observer</u> 14 (19 July):21.
           The essays are a potpourri of semantics, linguistics,
      psychology, and philosophy seasoned with a little lagniappe--"a
      certain joyful enthusiasm not often found in works so full, as
      this one is, of diagrams and equations." The best section is the
      middle one, which "veers almost against its will into matters
      purely literary. . . ." Marring the final sections, which con-
      tain "a highly technical discussion of semiotics," are his lapses
      in logic, failure to mention some important scholars, and unnec-
      cessarily abstruse writing.

32   VAUTHIER, SIMONE. "Title as Microtext: The Example of <u>The</u>
      <u>Moviegoer</u>." <u>The Journal of Narrative Technique</u> 5, no. 3:
      219-29.
           In the course of reading <u>The Moviegoer</u>, the reader slowly
      realizes that the title refers to an existential mode of being
      rather than to the designation of one who simply attends movies.
      "The text not only saturates the general name of the title with
      information, it blows it up into a complex metaphor for man's
      ambivalent relation to experience. . . ." This realization is
      somewhat startling because the title alone conveys so little in-
      formation and what is conveyed is ambiguous. Short and unallu-
      sive, the words <u>the moviegoer</u> seem to suggest the relationship
      between "an escapist . . . and the world of cinematographic
      illusion." Percy's original title, <u>The Confessions of a Movie-</u>
      <u>goer</u>, juxtaposing "intense inner life and seriousness of purpose"
      with "light entertainment and escapism," would have conveyed more
      information but also might have invited an unwarranted levity.
      Because "Binx uses the movies both negatively in flight from the
      concrete world, and positively to recover reality and see through
      the common delusions," his appelation as "the moviegoer" rein-
      forces his position as a pilgrim. Ultimately, the title suggests
      "that we are all of us moviegoers."

33   ZAIDMAN, BERNARD. Review of The Message in the Bottle. LJ
     100, no. 14 (August):1417.
          Percy analyzes the "consequences of man's use of the sym-
     bol," and maintains that we have no adequate theory of language;
     yet he also is "unable to uncover the [semological-phonological]
     link between the two elements of that core."

34   ZEUGNER, JOHN F. "Walker Percy and Gabriel Marcel: The
     Castaway and the Wayfarer." MissQ 28, no. 1 (Winter):21-53.
          Walker Percy has acknowledged the influence on his writings
     of French Catholic existentialist Gabriel Marcel, and this influ-
     ence is especially apparent in Percy's preoccupation with the
     concept of intersubjectivity. For Marcel, intersubjectivity is
     "the intimate, subjective relation between two persons"; in
     Percy's novels the relationship becomes "the ground of being, the
     basis of consciousness, the way out of alienation, and a path to
     salvation." In his writings on philosophy and language, Percy
     examines the intersubjective nature of communication, maintaining
     that it forms the basis of the symbolization process. From
     Marcel, Percy also appropriates the term wayfarer, using it in
     one sense to denote the person deprived of intersubjectivity and
     in a more theological context as a designation for man in his
     fallen state. Percy maintains, as Marcel did before him, that
     "to live authentically . . . was to realize that one was a cast-
     away awaiting news of salvation. . . ." Percy contends that one
     must recognize this wayfarer status before one can be receptive
     to the good news of salvation. The spiritual progress of Binx
     Bolling depicted in The Moviegoer "is a full illustration of the
     power of intersubjectivity to lead the wayfarer out of alienation
     into authenticity and salvation." Such a clear-cut progression
     is not evident in The Last Gentleman. Will Barrett fails to
     achieve intersubjectivity with either "the disillusioned hater
     of self-actualization," Sutter, or "the illusion-minded Kitty."
     Percy also is indebted to Marcel for the concept of abstraction,
     and "Love in the Ruins can be seen as a series of repudiating
     illustrations of the dangers of abstraction implicit in American
     culture." Percy has become increasingly political with each
     successive novel. In Love in the Ruins, he manifests a "Southern
     aristocratic condescension," which overshadows his spiritual con-
     cerns.

                              1976

1   ANON. "Walker Percy." In Contemporary Literary Criticism.
     Vol. 6. Edited by Carolyn Riley and Phyllis Carmel Mendelson.
     Detroit: Gale Research Co., pp. 399-401.
          Introduction asserts "the search for individual identity in
     the post-bellum South and the reconciliation of love as a grand
     ideal with modern moral confusion are abiding themes in Percy's
     distinguished fiction." Excerpts are from the following: The

Antioch Review [Anon.] (1971.5), Cleanth Brooks (1973.8), Lewis
Jerome Taylor, Jr. (1974.11), Thomas LeClair (1975.20-21), and
Jane Larkin Crain (1975.10). Also Eugene Lyons, Southwest Review
(Spring 1974), a review of Martin Luschei and John Carr not in-
cluded in this reference guide (see 1972.13, 1971.16).

2   APPLEYARD, J.A. "Critic's Choice for Christmas." Commonweal
    102 (5 December):597.
        Brief mention of The Message in the Bottle: "Percy's
graceful clarity makes [one] wish all books on language could be
written by novelists."

3   ARRINGTON, ROBERT L. "The Mystery of Language." SR 84, no. 4
    (Fall):cxxvii-cxxx.
        By relating problems which result from "rigorous profes-
sionalism" and the limits imposed on knowledge in the twentieth
century, the reviewer admits the seriousness of Percy's inquiry.
Alienation can be "related to and explained in terms of the fact
that man is a symbol-user"; however, many of Percy's suggestions
are not worked out, and Percy's major claim seems to rest "on an
obscure idealist conception of thought." In spite of reservations about the "ultimate philosophical value" of the book one
sees immediately what Percy is "trying to do."

4   AUER, MICHAEL JOSEPH. "Angels and Beasts: Gnosticism in
    American Literature." Ph.D. dissertation, University of North
    Carolina at Chapel Hill.
        Traces the religion of Gnosticism from its origins in the
first centuries after Christ and examines how the Gnostic concept
of self as something apart from flesh has reentered the modern
world in the Cartesian cogito. Poe and Emerson are examined as
Gnostics. Evidence of a Gnostic outlook is seen in Emily
Dickinson, Walt Whitman and Hemingway. This Gnostic point of
view is countered by writers such as Percy who are willing to
accept man as incarnate.

5   BORGMAN, PAUL C. Review of The Message in the Bottle.
    Christian Scholar's Review 6, no. 2-3:272-73.
        Parallels between Percy and Ortega y Gasset's theorizing
are mentioned. Both are concerned with formulating an adequate
theory of man, and while Percy's is a Christian search, Ortega's
thought parallels his in these "wonderful" essays. Percy describes the uniquely human act as the "ability to symbolize with
an intentional act of naming."

6   BROUGHTON, PANTHEA REID. "A Bottle Unopened, a Message Un-
    read." VQR 52, no. 1 (Winter):155-60.
        "These essays may not answer Percy's own questions, but
they go a long way toward answering Wittenstein [sic] . . . and
toward refuting (or at least undermining) both Skinner and
Chomsky." Percy analyzes the themes of alienation and language

as symbol from the stance of a detached observer, a perspective which has marred his novels but lends freshness to the essays.

7   BUKOSKI, ANTHONY. "The Lady and Her Business of Love in Selected Southern Fiction." Studies in the Humanities 5, no. 1 (January):14-18.
     Kate of The Moviegoer is mentioned as belonging to a class of female characters in Southern fiction dubbed "Love-Brokers" for their scheming exploitation of hapless men.

8   CASPER, LEONARD. Review of The Message in the Bottle. Thought 51, no. 201 (June):211-12.
     Recognizes importance of Percy's underlying argument that "the most reasonable explanation for man's madness" in this age is that "we must be castaways." The significance of the mind's power of association is basic for Percy whose musings and "logical/evidential refutations of Carnap and Skinner have to be ranked with the best of Cassirer, Langer, and Chomsky."

9   CULLER, JONATHAN. "Man the Symbol-Monger." YR 65 (December): 261-66.
     "Mr. Percy raises a series of problems which are central to contemporary thinking about signs, representation, and symbolic systems, and though he often does so without full awareness of their implications or of the distinctions which others have raised, his clear presentation and his skill in relating them to little dramas of ordinary experience make this a book to recommend." Also reviewed is Roland Barthes's The Pleasure of the Text.

10   DENT, HUNTLEY. Review of The Message in the Bottle. University of Denver Quarterly 10, no. 4 (Winter):141-42.
     Essays provide pleasure of watching an artist outside his field. Percy is, however, attuned to the centrality of his subject, one of importance for modern man. Percy's blend of "ideosyncrasy and theorizing" allows him to focus on problems of language so that he can express his hope that the study of signs will go beyond behavior and open for man a new road to consciousness.

11   DORAN, LINDA KAY DYER. "Naming as Disclosure: A Study of Theme and Method in the Fiction of Walker Percy." Ph.D. dissertation, George Peabody College for Teachers.
     Through his art Percy effects a reversal of alienation by allowing his reader to participate in the intersubjectivity of naming. This naming is threefold, being demonstrated in the indirect communication of the novel itself, in the emphasis on religious rite and observance as symbol, and in the reader's participation in the re-presentation of experience.

12   GASTON, PAUL L. Review of The Message in the Bottle. Journal
     of Modern Literature 5, no. 4 (Supplement):611-13.
          The Message in the Bottle illuminates the themes of Percy's
     fiction, "providing the best available introduction to the in-
     tellectual content of the three novels in print as well as an
     intimation of concerns likely to surface in future work." But
     the essays serve as much more than a gloss to the novels; "The
     Message in the Bottle is an instructive and provocative work of
     wide cross-disciplinary learning and syncretic imagination."

13   GRAY, PAUL. "Yoknapatawpha Blues." Time 108, no. 13
     (27 September):92-93.
          Within a survey of contemporary Southern literature,
     Percy's art is used to suggest a way to escape Faulkner's shadow
     for Percy has chosen to examine not the past, but the present.
     This method "strikes some as aesthetically disappointing." Percy
     is quoted as saying writers "have the challenge to bring the
     peculiar Southern quality to bear on whatever we write."

14   KIRBY, MARTIN. "Neither Far Out Nor in Deep." The Carleton
     Miscellany 16 (Fall-Winter):209-14.
          Although Percy seemingly is concerned with the study of
     linguistics in these essays, he apparently is "writing less about
     language than about religion." In his central argument that the
     phenomenon of language provides the key to the study of man, "he
     substitutes cryptomystic eloquence for the effective assembling
     of a logical case." Also, Percy errs in using Helen Keller's
     cognitive grasp of the word water as a paradigm for man's acqui-
     sition of language because her condition was complex and unusual.
     Percy further oversimplifies by attributing man's uniqueness
     solely to language. Moreover, Percy's contention that man could
     recover his sovereignty by seeking direct experience is basically
     a romantic notion. In short, "Percy's essays show him to be an
     admirable man: serious, kind-hearted, and genuinely worried
     about the state of human affairs. But he is fundamentally anti-
     rational, and, for the most part, he fails to convince."

15   KLINE, EDWARD A. "Words, Words, Words." Review of Politics
     38, no. 1 (January):139-41.
          Review of A Message in the Bottle. Since the book has been
     reviewed from a philosophical point of view by Thomas Nagel
     (1975.26), this review concentrates on the linguistic. Percy did
     not discover the "Delta Factor": he coins a name for something
     theorizers of language have known since the physis-nomos contro-
     versy. Percy does not really confront the issue of the nature of
     communication. His book is interesting and does lead us back to
     man himself, but so have many other linguistic theories developed
     in the last 300 years.

16   LAWSON, LEWIS A. "Walker Percy as Martian Visitor." SLJ 8,
      no. 2 (Spring):102-13.
          The chronology of Percy's life, together with his preoccu-
      pation with the concept of recovery of the self through ordeal,
      indicates that his personal ordeals, particularly his bout with
      tuberculosis, precipitated a dramatic change within his con-
      sciousness. He has shared his particular perspective as scien-
      tist cum phenomenologist in numerous journal articles (a number
      of which appear in The Message in the Bottle) which look pre-
      dominantly at the relation between man's behavior and his unique
      capacity for language. Because his extensive reading in philos-
      ophy as well as in science has convinced Percy that science can
      say nothing about an individual person, except in his resemblance
      to others, Percy has adopted a unique stance from which to view
      the phenomenon of man: "He realized that he would have to ap-
      proach man not as a scientist, but as a Martian." Accordingly,
      in addition to recording his observations in essays, he also
      began writing novels "as a means of testing out and verifying
      his theories according to their truthfulness to a human situa-
      tion." His investigations both in his essays and in his novels
      point to one conclusion: "the only thing man can know about him-
      self by symbolization has been implied, that if he is not content
      with the objective-empirical he can only be alienated, a cast-
      away." Consequently, he must seek "news from across the seas" as
      the title The Message in the Bottle indicates.

17   MACK, JAMES ROBERT. "Love and Marriage in Walker Percy's
      Novels." Ph.D. dissertation, Emory University.
          Love and marriage are focal points in Percy's investiga-
      tions of such philosophical concepts as symbolization, inter-
      subjectivity, loss of sovereignty, and apocalypse. Specifically,
      marriage represents a solution to existential angst since it em-
      bodies intersubjective communion and sacrament.

18   McLELLAN, JOSEPH. "Paperbacks." BW, 16 May, p. L4.
          A brief, favorable note about The Message in The Bottle.

19   MICHAELS, WALTER. Review of The Message in the Bottle. GaR
      29, no. 4 (Winter):972-75.
          While readers may be perplexed by the synthesis of European
      phenomenology and American empiricism, these essays, like "mu-
      tually exclusive desires," have a certain charm. Percy identi-
      fies meaning with an interpretive community, and because he never
      examines, for example, Saussure and Barthes, and seems to address
      American positivists only, his weakest points, such as acceptance
      of "'an empiricism which tacitly posits the world' . . . go un-
      challenged." There are still other paradoxical problems about
      interpretation and community because of Percy's insistence that
      to see, to understand, is to avoid falling into everydayness.

20   MILLER, NOLAN. Review of <u>The Message in the Bottle</u>. <u>AR</u> 34
     (Spring):369.
          This brief review notes that "for all the conundrums that
     remain unsolved in every theory about language, Percy satisfies
     us that unexplored territories of knowledge remain undis-
     covered. . . ."

21   NEILSON, KEITH. "The Message in the Bottle." In <u>Masterplots</u>
     <u>1976 Annual</u>. Edited by Frank N. Magill. Englewood Cliffs,
     N.J.: Salem Press, pp. 221-24.
          A "deeply serious" collection of essays; Percy is concerned
     with fundamental questions about modern man. He designates him-
     self an "amateur" in relation to linguistics, but his designation
     implies an assumption about experts who study language: they are
     all "partisan." Percy, as amateur, has a fresh point of view and
     he raises basic questions about language and human activity.
     Percy believes that language is a "divine gift." He sees para-
     doxes between the scientific and Christian views of man and his
     answers, such as in the "Delta Factor" about man's naming process,
     that suggest man's special place in the universe.

22   O'DONNELL, ROY. Review of <u>The Message in the Bottle</u>. <u>English</u>
     <u>Journal</u> 65, no. 5 (May):75.
          Perhaps the book would have been more coherent if the
     essays were revised. What unity there is comes from Percy's
     interest in the nature of human communications and the rejection
     of common linguistic theories such as descriptive (structural)
     linguistics. Percy advocates "the theory of abduction set forth
     by Charles Peirce" and talks about the "triadic" nature of lan-
     guage communication, but the "coupler" remains a mystery. While
     ignoring some important theory, Percy asks some of the correct
     questions.

23   PERCY, WALKER. "A Symposium on Fiction: Donald Barthelme,
     William Gass, Grace Paley, Walker Percy." <u>Shenandoah</u> 27,
     no. 2 (Winter):3-31.
          Percy indicates his views that literature conveys a pri-
     marily cognitive type of knowledge, that language must constantly
     be renewed because "words get worn out," and that the narrative
     element is an "essential ingredient" of the fictional process.

24   RUBIN, LOUIS D., Jr. et al. "Deep Delta." In <u>Mississippi</u>
     <u>Writers in Context: Transcripts of</u> "A Climate for Genius,"
     a Television Series. Edited by Robert L. Phillips, Jr.
     Jackson: Mississippi Library Commission, pp. 17-33, esp.
     21-22, 25-27.
          Participants included Shelby Foote, Ellen Douglas, Hodding
     Carter III, and Professors Louis Rubin, Lewis Simpson, and Thomas
     Daniel Young. Topics ranged from the influence of William
     Alexander Percy on the writers of Greenville to the economic
     conditions that produced a sense of the compression of history.

In particular, William Alexander Percy influenced his cousin and
adopted son, Walker. This influence is dramatized in the relationship between Aunt Emily and Binx Bolling in The Moviegoer.
Binx's reaction to the philosophy of his aunt creates the tension
and the drama of the novel. Additional topics of concern to
Delta writers include religion and interest in "the Southern
military tradition." "The final destruction of family and family
responsibility" is another important consideration. In The Last
Gentleman, this theme is compressed into the three generations
represented by Will Barrett, his father, and his grandfather.

25   RYAN, STEVEN TOM. "Chaotic Slumber: Picaresque and Gothic in
      Contemporary American Novels." Ph.D. dissertation, University
      of Utah.
          Consideration of novelists who have used the picaresque and
      gothic as responses to a breakdown of order in the modern world.
      Entropic disorder is central. The concluding chapter investi-
      gates language as the link between individual consciousness and
      the external world. While Gothic fiction seems to retreat from
      the reader, picaresque fiction embraces reader and language.
      Nevertheless, Percy's Last Gentleman and Love in the Ruins pre-
      sent a world where mind and body are separated, and in which
      lifeless equilibrium remains a threat.

26   SCOTT, ROBERT L. Review of The Message in the Bottle.
      Communication Quarterly 24, no. 1 (Winter):51-52.
          Percy's essays may leave the reader with many questions,
      but he does provide the correct ones. He raises questions about
      linguistics, language, semiotics, but implies there must be more
      to life than this. Percy's theories reveal that he is a "true
      intersubjectivist." While the essays are repetitive, the in-
      sights shimmer with value.

27   SIMS, BARBARA B. "Jaybirds as Portents of Hell in Percy and
      Faulkner." NMW 9, no. 1 (Spring-Winter):24-27.
          Although Walker Percy disclaims being a writer in the
      Southern oral tradition, folklore motifs appear in his fiction.
      In particular, like Faulkner in The Sound and the Fury, Percy
      uses jaybirds figuratively to reinforce his theme of moral and
      spiritual decay. Thus, he is alluding to the Southern Negro be-
      lief that the jaybird is "the devil's ally, spy, and messenger."
      It is significant that Percy twice uses jaybirds metaphorically
      in describing the hellish visit of Binx and Kate to Chicago.

28   SMITH, MARCUS. "Talking about Talking: An Interview with
      Walker Percy." New Orleans Review 5, no. 1:3-18.
          Percy is interviewed about concepts of language developed
      in The Message in the Bottle. He maintains that his approach to
      semiotics "is essentially behavioral, beginning with observable
      data" but includes "seeing how far an analysis of language would
      take us toward an understanding of . . . other equally unique

human traits." He insists that a mysterious element, "a
'coupler' . . . an 'I' which thinks" applies in explaining
linguistic behavior. Percy indicates that the book primarily
addresses man's paradoxical status of being at once a part of the
universe and detached from it, and examines such duality through
man's capacity for and dependence upon language. Elaborating on
the development of his thinking and writing, he contrasts the
view of man in modern literature as alienated and homeless with
that of the scientific view which seeks "to fit man into a body
of phenomena." He explains that The Message in the Bottle attempts "to reconcile these two views from a scientific point of
view." Additionally, he discusses his approaches to language and
character in his work in progress, Lancelot.

29   STUCKEY, W.J. "Percy, Walker." In Contemporary Novelists.
      2d ed. Edited by James Vinson. New York: St. Martin's
      Press, pp. 978-79.
          Included are a brief biography, a list of novels through
      1971, and a critical assessment. Percy is classified in the
      "'waste land' school of modern literature," sharing the world
      view of Eliot, Fitzgerald, and Faulkner. Though his concerns are
      ultimately religious, he skillfully delineates manners as well.
      "His rendering of characters and scenes is strikingly fresh,
      vivid and bitingly satirical," and his style is "sensitive and
      poetic."

30   SULLIVAN, WALTER. A Requiem for the Renascence: The State of
      Fiction in the Modern South. Athens: University of Georgia
      Press, 90 pp., esp. 64-69.
          Percy's first three novels progressively illustrate the way
      in which southern literature is diminished as southern culture
      dissolves. Binx Bolling's drama, while existential in nature,
      unfolds within a distinctively southern milieu; but Will Barrett,
      estranged from his present as well as his past, has a decidedly
      solipsistic view of the world. Percy's placing Love in the Ruins
      in the future "is indicative of his divorce as an artist from his
      own culture."

31   SULLIVAN, WILLIAM A., Jr. "Walker Percy." Jackson:
      Mississippi Library Commission, 8 pp.
          Although Percy was not well-known until he won the National
      Book Award for Fiction in 1962, he had been writing linguistic
      and philosophical essays since the fifties. The formative years
      of his life were spent under the guidance of William Alexander
      Percy, his second cousin. Walker Percy gained "'a vocation and
      in a real sense a second self'" through their association. A
      conflict between generations—one that espoused stoicism and one
      that saw it as "an impediment to social progress in the South"—
      was not a reality for Walker Percy. Instead, he saw the possi-
      bilities of each individual as a tribute "'to the best people we
      know to use them as best we can, to become not their disciples,

but ourselves.'" The relationship between W.A.P. and Walker
Percy is reflected in the characters of Aunt Emily and Binx in
The Moviegoer. Walker both echoes and mocks William Alexander's
Stoic posture.
    Percy's work is often considered existentialist or Chris-
tian existentialist. The rigid ethics implicit in existentialism
are compatible and adaptable to Christian principles--man must
"accept moral responsibility for other men, because in choosing
or willing himself, he chooses or wills man." The structure of
Percy's novels is not classical. Replacing the linear development of a plot and its resolution, Percy begins with a situation
and explores "the reactions that take place between a character
and his environment and the people he meets." Essay continues by
examining the singular consciousness of The Moviegoer, The Last
Gentleman, and Love in the Ruins. The role of the protagonist is
often a vehicle for the author's voice or the recipient of the
author's satire. As satirist Percy makes frequent use of irony
and "the juxtaposition of illusion and reality."
    In addition to existentialism, Percy's fiction is relevant
to the philosophy presented in Science and the Modern World by
Alfred North Whitehead. Science, however, is not without its
flaws. Percy therefore deals with the concept of mistaking the
idea for the real in his novels and in the essay "The Loss of the
Creature." His "corrective" for modern man's alienation is in
the questions that he asks: "'the question is not whether the
Good News is no longer relevant, but rather whether it is possible that man is undergoing a tempestuous restructuring of his
consciousness which does not allow him to take account of the
Good News.'" Because he communicates hope and possibility to the
modern world, Walker Percy is an appropriate spokesman.

32   TELOTTE, JAY PAUL. "To Talk Creatively: A Study of the
     Writings of Walker Percy." Ph.D. dissertation, University of
     Florida.
    Percy's novels illustrate the importance of rediscovering
the creative possibility of language as a remedy to despair. His
heroes discover renewed meaning in their lives and approach sovereign wholeness when they begin to communicate authentically
with others. The novels themselves represent the effectiveness
of intersubjectivity as realized through the affirmative act of
naming.

33   TENENBAUM, RUTH BETSY. "Walker Percy's 'Consumer-Self' in The
     Last Gentleman." LaS 15, no. 3 (Fall):304-9.
    Will Barrett is "the last gentleman" indicated in the
novel's title and therein lies his problem. He is last in both a
final and an ultimate sense, and he is a gentleman with all that
appelative's connotations of refined docility. Thus, "the preg-
nant title carries within itself not only the thematic germs of
the novel but the story's denouement as well." A gentleman of
his ilk cannot survive the consumer mandates of a technological

society, "a capitalistic world gone haywire." Not only are
Will's chief acquaintances, the Vaughts, obsessed with getting
and spending; but also "Percy deliberately drenches both landscape and characters with commercially named products." Will's
own attempt to facilitate his quest for selfhood with a piece of
expensive equipment, the high-powered telescope, yields nothing
more revealing than the label on a can of beer. Finally, with
his decision to work in the automobile agency, "the last gentleman becomes a consumer-self and a self consumed."

34   WINEAPPLE, BRENDA. "Neo-Romanticism in Contemporary American
     Fiction." Ph.D. dissertation, University of Wisconsin,
     Madison.
          Provides a definition of neo-romanticism which argues that
     this phenomenon exists across time; Emerson, Faulkner and Mailer
     are used to generate a model of neo-romanticism which diverges
     from modernism. The fiction of the postwar era presents a wide
     range of writers who in their neo-romanticism react to contempo-
     rary culture. The most well known exemplifiers of neo-romanticism
     are Percy, Kesey, Kerouac, Beagle, Elkin, and Vonnegut.

35   WOOD, RALPH. Review of The Message in the Bottle. CC 92
     (3 December):1115.
          The reviewer contends that the "repetitive arguments and
     barbarous neologisms [of the essays] will offend even those pre-
     pared to follow Percy's complex logic." But he also credits
     Percy with having "developed a truly profound anthropology."

                              1977

1   ANON. "A Christmas Potpourri of Books." Wall Street Journal,
     15 December, p. 20.
          Lancelot is "a witty, savage story of a man's failure."

2   ANON. Review of Lancelot. Booklist 73, no. 12 (15 February):
     879.
          A brief note: Episodes range "far and wide" and "cumulate
     into a moving and leisurely self-portrait."

3   ANON. Review of Lancelot. CC 94 (6 July):634-36.
          Though jarring upon first reading, Lancelot serves to "con-
     front us mercilessly with the nature of damnation in our time."
     In short, "it is not a cheery book, and those of us who would
     make Percy out to be a safe Christian novelist had better
     beware."

4   ANON. Review of Lancelot. Choice 14, no. 4 (June):536.
          Lancelot's "rage" seems as ridiculous as his "tirades"
     against the evils of the times. Percy's heroes seem more atrac-
     tive in their earlier forms; nevertheless he is a writer "of
     power and stature."

5   ANON. Review of <u>Lancelot</u>. <u>Kirkus</u> 45, no. 1 (1 January):16.
       "Percy / Jeremiah," as if disappointed that America did not
right itself after the "comic forecasts of <u>Love in the Ruins</u>,"
returns with "less funny stuff . . . and much more resolve."
Lancelot's tirades will keep the reader from sleep; Percy is "a
great novelist working in the public interest."

6   ANON. Review of <u>Lancelot</u>. <u>PW</u> 211, no. 2 (10 January):66.
       "Powerful" novel in which the questions of Lancelot raise
still other questions about values. Percy's "outrage" at the way
we live is strong, but effective.

7   ANON. Review of <u>Lancelot</u>. <u>Rolling Stone</u>, 7 April, p. 87.
       This brief note represents the novel as "absurd mutterings
. . . on the general loathsomeness of the human condition. . . ."

8   BAKER, J.F., ed. "PW Interviews." <u>PW</u> 211 (21 March):6-7.
       Percy openly responds to questions pertaining mainly to his
latest novel, <u>Lancelot</u>, but also to those about the state of the
South and his position as a Southern novelist. He reveals that
rather than the dramatic monologue <u>Lancelot</u> eventually became, he
originally conceived it as a dialogue between "Lancelot representing . . . 'the Southern Greco Roman honor code' and
Percival . . . the Judeo-Christian tradition." Additionally,
Percy indicates that the South has lost its sense of a special
identity: "Louisianans seem to respond more vitally to the use
of their historic settings for movies than they do to their
actual historical resonance." He laments his isolation from
other writers and admits that he would "really love to meet
[John] Cheever and talk to him."

9   BARNES, JULIAN. "Pantyhose." <u>New Statesman</u> 94, no. 2431
       (21 October):556-57.
       Like pantyhose, the novels dominating the American mass-
market come in one size and fit nearly everybody. Three novels
are dismissed; "which leaves the real novel" by Percy. <u>Lancelot</u>'s
main character "is excellently done." The novel "survives its
silly mythic impositions," and this is a tribute to Percy's
strength as "a naturally wry and ordered novelist."

10   BIGGER, CHARLES P. "Logos and Epiphany: Walker Percy's
       Theology of Language." <u>SoR</u> 13, no. 1 (January):196-206.
       An anomaly in the American tradition of writing, Percy
resembles European writers in his emphasis on man as a spiritual
and historical self. Thus, Percy also runs counter to the American current of eighteenth-century Rationalism, which is still
extant and which has accumulated the detritus of "Protestantism,
capitalism, barren distances, and the social and behavioral
sciences. . . ." Percy has taken on the scientific tradition
and subjected it to the searching light which is the coming-into-
being of the <u>logos</u> itself and has, on the whole successfully,

showed its incapacity to yield understanding." In his investigation of the relationship between language and being, Percy particularly emphasizes the importance of metaphor. One flaw in
Percy's philosophy "is that he has, in freeing us from [the]
naturalistic jargon of the social sciences, unwittingly laid
claim to the sterile jargon of despair we have inherited from
Kierkegaard and romantic existentialism."

11   BLEWITT, CHARLES G. Review of Lancelot. BS 37 (June):73.
        Brief comment about strength of Lancelot as "strongest,
angriest" Percy to date, "nothing less than superb."

12   BROOKS, CLEANTH. "Walker Percy and Modern Gnosticism." SoR
        13, no. 4 (Autumn):677-87.
        In what the author deems a "mini-essay" and elsewhere
"notes for an essay to be written," he draws parallels between
the views of Walker Percy and those which Eric Voegelin propounds
in his five-volume series Order and History. Both Percy and
Voegelin depict modern man as being deluded by the gnostic belief
that he can achieve bliss and fulfillment on earth, in contrast
to the Judeo-Christian tradition that man is destined to feel
homeless and alienated while on earth. Whereas Percy primarily
contends that present-day scientists and humanists are the engi-
neers of this modern gnosticism, Voegelin traces the current
faith in utopia back to the original gnostic cults. The parallels between Percy's novels and Voegelin's study indicate that
the former are "certainly not to be regarded as the privileged
crankiness of a somewhat eccentric Roman Catholic intellectual,"
but rather that "they have a close relation to a powerful and
searching criticism of the modern world." Reprinted: 1979.3.

13   CASHIN, EDWARD J. "History as Mores: Walker Percy's
        Lancelot." GaR 31, no. 4 (Winter):875-80.
        Because Walker Percy reveals a "felt" history rather than
a factual one, he illuminates Southern heritage more accurately
than does a historian. Such an internalized history includes the
mores and mythology that a people live by. Despite the influences of the mercantile tradition of Charleston and the evangelical tradition of the Great Awakening, the planter mentality
of Virginia with its chivalric code prevails in the South. Included in the Virginia tradition are "a widespread dedication to
public responsibility, a scorn for moneygrubbing as an end in
itself, an emphasis on honor, a conviction that those in govern-
ment should not cheat or steal, [and] a competition for self-
improvement. . . ." Percy expounds such an ethos in Lancelot,
failing "to recognize the commercial tradition as genuinely
Southern" and acknowledging, but disdaining, the evangelical
tradition. Thus, Percy "emphasizes and glorifies the Virginia
ideal. . . ."

14   CHESNICK, EUGENE. "De Contemptu Mundi." <u>Nat</u> 224, no. 17
     (30 April):533.
          By focusing on Percy's continuing interest in film and the
     gap between what movies prepare us to expect and reality, the
     plot, and especially the plot of the movie being made in <u>Lancelot</u>,
     are related to Percy's intellectual interests. In the novel
     Percy "dissects our feelinglessness" and thereby reflects some of
     his own attitudes toward the quality of modern life.

15   CHRISTOPHER, MICHAEL. "Days of Thorn and Roses." <u>U.S.</u>
     <u>Catholic</u> 42, no. 8 (August):49-51, esp. 49-50.
          Percy is described as a "fine" Catholic writer "whose
     specialty is the novel of introspection and social vision."
     <u>Lancelot</u> (reviewed with several other novels) is described as a
     "study in madness." This allegory about what is happening to the
     Southern and national moral landscape is "so freighted with mean-
     ing that . . . it topples from the weight" and simply becomes
     absurd. It is noted, however, the novel has received "lavish
     praise" elsewhere.

16   COOK, BRUCE. "The Last Man in America Who Believes in Love."
     <u>SatR</u> 4 (19 March):28-29.
          Percy is sometimes overlooked because of all contemporary
     novelists he is the most difficult to fix; he is "essentially a
     philosophical novelist." <u>Lancelot</u> can be related to Percy's
     "Notes for a Novel About the End of the World" for what happens
     in the novel, Lance's recitation of troubles, finally makes the
     book "work a kind of magic." The novel seems bigger on the in-
     side than on the outside and Percy, speaking through his "mad-
     man," is eloquent.

17   COSER, LEWIS A. "Culture and Society." <u>Society</u> 14, no. 4
     (July-August):85-87.
          Cheever's <u>Falconer</u> and <u>Lancelot</u> are examples of writers
     restricting art severely. There are similarities in their main
     characters. Percy has provided a portrait of a "modern fascist"
     character, and has pointed to some of the social and psychologi-
     cal factors that combine to create such personalities, yet
     Cheever's character is treated with empathy and his portrait
     contains hope. Percy's attitude is not immediately clear; he
     seems to suggest the end of our civilization is near.

18   CUFFE, E.D. "Percy and Cheever: Prison as Prism." <u>America</u>
     136 (12 March):220-21.
          The reviewer commends the novel for "some brilliant epi-
     grammatic eloquence and dazzling bits of description," and also
     for its "narrative power and the tantalizing suspense of its
     structure."

19   DAVIS, HOPE HALL. Review of Lancelot. NL 60, no. 9
      (25 April):14-15.
         Lancelot reviewed with John Cheever's Falconer; Cheever's
      book has met with critical acclaim, perhaps because he is able
      to give a view of an outsider who must make sense of life in the
      difficult circumstances of prison life. Percy's book, however,
      is problematic because the harangues of Lancelot are so extreme.
      Percy seems to have forgotten that there cannot be a literature
      of alienation because alienation "is transformed in the act of
      writing."

20   DUBUS, ANDRE. "Paths to Redemption." Harper's 254, no. 1523
      (April):86-88.
         While there may appear to be repetitions in the novel from
      earlier novels by Percy, what we have is the "resonant sound of a
      writer grappling with his theme." All of Percy's heroes ask
      questions about the meaning of life, but they cannot obtain abso-
      lute answers and in successive novels Percy's heroes are por-
      trayed less comically as the world closes in on them. In
      Lancelot Percy depicts a world where one can no longer be content
      with "amused tolerance," and Lancelot's radical actions which
      bring destruction are Percy's "counterattack" against the forces
      which threaten life.

21   EGERTON, JOHN. "Memorable Madman." Progressive 41 (June):
      40-41.
         The reviewer finds the novel "to be as skillfully crafted
      as [Percy's] other books, as compelling, as complex--but in the
      end less interesting," primarily because it is difficult to take
      seriously the mad ravings of Lancelot.

22   FOOTE, BUD. "A New Lancelot Seeks His Knighthood." National
      Observer, 12 March, p. 19.
         Lancelot is so unerringly justified in his moral outrage
      that one can easily lose sight of his insanity. The ending is
      indeterminate, but the book abounds with perceptive and symbolic
      matter.

23   FORD, RICHARD. "Walker Percy: Not Just Whistling Dixie."
      NatR 29 (13 May):558, 560-64.
         Percy's sentences are masterfully written and that mastery
      of the moment-to-moment suggests the strength of his accomplish-
      ment. Percy's concern with the change from a South which was
      recognizable to a place of anonymity is outlined. Yet in
      Lancelot Percy seems to want to teach readers, and he attempts
      to do so through a mad scheme. If the novel is a parody, it does
      not work; it only works part of the time and at others it is just
      sad. Still another deficiency in the novel is that Percy seems
      to have been so intent on providing ideas that he often seems to
      have lost his facility for writing good prose.

24   FRENCH, PHILIP. "Communing with Camus." TLS, 28 October,
     p. 1259.
         Like Percy's other novels, Lancelot bears resemblances to
novels of Camus. Lancelot is another of Percy's "deceptively
passive men" and "like the narrator of La Chute, Lance is a mono-
loguist with a captive audience. . . ."

25   FULLER, EDMUND. "A Cutting Satire on Modern Life." Wall
     Street Journal, 17 March, p. 18.
         In what "seems the most pessimistic of his books," Percy
delineates "with cutting satire many of the worst, falsest aspects of modern living."

26   GARDNER, JOHN. Review of Lancelot. NYTBR, 20 February,
     pp. 1, 16.
         While Percy cares about plot and character, raises signifi-
cant philosophical questions, and cares about technique, reservations are expressed about Lancelot, which does not succeed as "a
philosophical novel." This "confession [the novel] . . . sounds
written, not spoken," and this seems to show that the writer is
not "serious about creating a fictional illusion." Worse,
Gardner believes the important moral "issue has been avoided,"
for Lancelot simply "rages." Percy is not a very good novelist;
Lancelot is bad art. See also 1978.1.

27   GLASSMAN, PETER. "American Romances: Fiction Chronicle."
     HudR 30, no. 3 (Autumn):437-50.
         Lancelot is analyzed in relation to Warren's A Place to
Come To, Grau's Evidence of Love, and John Casey's An American
Romance, and others, which "speak to the condition and the pres-
tige of love in our society." Not Percy's best novel, Lancelot
is a "conscientious and engaging entertainment," yet his characters, less moral agents than characters who propose themselves
"as momentary accretions" do not seem to advance.

28   GRAY, PAUL. "Questing after an Unholy Grail." Time 109
     (7 March):86-87.
         With "inventiveness and rapid pacing," Percy records
Lancelot's "confession," which is "both a funny and a scarifying
jeremiad on the modern age."

29   GREELEY, ANDREW. "Novelists of the Madhouse." Chicago
     Tribune, 9 June, sec. 4, p. 4.
         Rather mindless article attacking Robert Penn Warren's A
Place To Come To, John Cheever's Falconer, and Walker Percy's
Lancelot. Warren and Cheever are described as talentless writers.
Percy is "clever," but "he is wasting his talents being angry at
the Catholic Church for changing." All three are engaged in
foisting alienated characters on the reading public and in pre-
senting the world in madhouse imagery. If they are so dissatis-
fied with modern society, why are they willing to profit from it?

30   GRIFFITH, THOMAS. "Moral Tales For a Depraved Age."
     Atlantic 240, no. 1 (July):20-21.
          Percy's Lancelot is reviewed with John Cheever's Falconer
     (which is declared better), but Percy's novel is still considered
     one of the "year's two best novels." These authors are not
     moralizing, yet they seem to bear a grudge against the middle
     class, perhaps even an aesthetic one. Writers like Cheever,
     Percy, and Bellow "no longer seem to expect society to change,"
     yet the optimistic side of such writers seems to believe that
     Americans are better than the culture in which they are trapped.
     They counsel us to live lives that "have their own rhythm."

31   GUIDRY, FREDERICK. "Walker Percy's 'Lancelot.'" CSM,
     2 March, p. 23.
          Percy "fingers what he perceives as the rotting fabric of
     Southern aristocratic life, and describes it with vividness and
     a kind of affection, even as he starts to shred it."

31   KENDALL, ELAINE. "The Degradation of Lancelot in an Uncourtly
     Age." The Los Angeles Times Book Review, 13 March, p. 6.
          Favorable review summarizes the novel's major episodes and
     commends Percy's moral vision.

33   KISSEL, SUSAN S. "Walker Percy's 'Conversions.'" SLJ 9,
     no. 2:124-36.
          The religious implications of Walker Percy's novels, par-
     ticularly evidenced in the dramatic reversals in the major char-
     acters' lives, have largely been ignored. "Many readers continue
     to resist interpreting Percy's novels as expressions of his
     Catholic existentialist faith." Yet his first three novels
     clearly end with the protagonists' undergoing religious conver-
     sions" that alter the direction of their lives. These conver-
     sions occur after, and indeed result from, the protagonists'
     self-imposed exiles from the demoralizing influences of contem-
     porary American life. Such alienation proves to be "destructive
     rather than constructive as [the characters] have supposed."
     Significantly, their rejection of exile is accompanied by rejec-
     tion of "their pursuit of nonintimate sexual relationships as a
     means of escaping their pain. . . ." As a result of these con-
     scious rejections of debilitating existential modes, "the pro-
     tagonists learn to accept their unfulfilled desires, their in-
     ability to 'figure out' the mystery of existence, and their
     personal suffering as the necessary conditions of man's earthly
     exile from God."

34   LARDNER, SUSAN. Review of Lancelot. NY 53 (2 May):141-44.
          In this review of both Lancelot and Falconer, the writer
     contrasts the dark view of Percy with Cheever's sanguine percep-
     tion of the world. Noting that the phenomenological concerns of
     "The Delta Factor" are the prevailing themes in the novels of
     Percy, she observes that his dramatization of ideas "works fine"

in The Moviegoer and Love in the Ruins, but fails in The Last
Gentleman and Lancelot. Lancelot suffers in part from an "in-
cessant raising of questions and lowering them without answers,"
but mainly in that the title character, "a crackpot," lacks
proper "credentials as an existential spokesman." Consequently,
"Percy seems to have backed himself into an empty corner."

35   LeCLAIR, THOMAS. "Walker Percy's Devil." SLJ 10, no. 1
     (Fall):3-13.
        Despite his pronouncement that the "conventional novel no
longer makes sense" because it does not reflect the disintegration of the post-modern world, in Love in the Ruins Percy frames
his existentialist tenets in a conventional novel form. Further-
more, he allows his characters to become abstractions and his
language to be devalued. A direct analogy can be drawn between
the relationship of Tom More to Art Immelmann, and that of Percy
to his art. Just as in the novel More is seduced by Immelmann's
promise of "fame, a chance to do good for others, and the conven-
tionalized joy of love in the ruins," Percy succumbs to the lure
of "popularity, edification, and conventionality of form." The
implication is that this book does not live up to the promises
that Percy makes in essays, interviews, and earlier novels.
Reprinted: 1979.19.

36   LEHMANN-HAUPT, CHRISTOPHER. "Camelot Lost." The New York
     Times, 17 February, p. 37.
        Unfavorable review condemns the novel for its multiplicity
of voices, for its awkward use of Arthurian legend, and especially, for its lack of a convincing fictive framework.

37   LOCKE, RICHARD. "Novelists as Preachers." NYTBR, 17 April,
     pp. 3, 52.
        In a discussion of fiction and the current "decadent era,"
Percy is considered with Joan Didion, Thomas Berger, and John
Cheever. While Cheever's Falconer is forced, Percy's Lancelot
is a book guilty of "sermonizing." "It's hard to take
[Lancelot's] ranting seriously. Bellow's Herzog did it so much
better." Percy's book therefore makes dreary reading. All four
writers exhibit weaknesses and "the extremeties of plot and style
to which [they] are committed have conservative if not conventional aims."

38   McNASPY, C.J. "Sick World Diagnosed." National Catholic
     Reporter 13 (6 May):16.
        Lancelot is a story of self-revelation, yet told in such a
way that we can sometimes laugh. Percy's humor is like Evelyn
Waugh's for he makes the reader aware that the laugh is often on
us. Lancelot's "dialogue" with his friend is rich in its implications for Percy is a major "diagnostician" of the modern world.

39   MALIN, IRVING. Review of <u>Lancelot</u>. <u>VQR</u> 53, no. 3 (Summer):
     568-71.
         Percy as Christian novelist refuses to write "mere ser-
     mons." Through metaphors of enclosure and opening he provides a
     narrator in <u>Lancelot</u> who "is trapped in consciousness," yet one
     wants his "'narrow view'" to be shared. While some critics have
     emphasized the destructive tendencies here, the novel is "an <u>open</u>
     book." It offers faith as a possible answer.

40   MILTON, EDITH. "Seven Recent Novels." <u>YR</u> 67, no. 2
     (December):260-71, esp. 268-70.
         Insightful appreciation of the novel which is "about the
     death of a legend" and "the removal . . . of things of the mind,
     of literature and art, from the reality which they are intended
     to reflect." In the novel communication has become impossible,
     yet <u>Lancelot</u> is "splendidly intelligent . . . as serious in its
     wit as it is inventive in its humor." Its use of language makes
     it possible for Percy to raise questions which trouble his hero.

41   MITGANG, HERBERT. "A Talk With Walker Percy." <u>NYTBR</u>,
     20 February, pp. 1, 20.
         Percy acknowledges his debt to the French and Russian
     novelists and mentions Camus's <u>The Fall</u> as a book which in
     structure resembles <u>Lancelot</u>, "something like a dramatic morality
     play." The failure of communication is one of the things Percy
     tries to get across. Information about Covington, Louisiana,
     Percy's ideas about race and culture, his years at Columbia, and
     recuperation in the Adirondacks are included.

42   MULLIGAN, HUGH A. "Doctor Is In--at the Typewriter." <u>Los
     Angeles Times</u>, 4 December, sec. V, pp. 18-19.
         Laudatory column gives biographical background on Percy and
     explores some of his prevailing themes, especially his preoccupa-
     tion "with sin and evil."

43   OATES, JOYCE CAROL. Review of <u>Lancelot</u>. <u>NewR</u> 176, no. 6
     (5 February):32-34.
         While Percy has acquired the reputation of being a
     "'philosophical thinker,'" his first two novels were rich and
     "beautifully crafted." <u>Love in the Ruins</u> was "a rather shrill
     venture" and <u>Lancelot</u> continues in this satiric vein. Objecting
     to the story, and to the characterization, Oates asserts the
     "central problem" is a confusion of tones, and thus the function
     of Percival as well as Lance's attitude toward his wife is not
     clear. Yet to be disappointed with this novel is to pay tribute
     to Percy's earlier work.

44   PEARSON, MICHAEL PATRICK. "The Rhetoric of Symbolic Action:
      Walker Percy's Way of Knowing." Ph.D. dissertation,
      Pennsylvania State University.
          The essays in The Message in the Bottle are examined in
      relation to the concepts of language, philosophy, and aesthetics
      that are dramatized in the novels. Central to Percy's fiction is
      his belief that "symbolic action is an intersubjective process,
      a communication in the root sense of 'making common.'"

45   PRESCOTT, PETER S. "Unholy Knight." NW 89 (28 February):
      73-74.
          Percy represents a rarity among current novelists in that
      he "writes about Christian concerns," and in his fourth novel he
      has added a note of "urgency" to his prevailing theme of moral
      dilemmas that can be solved only through the power of Christian
      love. Indeed, the protagonist of the novel fails in his quest
      for a "revolution in morality" because he does not realize that
      it must be effected by such love. Lancelot is an "ambitious"
      novel, but not beyond the control of Percy, "a seductive writer,
      attentive to sensuous detail, and such a skillful architect of
      fiction that the very discursiveness of his story informs it
      with energy and tension." In short, "this is a fine novel, not
      so much a departure from what Percy has done before as an exten-
      sion of it. . . ."

46   PRICE, REYNOLDS. "God and Man in Louisiana." BW,
      27 February, pp. E7, E10.
          Favorable review of Lancelot analyzes Lancelot's rage as a
      cri de coeur to a silent God and indicates the conclusion should
      have been made more explicit for a post-Christian readership.

47   QUAGLIANO, ANTHONY. "Existential Modes in The Moviegoer."
      Research Studies 45, no. 4 (December):214-23.
          Critics most closely attuned to what Percy attempts in The
      Moviegoer are those who interpret the novel in light of his
      essays on philosophy and psychology. Particularly useful are
      Percy's arguments on man as a symbol-user and on the existential
      modes of alienation, rotation, and repetition. Binx Bolling con-
      fronts his sense of alienation "by seeking out moments of rota-
      tion and repetition," particularly through his moviegoing. Binx
      transcends his alienation most decisively through his commitment
      and ultimate marriage to Kate.

48   SIVLEY, SHERRY. "Percy's Down Home Version of More's
      Utopia." NConL 7, no. 4 (September):3-5.
          Tom More's life in the bayou described in the epilogue of
      Love in the Ruins conforms closely to the type of utopian exis-
      tence encouraged by his ancestor St. Thomas More. Abandoning the
      "illusory pleasures" Thomas More warned against in favor of the
      "natural pleasures" that he urged, Tom More demonstrates through
      his simple pursuits and concerns just how accessible Utopia is.

"Tom More's life in the epilogue of <u>Love in the Ruins</u> comes as
close as one could in mid-twentieth century America to living
according to the suggestions Sir Thomas More made in <u>Utopia</u> for
finding a happy and virtuous life."

49   SMITH, LAURENCE. Review of <u>Lancelot</u>. <u>Critic</u> 35, no. 4
      (Summer):86-89.
         Neither "moralist" nor "mimic," Percy as Christian writer
      asks what a man does when he finds himself living after an age
      has ended and the theories of a former age do not suffice. Such
      is Lancelot Lamar's case. In the nightmarish story told by him,
      the priest Percival plays an important role. This silent ob-
      server represents Percy's viewpoint, and the expression of
      Percival's conviction that "salvation is found in the search
      for salvation," ironically concludes the novel.

50   STELZMANN, RAINULF A. "Das Schwert Christi: Zwei Versuche
      Walker Percys." <u>Stimmen der Zeit</u> (Freiburg) 195, no. 9
      (September):641-43.
         Percy's world view has been influenced by European existen-
      tialism. One of the few American writers familiar with the Ger-
      man language, he has confirmed that as a student in 1934 he
      traveled to Germany, lived in Bonn, and already then became aware
      of the inhumanity of man when he witnessed a Jewish person beaten.
      Percy's <u>Lancelot</u> relates an attempt at a "new order," after
      Lancelot has discovered evil and sought to destroy it. While in
      the earlier novels we find discussion of therapy and spiritual
      healing, Lancelot demands more radical solutions for he does not
      think that the Church provides clear distinctions. Lancelot
      hopes to build his own world. Percy has confirmed his own belief
      in the necessity of an active Christian faith, and also investi-
      gated the uniqueness of man in relation to speech. In <u>The Message</u>
      <u>in the Bottle</u>, he outlines his belief that the gospel message is
      one that speaks to the shipwrecked, and only those shipwrecked
      who realize that they are so. Such realization, he maintains,
      rests on man's nature as "the animal with language"; hence his
      investigation of the relationship between man's existential situ-
      ation and language in <u>The Message</u>. In these two recent books
      Percy stresses the importance of the religious decision; just as
      in O'Connor's stories, he reminds us the "powers of heaven are
      prevailed against."

51   T., A. Review of <u>Lancelot</u>. <u>West Coast Review of Books</u> 3
      (May):33.
         While "getting into the mind of a madman might make fasci-
      nating reading," this stream of consciousness writing fails.
      Plot and characters are so confusing that it is necessary to use
      the dust jacket to follow the action.

52   TODD, RICHARD. "Lead Us into Temptation, Deliver Us Evil."
Atlantic 239, no. 3 (March):113-15.
     Percy, as Christian novelist, has provided a novel,
Lancelot, which is about "a problem of faith"; Lance Lamar "is
awakening from the sleep that . . . Percy believes to be endemic
in the modern world." Lance's tirades are "in their way glori-
ous," but the "burden of the novel lies elsewhere." All of
Percy's fiction has been written "in the service of the same
theme that animates Lancelot," a search for what will "banish"
despair. The strength of Percy's work is that he reflects the
"moral and emotional confusion" of the landscape but he refuses
"handy" wisdom; he calls attention to the possibility of faith.

53   TOWERS, ROBERT. "Southern Discomfort." NYRB 24 (31 March):
6-8.
     Percy's aristocratic southern heritage coupled with his
status as an anglo-saxon Catholic convert affords him a unique
perspective, one as both alien and native, from which to chronicle the transformation of the South to the "Sunbelt." This dual
perspective informs all of his novels, whose protagonists refuse
to seek shelter in traditional southern culture when confronted
by the changing mores of their region. Percy presents a Catholic
alternative to the experience of psychic dislocation. In
Lancelot Percy creates in his depiction of the plantation Belle
Isle "a miniature allegory of the New South."

54   WATKINS, SUZANNE BLACKMON. "From Physician to Novelist: The
Progression of Walker Percy." Ph.D. dissertation, New York
University.
     Percy's extensive reading in European existentialism during
his recovery from tuberculosis was formative in his progression
from physician to novelist. His writing also reflects his southern heritage and the influence of his adoptive father, William
Alexander Percy. Additionally, his satire and social commentary
focus upon American culture as a whole. What has evolved from
these multifarious perspectives is Percy's Catholic vision of man
as a wayfarer and a concomitant emphasis on sin, faith, and
redemption.

55   WIEHE, P.L. Review of Lancelot. LJ 102, no. 5 (1 March):633.
     This work can be praised only by calling it "'another good
book by Walker Percy,'" and while it lacks "the ebullience" of
Love in the Ruins, and there are problems with the symbolism,
Percy remains "a fine writer."

56   WILL, GEORGE F. "In Literature and Politics, a Quest for
Values." BW, 31 March, p. A15.
     The reviewer lauds Percy's spiritual vision, particularly
as it is evidenced in his latest novel, Lancelot, "a cautionary
tale about the forces that may flood into the moral vacuum we

dignify as 'tolerance.'" Also cited for expressing similar concerns are Joan Didion's A Book of Common Prayer and John Cheever's
Falconer.

57   WOLFF, GEOFFREY. "The Hurricane or the Hurricane Machine."
     New Times 8, no. 6 (18 March):64-66.
         Summary does an injustice to the novel, for Percy's purpose
     is serious. Ultimately "hostile to theatrics and entertainments,"
     Percy's novels reflect his reading; but more importantly, Lancelot
     reflects the writer's own expression of an inner struggle charac-
     teristic of the age, a struggle to avoid abstraction. Sin is per-
     ceived here as the reduction of people to objects. Percy pro-
     vides a particular portrait of a character who struggles within
     his "unexemplary" circumstances.

58   WOOD, RALPH. "Damned in the Paradise of Sex." CC 90
     (13 July):634-36.
         Percy is to be commended for confronting us with the nature
     of contemporary damnation in Lancelot. The power and terror of
     the novel is that it provides no clear "first step" toward salva-
     tion as do his preceding novels. The startling use of Lancelot's
     obsessions with sex provides a way for Percy to imply that in our
     "liberated age" we will either be damned seeking a sexual abso-
     lute or "saved in pursuit of Eternal Love."

59   YOUNT, JOHN. "Walker Percy's Funhouse Mirror: More True than
     Distorted." Chicago Tribune Book World, 27 February, p. 1.
         Review of Lancelot. The Moviegoer was a true existential
     novel with a protagonist who resembled Meursault in Camus's The
     Stranger. Percy's later novels, however, seem more interested
     in the dilemmas of society than the problems of the individual.
     The novels are becoming more like philosophical essays: his
     characters have flattened into stereotypes, and his themes have
     simplified into propaganda. Percy does not allow his reader
     enough alternatives and his characters are not always credible.
     Despite these reservations, Lancelot is still recommended. It
     will remind the reader more of Faulkner (The Sound and the Fury)
     than Camus or Dostoyevsky. Although there is some distortion,
     the novel reflects a truer world than we would like to admit.

                              1978

1   ANON. Review of Lancelot. NYTBR, 23 April, p. 43.
        Short comment summarizing plot and quoting from earlier
    John Gardner review. See 1977.26.

2   ANON. "Walker Percy." In Contemporary Literary Criticism.
    Vol. 8. Edited by Dedria Bryfonski and Phyllis Carmel
    Mendelson. Detroit: Gale Research Co., pp. 438-46.

Introduction maintains Percy's "fictive concerns are
serious and ambitious; ranging from existentialism to episte-
mology to language and ways of communication." Excerpts are
from the following: John Boatwright (1975.8), Pearl K. Bell
[sic, correct author is Richard H. King] (1975.18), Jonathan
Culler (1976.9), Martin Kirby (1976.14), Charles P. Bigger
(1977.10), Reynolds Price (1977.46), John Gardner (1977.26),
Richard Todd (1977.52), Robert Towers (1977.53), Andre Dubus
(1977.20), and Irving Malin (1977.39).

3   BATES, MARVIN RANDOLPH. "Walker Percy's Ironic Apology."
    Ph.D. dissertation, Tulane University.
        This critical assessment of Percy's artistry concludes that
    he has written one fine novel, The Moviegoer, and several valu-
    able essays on the mystery of language.

4   BECKER, TOM. Review of Lancelot. New Orleans Review 5,
    no. 4:363-64.
        Percy's interest in language, which includes "non-verbal
    indexical elements of behavior," must be taken into account for
    the implied text allows us to find out Percival's critique of the
    monologue, Percival's moral and spiritual development, and the
    unstated conclusion of the novel. Both characters are on the
    same search, but Lancelot is one step behind Percival. The nar-
    rative takes the form of Roman Catholic confession, and the ex-
    change assists the priest to clarify points for himself. Lancelot
    can be thought of as an "expanded expression" of semiotic theory.

5   BRINKMEYER, BOB. Review of Lancelot. Southern Exposure 5,
    no. 1 (Spring):95-96.
        In Lancelot Percy has created his most "intense and up-
    setting" novel to date. He assumes a role as prophet in order to
    issue both "a challenge, a call to war against the putrefaction
    of modern civilization" and a summons "for a simpler and more
    honorable way of living."

6   COGELL, ELIZABETH CUMMINS. "The Middle-Landscape Myth in
    Science Fiction." Science-Fiction Studies 5, no. 15, pt. 2
    (July):134-42.
        Like George Stewart's Earth Abides and Ursula K. Le Guin's
    The Lathe of Heaven, Love in the Ruins combines two archetypal
    myths--that of the apocalypse and that of the middle landscape--
    and demonstrates their application within a contemporary milieu.
    Percy uses Christian humanism as a norm from which to render
    judgment "against the psyche of Western man, the false middle
    landscape [Paradise Estates] he has created, and the substitute
    ideology he has offered, i.e. scientism."

7   COLES, ROBERT. "Profiles: The Search (Walker Percy I)." <u>NY</u>
      (2 October):pp. 43-44, 47-48, 50, 52, 57-58, 60, 62, 67, 68,
      70, 72, 74, 79, 80, 82, 84, 86, 91-96, 98-106, 109, 110.
         A somewhat abbreviated and differently arranged version of
Cole's subsequent book. See 1978.8-9.

8   _____ . "Profiles: The Search (Walker Percy II)." <u>NY</u>
      (9 October):pp. 52-54, 57-60, 65, 66, 68, 71, 72, 74, 77-79,
      82, 84, 88, 90, 92, 94, 99, 100, 102-4, 106, 109-16, 119-22,
      125.
         A somewhat abbreviated and differently arranged version of
Cole's subsequent book. See 1978.7, 9.

9   _____ . <u>Walker Percy: An American Search</u>. Boston: Little,
      Brown & Co., 270 pp.
         This study of Percy is divided into three major sections:
the first investigates Percy's philosophical roots; the second,
the essays; and the third, the novels. Also included are details
about Percy's biography. Throughout the book, the author inter-
jects personal commentary about his own response to Percy's work
and also reflects on the way in which Percy's existential ideas
are echoed in the observations of Coles's sociological subjects.
In the first section, the author discusses the thought of Percy's
philosophical progenitors, such as Kierkegaard, Marcel, and
Heidegger. In his examination of Percy's essays, Coles traces
the development of Percy's writing as it simultaneously widened
to encompass broad subject matter (such as psychiatry, the South,
and national problems) and narrowed for a close look at the language phenomenon, notably the field of semiotics. Additionally,
Coles examines the articles Percy wrote which are specifically
"devoted to an exploration of Being in the tradition of philoso-
phers like Heidegger, Karl Jaspers, and Marcel." Coles finds
that Percy "wants an existentialism that keeps in touch empiri-
cally with people and the kinds of communion they seek and find
with one another." Coles emphasizes the Christian nature of
Percy's existentialism: "Christ's 'good news' happens to be the
'message in the bottle' which Percy happens to find most responsive to his situation."
         Coles views Percy's turn to novel writing as an "ambitious
effort to combine an interest in philosophical explication with
the traditional requirement of the novel." Accordingly, he
examines the novels as concrete modes for Percy's delineation of
his philosophical preoccupations. Emphasized are the ideas of
Kierkegaard, Heidegger, and Marcel as they are personified in the
struggles of Percy's protagonists. See also 1978.7-8.

10   CUNNINGHAM, LAWRENCE. "Catholic Sensibility and Southern
      Writers." <u>Bulletin of the Center for the Study of Southern
      Culture and Religion</u> 2 (Summer):7-10.
         As Catholic writers, Flannery O'Connor and Walker Percy
present a "pre-modern" sensibility. Greatly vitiated today by

the effect of the Reformation's emphasis on the polarity of God
and nature, such sensibility sees the operation of the sacred
within the world of matter. In this respect, Percy's vision
resembles that of Gerard Manley Hopkins more than that of
Kierkegaard. Love in the Ruins is used as an exemplar of the
way this sensibility obtains in Percy's fiction.

11   DALE, CORRINNE HOWELL. "The Lost Cause: Myth, Symbol, and
     Stereotype in Southern Fiction." Ph.D. dissertation, Univer-
     sity of Michigan.
          Percy is mentioned as a contemporary Southern writer who,
     like Faulkner, emphasizes "commitment to the human community"
     over the "doomed idealism" of the Southern aristocrat.

12   DANIEL, ROBERT D. "Walker Percy's Lancelot: Secular Raving
     and Religious Silence." SoR 14, no. 1 (January):186-94.
          Percy's novel is an examination of Lancelot's illness as
     "full-fledged secularism," yet even in this advanced state the
     hero realizes the need to be watchful and to wait. Unfortunately
     Lancelot hopes to come to an understanding of his situation
     through an understanding of the physical. Such a method is mad-
     ness; and finally Lancelot's extremism forces Percival to stop
     straddling the chasm between secular humani m and Christianity.

13   EPSTEIN, SEYMOUR. Review of Lancelot. Denver Quarterly 12,
     no. 4 (Winter):97-98.
          Discusses Lancelot as the melodramatic outpourings of a
     Southern gentleman, and Percy's novels as the definitive posture
     of that gentleman toward the coming Apocalypse. Lancelot's
     ravings, and the dramatizing of the world from which he recoils,
     cannot be taken with seriousness because Percy spells out so
     much. While Percy's books seem to take a serious approach to
     moral problems, this novel "is the most trivial" of all.

14   GARDNER, JOHN. "Moral Fiction." SatR 5, no. 13 (1 April):
     29-30, 32-33, esp. 29.
          This sweeping review of several modern authors and their
     fiction attempts to define "true morality" and the responsibility
     of the artist. A function of the serious artist continues to be
     "the celebration of true morality." Recognizing that true art
     cannot exist without love, the artist tries to recreate this emo-
     tion through fiction. Percy succeeds in The Moviegoer; however,
     in Lancelot he does little more than reiterate the ideals of
     Nietzsche and Dostoevsky on "the moral outsider."

15   GRAY, RICHARDSON K. "A Christian-Existentialist: The Vision
     of Walker Percy." Ph.D. dissertation, Ohio University.
          Percy's characters experience a sense of "spiritual home-
     lessness," the malaise he examines at length in his essays.
     Their discomfort sends them searching for their "spiritual home
     with God."

16   HALL, CONSTANCE. "The Ladies in The Last Gentleman." NMW 11,
      no. 1 (Spring):26-35.
          Although critical analyses of The Last Gentleman generally
      neglect the female characters--Rita, Val, and Kitty--the women
      play key roles in determining Will Barrett's development and
      ultimate life decision. "Rita's abstraction, Kitty's everyday-
      ness, and Val's faith" present existential choices to Will; and
      Kitty's failure to enter into an intersubjective relationship
      with him partially accounts for his ultimate rejection of faith.
      Rita, ostensibly committed to love, actually approaches life by
      abstracting herself and others. Val presents to Will a thoroughly
      committed by decidedly unorthodox Christianity. Her consuming
      hatreds, unattractiveness, and abrasive personality may suggest
      the multiplicity of God's works. She doubtless embodies familiar
      Percyan concepts: she is the quintessential "hearer" of the Good
      News described in the essay "The Message in the Bottle," and she
      delights in her students' ontological breakthrough into language.
      Finally, Kitty represents "the way of everydayness . . . living
      a life that is bound by convention and blurred by the familiar."
      Her preference for form over substance "precludes the inter-
      subjective relationship and points instead to the inauthentic
      life." Despite the shallowness she offers, Will seemingly
      chooses Kitty and a conventional career at a Vaught automobile
      dealership, but even in these decisions a hint of affirmation
      resides.

17   HAYDEL, DOUGLAS JOSEPH. "From the Realistic to the Fantastic:
      Walker Percy's Expanding Vision." Ph.D. dissertation, Florida
      State University.
          This "three-part sequence of essays" examines first the
      imagery of Percy's fiction, secondly "his view of religion," and
      lastly the "confessional narrative technique" used in Lancelot.

18   HELTERMAN, JEFFREY, and LAYMAN, RICHARD, eds. "Walker Percy."
      Dictionary of Literary Biography. Vol. 2, American Novelists
      Since World War II. Detroit: Gale Research, pp. 390-97.
          Presented are a biographical sketch, including factors in-
      fluencing Percy's development as a novelist; his chief philosoph-
      ical tenets; and synopses of his first four novels. "The thinly
      veiled religious jeremiads of his novels have caused them to be
      frequently grouped with modern secularized apocalyptic novels,
      and Percy admits that his main writing motivation is usually to
      correct wrongs." Also included is a selected bibliography.

19   IYER, PICO. "A Sad Tidiness: Walker Percy and the South."
      London Magazine 18, no. 1 (April):62-66.
          Lancelot resembles Percy's other novels and the general
      trend of American writing in its preoccupation with the dull
      subjects of suburban boredom and neurosis. "In all fairness,
      Lancelot is somewhat richer than an income-tax file." Of some

note are Lancelot's plan for society's reform and the "ingenious"
unfolding of the plot. Particularly jarring is Percy's graceless
prose.

20   KIRBY, JACK TEMPLE. Media-Made Dixie: The South in the Amer-
      ican Imagination. Baton Rouge and London: Louisiana State
      University Press, pp. 160, 164-65.
         The characters of Walker Percy ("Faulkner's successor as
      the most significant novelist from the Lower South" and "of all
      things--a southern existentialist") reflect the ethos of the New
      South in that they "are alienated from the past and have no par-
      ticular feelings for place."

21   KREYLING, MICHAEL. "Crime and Punishment: The Pattern
      Beneath the Surface of Percy's Lancelot." NMW 11, no. 1
      (Spring):36-44.
         Although reviews of Lancelot, even unfavorable ones, cor-
      rectly call attention to the obvious parallel between this con-
      temporary quest and that of chivalric romance, a more critical
      pattern has been overlooked. Lancelot shares a pattern with
      Dostoyevsky's Crime and Punishment. They coincide particularly
      in plot, but "in the different resolutions . . . lies the prin-
      cipal and significant difference." Both protagonists encounter
      "a social environment peopled with aliens" and seek to impose a
      new order through acts of violence. Crime and Punishment "cul-
      minates in a moral resurrection" for Raskolnikov not because of
      his efforts but because he recognizes "the old order (the human
      network made supernatural by Christ--the story of the New Testa-
      ment) has always been present in spite of Raskolnikov's attempts
      to deny it." But both a successful quest and a spiritual resur-
      rection elude Lancelot; he remains "a moral extremist."

22   LAWSON, LEWIS A. "The Gnostic Vision in Lancelot."
      Renascence 32, no. 1 (Autumn):52-64.
         Going beyond suggestions made by Cleanth Brooks about Percy
      and "Modern Gnosticism," Lawson traces Percy's awareness of Eric
      Voegelin to an interview in 1967. Voegelin's essay on Gnosticism
      is examined in detail as a means of enhancing understanding of
      Lancelot. Lance's view of his world is a "visionary construction"
      and that vision, with its "predictable processes, replaces God as
      the eidos of history." Lance is a "Gnostic prophet" whose ver-
      sion of history revises, or ignores, key features of the tradi-
      tional Christian story. Employing his unique interpretation of
      his experience to prophesy history, Lance dreams of a future
      "millennial epoch" where politics will vanish. Each major char-
      acteristic of his thought can be examined as parallel to basic
      data provided in Voegelin's The New Science of Politics.

23   LEE, HERMIONE. "Poe Faced." New Review 4, nos. 45-46
     (December-January):73-74.
        Lancelot shares characteristics with other narrators
     created by authors from Poe to Bellow; the irony of his possible
     madness, however, lessens the effectiveness of the novel. Never-
     theless, the fusion of "the macabre and apocalyptic" is impres-
     sive. Parallels between Lancelot and "The Purloined Letter" and
     "House of Usher" seem to fuse the narrator into Dupin and Usher.

24   _____. Review of English reissues of The Last Gentleman and
     Love in the Ruins. New Statesman 95 (3 March):294-95.
        Comparison of Percy must be made with Faulkner and his
     "baroque South." Percy's novels seem to be overdone and finally
     The Last Gentleman comes adrift, the comedy sunk under the mes-
     sage. Similarly Love in the Ruins is "very funny," but the
     "harangues" make one come away "with the glazed eyes of a Wedding
     Guest."

25   LISCHER, TRACY KENYON. "Walker Percy's Kierkegaard: A Read-
     ing of The Moviegoer." Cresset 41, no. 10 (October):10-12.
        Kierkegaard's three stages of life--aesthetic, ethical,
     religious--are incorporated in this novel which ends suggesting
     Binx may possess the potential to make the leap of faith to the
     religious life. First caught in the "boredom of aestheticism,"
     Binx is presented early in the narrative as close to despair,
     which he calls malaise. Binx's commitment to Kate, which repre-
     sents the ethical stage, is a synthesis of possibility and neces-
     sity. Only Lonnie reaches the final stage, but at the novel's
     conclusion Binx seems close to faith.

26   SHEED, WILFRID. "Walker Percy Redivivus." In The Good Word
     and Other Words. New York: E.P. Dutton, pp. 127-31.
        Reprint of 1971.43.

27   SIMPSON, LEWIS P. "The Southern Aesthetic of Memory." Tulane
     Studies in English 23:207-27, esp. 221-27.
        The contemporary southern literary impulse embraces not
     only the resistance of memory to historicism best exemplified by
     Faulkner's work, but also Flannery O'Connor's resistance to
     memory and concomitant emphasis on revelation. Percy's perspec-
     tive encompasses both points of view: he "dramatizes a relation
     among history, memory, and prophecy." Alone of Percy's protago-
     nists, Binx Bolling resists the seductive lure of abstraction by
     history and makes a Kierkegaardian leap into faith. Will
     Barrett's internalization of southern history creates pathologi-
     cal consequences for him. In Love in the Ruins, "the scientific
     management of the psyche," with its predictably deleterious
     effects, ironically depends for its justification upon "the
     classical-Christian concepts of the culture of memory." Addi-
     tionally, Love in the Ruins illustrates the confusion generic to
     the American mind in imagining utopia as a place to be realized

on earth. In Lancelot, such utopian idealism and its resultant
"internalization of American history as the memory of the future"
reaches apocalyptic conclusions.

28   SMITH, LARRY. "Catholics, Catholics Everywhere . . . A Flood
      of Catholic Novels." Critic 37, no. 11 (December 1-2):1-8,
      esp. 6-7.
         Lancelot continues Percy's exploration "of God's presence
      in the everyday world. . . ." Such awareness occurs to Percival,
      who "stirs from his moral inertness to recognize that the true
      quest for this age is in the search of everyday life for the
      grace and the mystery of God. . . ."

29   SULLIVAN, WALKER. "The Insane and the Indifferent: Walker
      Percy and Others." SR 86, no. 1 (January):153-59.
         Along with several novels published contemporaneously,
      Lancelot is analyzed for its commentary on modern values. Among
      the novels discussed, Lancelot is unique for its insistence on
      the necessity for a "system of values by which human gains and
      frailties can be measured." Percy forces the reader to reflect
      on whether Lancelot or the world is insane. It then becomes in-
      cumbent upon the reader to "see as clearly as Lance does that the
      end of the old way is upon us."

30   TELOTTE, J.P. "Walker Percy's Language of Creation." SoQ 16,
      no. 2 (Winter):105-16.
         The essays in The Message in the Bottle reenforce a theme
      found within all of Percy's novels: language, because of its
      symbolic and intersubjective nature, is both a key to and a cure
      for man's alienated spirit. The protagonists of the novels il-
      lustrate the transformational powers of language. From "a despair
      marked by 'silence,' an inability to express their feelings or
      talk about their situations to others . . . they emerge, . . .
      using their natural communicative abilities to open up new lives
      for both themselves and others." Percy underscores in the essays
      the mysterious nature of this symbolic process and concomitantly
      emphasizes that "man's limited nature inevitably bars him from
      any total comprehension of reality." Such an approach differs
      from that of the scientific method, which puts man outside of
      himself as an observer, thereby contributing to his sense of
      alienation. Also, the scientific method contributes to the cor-
      ruption and trivialization of language by leading one "to desig-
      nate a thing according to what it does, not what it is." As an
      antidote to this debilitation of language, Percy prescribes an
      increased awareness of the "metaphoric potency involved in every
      act of symbolization . . . a feeling for the portentousness in-
      volved in every relation asserted between name and referent."

31   VAUTHIER, SIMONE. "Narrative Triangle and Triple Alliance: A
     Look at The Moviegoer." In Les Américanistes: New French
     Criticism on Modern American Fiction. Edited by I.D. Johnson
     and C. Johnson. New York: Kennikat Press, pp. 71-93.
         Although criticism of The Moviegoer has focused mainly on
     the central character, analysis of the aesthetics of the novel is
     also revealing. In particular, scrutiny of "the relations within
     the narrative triangle between narrator, narratee, and narration"
     indicates the complexity of Binx's consciousness. "The combina-
     tion of a narrative stance in which narrating 'I' and experienc-
     ing 'I' seem to coincide, and of occasional addresses to a self-
     narratee, dramatizes the nature of consciousness and the cleavage
     on which it depends." Binx shares with his narratee thoughts on
     his alienation that he finds inexpressible to others; but at
     times he injects an urgency into his narration, indicating an
     underlying doubt that his complex consciousness can really be
     understood. The narrative act also undergoes permutations, par-
     ticularly in the epilogue which places the preceding narration,
     seemingly in the present, in retrospect. Such narrative shifts,
     particularly in tenses, reveal "a fictive consciousness engaged
     in the unlocated and unlocatable--virtual--task of apprehending
     itself through the matrix of language."

                                   1979

1   ANON. Review of Lancelot. Critic 37 (December):6-7.
         The epiphany of the novel occurs for Percival, whose silent
     listening reveals to him "that the true quest for this age is in
     the search of everyday life for the grace and the mystery of God,
     that salvation is found in the search for salvation. . . ."

2   BINDING, PAUL. "Walker Percy." In Separate Country: A Lit-
     erary Journey through the American South. New York:
     Paddington Press, pp. 33, 69-76, 147, 199, 209, 213.
         Presented are a few remarks by Percy, a profile of his life
     and personality, and brief analyses of the novels. Percy acknowl-
     edges his distinction from other Southern writers in having been
     influenced by European existentialists. His protagonists are
     assessed as "reluctant, confused outsiders whose often tormented
     consciousnesses receive [Percy's] sympathetic and intense con-
     sideration." His novels are informed by his Roman Catholic faith
     and by the Greco-Roman stoicism of William Alexander Percy. Al-
     though Percy eschews local color and regionalism in his fiction,
     the South figures prominently as setting.

3   BROOKS, CLEANTH. "Walker Percy and Modern Gnosticism." In
     The Art of Walker Percy: Stratagems for Being. Edited by
     Panthea Reid Broughton. Baton Rouge: Lousiana State Univer-
     sity Press, pp. 260-72.
         Reprint of 1977.12.

4   BROUGHTON, PANTHEA REID, ed. The Art of Walker Percy:
      Stratagems for Being. Baton Rouge: Louisiana State Univer-
      sity Press, 330 pp.
          Includes essays by Max Webb (1979.34), Martin Luschei
      (1979.20), Janet Hobbs (1979.13), Richard Pindell (1979.21),
      Simone Vauthier (1979.33), Panthea Reid Broughton (1979.6),
      J. Gerald Kennedy (1979.14), William Leigh Godshalk (1979.9),
      Thomas LeClair (1977.35), Weldon Thornton (1979.31), William H.
      Poteat (1979.22), Lewis A. Lawson (1979.15), William J. Dowie
      (1979.7), Cleanth Brooks (1977.12), and Ted R. Spivey (1979.27).

5   _____. Introduction to The Art of Walker Percy: Stratagems
      for Being. Baton Rouge: Louisiana State University Press,
      pp. xiii-xix.
          Ultimately, the stratagem of the book is to offer the
      pleasure of "returning to [a work of art], knowing it well, and
      deciphering its complications."

6   _____. "Gentlemen and Fornicators: The Last Gentleman and a
      Bisected Reality." In The Art of Walker Percy: Stratagems
      for Being. Baton Rouge: Louisiana State University Press,
      pp. 96-114.
          Ironically, Walker Percy's fiction is infused with the
      dualism that he deplores in his philosophical writings. His
      characters invariably confront "alternatives which tend to be
      either/or choices: either body or mind, bestialism or angelism,
      immanence or transcendence." In The Last Gentleman especially,
      complex moral dilemmas are reduced to either/or decisions over
      sexual mores: Will Barrett, for example, reasons that he must
      be either a gentleman or a fornicator. Similarly, the other
      characters seem incapable of regarding sexual union as the con-
      junction of "the secular and the sacred, the flesh and the
      spirit, . . . a union which is ineffable and transcendent."
      Percy rather patly resolves Will's dissatisfaction with such
      dichotomy by letting him take Kitty as a wife and retain Sutter
      as a mentor, "as if having both of them will enable Will to com-
      plete his own personality." Consequently, The Last Gentleman
      reflects a pervasive problem in Percy's fiction: a "vision of
      the integrated self [that is] not whole but split."

7   DOWIE, WILLIAM J. "Lancelot and the Search for Sin." In The
      Art of Walker Percy: Stratagems for Being. Edited by Panthea
      Reid Broughton. Baton Rouge: Louisiana State University
      Press, pp. 245-59.
          Lancelot's quest for the unholy grail, the existence in the
      post-modern world of actual sin (as opposed to "aberrant behav-
      ior"), is doomed from the start because the protagonist mistakenly
      seeks sin outside himself. Thus, "Lancelot was looking for the
      impossible, for sin is a subjective occurrence existing only
      within an individual's psyche." The "true thematic center of the
      novel" resides in Percival, whose thoughtful silence and active

listening lead him to "consideration and ultimately confidence in
his own way." Therefore, Percival's decision to return to a
simple Christian ministry serves as the moral crux of the novel
since it provides a foil to Lancelot's moral insensibility.

8   FOX, WILLIAM HENRY. "Opposition to Secular Humanism in the
     Fiction of Flannery O'Connor and Walker Percy." Ph.D. disser-
     tation, Emory University.
        The fiction of Percy, like that of Flannery O'Connor,
     demonstrates opposition to "the evil obstacles of secular human-
     ism" rampant in contemporary society.

9   GODSHALK, WILLIAM LEIGH. "Love in the Ruins: Thomas More's
     Distorted Vision." In The Art of Walker Percy: Stratagems
     for Being. Edited by Panthea Reid Broughton. Baton Rouge:
     Louisiana State University Press, pp. 137-56.
        In Love in the Ruins, Walker Percy follows the prescriptions
     for writing an apocalyptic novel that he had established earlier
     in his essay "Notes for a Novel about the End of the World,"
     except for the critical modification that he chooses a "narrator
     whose point of view is both odd and unreliable." Thomas More's
     vision is "distorted by alcohol, neurosis, and guilt." As a
     result, his "ability to discriminate and to narrate simple facts
     accurately is decidedly suspect." In order to cope with his
     world, More mythologizes it: Samantha's death becomes a link to
     Christ's death, America the New Eden, More himself the savior of
     the post-modern world. Further, "the Tom More we see throughout
     most of the novel is a man preoccupied with destruction. Given
     More's preoccupation, it is not surprising that he sees an apoca-
     lyptic world." By implication, the reader sees his own distorted
     vision in that of Thomas More.

10   GORDON, CAROLINE. Correspondence to Flannery O'Connor. In
     "A Master Class: From the Correspondence of Caroline Gordon
     and Flannery O'Connor." Edited by Sally Fitzgerald. GaR 33,
     no. 4 (Winter):827-46, esp. 830.
        Comment by Gordon in letter of May 1951 about correspondence
     with Walker Percy, who informs her that he has written a novel
     "which he guesses is 'a Catholic novel. . . .'" Along with this
     is a statement that O'Connor and Percy would find it interesting
     to know each other.

11   HAMMOND, JOHN FRANCIS. "The Monomythic Quest: Visions of
     Heroism in Malamud, Bellow, Barth, and Percy." Ph.D. disser-
     tation, Lehigh University.
        Lancelot is examined along with three other contemporary
     novels for its demonstration of the "monomythic" quest pattern of
     "separation-initiation-return."

12 HICKS, JACK. "The Lesions of the Dead: Walker Percy's The Last Gentleman." Études anglaises 32, no. 2 (Avril-Juin): 162-70.

Like his French predecessors, Walker Percy ponders "'What is it like to be a man in a world transformed by science?'" From Marcel and other Christian existentialists, Percy conceives of man as a "spirit within flesh." Through his fiction, in particular, Percy explores "the effects of the scientific outlook on contemporary consciousness." Will Barrett's pilgrimage especially is informed by the "vision and language" of Gabriel Marcel. Barrett's displacement is "'the lostness of the American in America'" caused by "the failure to understand the limitations of science and technology." The pilgrimage that Will Barrett and Jamie Vaught share enables Jamie to prepare for an "inescapable transcendence out of the body." For Barrett, "simple love and human affection" allow him "re-entry into the world of immanence." For Percy, "the pilgrimage itself . . . is the means of that restoration of order."

13 HOBBS, JANET. "Binx Bolling and the Stages oⁱ Life's Way." In The Art of Walker Percy: Stratagems for Being. Edited by Panthea Reid Broughton. Baton Rouge: Louisiana State University Press, pp. 37-49.

Binx's search for authenticity involves a progression in the Kierkegaardian stages of existence, from aesthetic to ethical to religious. Binx is able to reach the last and most important stage by observing the existential modes of the other characters and by evaluating his experience. The secondary characters in The Moviegoer remain trapped in the aesthetic mode, unwilling to exchange the comforts of familiar everydayness for the pain of uncertainty and growth. Kate, though, is "aware of the ineffectiveness of aesthetic choices" and thereby helps Binx "to renew the search." In the epilogue, Binx "seems to know now that the search for one sphere cannot be satisfied with answers from another." Analysis of Binx's Kierkegaardian progression serves "to illumine the modal design of the [first] three novels that may be described as Walker Percy's Kierkegaardian trilogy. . . . Though Percy's fourth novel is radically different from his first three, Lancelot does make use of this same Kierkegaardian frame."

14 KENNEDY, J. GERALD. "The Sundered Self and the Riven World: Love in the Ruins." In The Art of Walker Percy: Stratagems for Being. Edited by Panthea Reid Broughton. Baton Rouge: Louisiana State University Press, pp. 115-36.

A parallel exists between More's diagnosis and attempted cure of the mind-body split that has ailed man since Descartes, and Percy's diagnosis and proposed treatment of the modern condition as evidenced by the novel. Just as More reduces man's fall from grace to a tug of war between angelism and bestialism, Percy reduces his characters to caricatures so simply and largely drawn that they fail to be convincing. Also, Percy ultimately

"deprecates the common man for his gullibility" and "in
effect . . . absolves the scientist." Consequently, the novel,
seen as a product of Percy's scientific training, philosophical
musings, and religious inclinations, "comes to us finally not as
the confession of a fellow sufferer but as the clinical diagnosis
of an angel orbiting the earth."

15   LAWSON, LEWIS A. "The Fall of the House of Lamar." In The
      Art of Walker Percy: Stratagems for Being. Edited by Panthea
      Reid Broughton. Baton Rouge: Louisiana State University
      Press, pp. 219-44.
           Unlike Percy's earlier novels, which explore the protago-
      nists' phenomenological awakening to consciousness and eventual
      communion with an empathic and significant other, Lancelot "be-
      gins with an association of the consciousness with another being
      capable of understanding." Lancelot and his auditor, Harry
      [Father John or Percival], had been so close in their youth "that
      Lance thinks their past is identical, that to see Harry is to see
      himself." Thus, in addition to his own recollections, Lancelot
      also recalls the experiences of Father John, particularly the
      priest's Kierkegaardian leap of faith. The priest, therefore,
      "serves as an intersubjective medium, a means through which Lance
      can retrieve and order the data of his past." But because
      throughout his life, Lance had attempted to meld the ideal with
      the real, in his communication he still "is trying to restore the
      past to a purity which it apparently never had." At the close of
      the novel, Lancelot rejects the priest's suggestion of a life
      devoted to caritas, preferring instead to view "his life as an
      apocalypse, with himself as the agent of a . . . revelation."

16   _____. "The Moviegoer and the Stoic Heritage." In The Stoic
      Strain in American Literature: Essays in Honour of Marston
      LaFrance. Edited by Duane J. MacMillan. Toronto and Buffalo:
      University of Toronto Press, pp. 179-97, esp. 180-91.
           Many Southerners besides Binx's Aunt Emily have been ad-
      herents of the Stoic tradition, including Thomas Jefferson and
      Robert E. Lee. To his esteem for the Stoics' emphasis on respon-
      sibility toward self, Jefferson added admiration for Christ's
      adjuration to serve others. Most other Southerners, however,
      viewed Jesus as "a focus for personal piety" and preferred to
      apply the principles of stoicism to their daily lives. Much of
      Southern literature reflects how flaccid this stoicism has become
      in the twentieth century. In contrast, the stoicism of William
      Alexander Percy in Lanterns on the Levee resonates the strength
      of a Jefferson or a Lee. Such stoic ideas, as personified in the
      figure of Aunt Emily, seem acceptable to Binx, until he encoun-
      ters the reality of war in Korea. There "he discovers, through
      the intrusion of fear, that he is condemned to be an individual,
      not an idealized manikin in a gallant historical series." After
      that experience, he is "cut off from the sustenance provided by
      a myth," no longer able to "organize his world to resemble his

aunt's. . . ." In his estrangement from her "calcified tradition" lies his salvation.

17   _____. "Walker Percy." In Southern Writers: A Biographical
        Dictionary. Edited by Robert Bain; Joseph M. Flora; and
        Louis D. Rubin, Jr. Baton Rouge and London: Louisiana State
        University Press, pp. 346-47.
              Basic information about Percy's life, education, and sub-
        sequent writing career. Some minimal background about his read-
        ing of the existentialists is also provided. In all his writing,
        Percy is concerned with the individual in conflict with a culture
        which defines him as datum or consumer. Works are listed through
        1977.

18   _____. "Walker Percy's Wonder-Working Powers." SLJ 12, no. 1
        (Fall):109-14.
              Review of Walker Percy: An American Search, by Robert
        Coles. Coles's three part structure (philosophical roots,
        essays, novels) imposes limitations on the study, yet within that
        structure "perceptive and balanced" readings are provided. The
        first chapter is sketchy and the "derivation from Catholic ortho-
        doxy" is not given sufficient stress. In the treatment of the
        novels Coles provides valuable insights, but he seems to refuse
        to make generalizations. Also, Coles seems to devalue Percy's
        own life as child and adolescent. What still seems to be needed
        is to include Percy the person within a study of his novels. See
        1978.9.

19   LeCLAIR, THOMAS. "Walker Percy's Devil." In The Art of
        Walker Percy: Stratagems for Being. Edited by Panthea Reid
        Broughton. Baton Rouge: Louisiana State University Press,
        pp. 157-68.
              Reprint of 1977.35.

20   LUSCHEI, MARTIN. "The Moviegoer as Dissolve." In The Art of
        Walker Percy: Stratagems for Being. Edited by Panthea Reid
        Broughton. Baton Rouge: Louisiana State University Press,
        pp. 24-36.
              Percy has produced a book rich in visual effects, but one
        that would be difficult to film. Dissolution of personality and
        of painful reality is a central thematic concern in The Movie-
        goer. Notably, Binx Bolling struggles against such dissolution,
        but "most of the characters in The Moviegoer seek to dissolve the
        individuality of themselves and of those around them." Accord-
        ingly, Percy uses the cinematic technique of dissolve to reinforce
        this theme; "virtually the entire novel is structured as a linger-
        ing dissolve." Nevertheless, the novel would present significant
        problems to a moviemaker because Percy's primary concerns, those
        of being and non-being, are among the most difficult to film.

21   PINDELL, RICHARD. "Toward Home: Place, Language, and Death
     in <u>The Last Gentleman</u>." In <u>The Art of Walker Percy: Strata-</u>
     <u>gems for Being</u>. Edited by Panthea Reid Broughton. Baton
     Rouge: Louisiana State University Press, pp. 50-68.
           Will Barrett is suspended in an existential limbo between
     the entropy of modern life and the epiphany of the Good News.
     But out of "the prime world-making <u>materia</u> of place, language,
     and death . . . Percy bodies forth <u>Will</u>'s inwardness and tracks
     his possibilities, and failures, of progress toward receptivity
     to news," especially "within an imagination of home." Three
     critical scenes in the novel particularly "exemplify the workings
     of the imagination of home: Will and Kitty's failed love-making
     in the Central Park 'sniper's den'; Will's visit to Valentine
     Vaught's piney-woods mission school; and Will's attendance at the
     deathbed baptism of Jamie Vaught." Notably in the latter scene,
     Will cannot orient himself either in space or through language,
     and thus reduces Jamie's death to "a problem in manners." But
     though he seemingly fails to recognize the unrelenting and neces-
     sary homelessness of his mortal state, ironically he may realize
     his condition in the home that he plans to occupy with Kitty,
     that of Cap'N Andy. The house's likeness to a ship, its bridge,
     and its ever-circling buzzards and crows may make Will aware that
     he is a "sovereign pilgrim stranger." The wider implications of
     Will's tentative progress toward recovery is that perhaps "the
     astonishing failure of the things in which man has misplaced him-
     self may lead to his self-recovery."

22   POTEAT, WILLIAM H. "Reflections on Walker Percy's Theory of
     Language: <u>Or, It is Better to Stay with Helen Keller at the</u>
     <u>Well-House in Tuscumbia, Alabama, than to Venture to Mars and</u>
     <u>be Devoured by the Ravening Particles</u>." In <u>The Art of Walker</u>
     <u>Percy: Stratagems for Being</u>. Edited by Panthea Reid
     Broughton. Baton Rouge: Louisiana State University Press,
     pp. 192-218.
           Although Percy is "so absolutely right in all his philo-
     sophical insights" on language and its relation to the human con-
     dition, he betrays these insights in his essay "A Theory of Lan-
     guage" by lapsing into the abstraction he decries in others. As
     a result, "Percy's profoundest and most original contribution
     . . . is to be found not in those essays in which he is being
     dialectically most explicit and rigorous as in 'A Theory of
     Language,' but in those in which he is being least so, as in
     'The Delta Factor.'" In the latter essay, such elements as
     first-person narrative, concrete images, and pathos "keep Percy
     close to his own incarnate reality as a speaker . . . and close
     therefore to the irreducible and radical truth about language
     which he sees." Consequently, among the essays, "The Delta
     Factor" rather than "A Theory of Language" functions as Percy's
     most powerful response to notable explorations of language and
     behavior, such as those of "Chomsky, the transformationalists,
     the semioticists, and Skinner."

23   RUBIN, LOUIS D., Jr.   "The Boll Weevil, the Iron Horse, and
     the End of the Line: Thoughts on the South." VQR 55, no. 2
     (Spring):193-221.
          The author draws a parallel between his experience of the
     demise of a passenger train, named the "Boll Weevil," and Will
     Barrett's recognition in The Last Gentleman of the concrete
     reality of the iron horse's head shortly before his father's
     suicide. Both experiences illustrate the mutability of the world
     and the danger of idealizing a past time for its imagined perfec-
     tion. Rather than departing from Southern literary tradition,
     Percy instead redefines it, indicating how one must incorporate
     individual value into an ever-changing community of men and
     women.

24   _____. "The South's Writers: A Literature of Time and
     Change." Southern World 1, no. 2:26-27.
          A consideration of why so much modern American literature
     is Southern, and what the future holds as the South changes.
     Major writers, including Percy, grew up in a South "rural but
     swiftly changing." Percy's work, while it considers that new
     South, is a world wherein the protagonists conduct their quests
     very much along traditional "Southern literary lines," and until
     writers such as Percy cease to ask questions about the relation-
     ship of the present to the past and accept the status quo, the
     Southern literary mode remains of importance.

25   SCHOTT, WEBSTER. "Marriage of Two Minds." WP, 18 February,
     sec. E, p. 50.
          A generally favorable review of Walker Percy: An American
     Search by Robert Coles indicates that the book is essential for
     Percy readers, but wishes for more biographical detail and less
     of Coles's philosophical musings. See 1978.9.

26   SIMPSON, LEWIS P. "Southern Fiction." In Harvard Guide to
     Contemporary American Writing. Edited by Daniel Hoffman.
     Cambridge, Mass. and London: Harvard University Press,
     Belknap Press, pp. 153-90, esp. 180-83.
          Although their fates as individuals rest upon the outcomes
     of their quests for personal salvation, Percy's protagonists
     cannot divorce themselves from their society and its history.
     "Binx Bolling in The Moviegoer and Williston Barrett in The Last
     Gentleman not only suggest the aura of ineffable loneliness as-
     sociated with the modern experience of radical individuation,
     they embody the experience." On the other hand, Dr. Thomas More
     of Love in the Ruins "seems so far divorced from his past" that
     his recommitment to traditional religious values remains uncon-
     vincing. The clash of history and individuation is present even
     more graphically in Lancelot: "the closure of history in the
     self has left no way open for salvation save self-will."

27 SPIVEY, TED R. "Walker Percy and the Archetypes." In <u>The Art</u>
    <u>of Walker Percy: Stratagems for Being</u>. Edited by Panthea
    Reid Broughton. Baton Rouge: Louisiana State University
    Press, pp. 273-93.
        The most profound influence that Kierkegaard exerted on the
    thought and writings of Walker Percy was to bring him "face to
    face with one or more of the archetypes." Both Binx Bolling and
    Will Barrett personify the archetypal heroic quester, or, in
    Kierkegaardian terms, the knight of faith. Will Barrett's quest
    is more fully developed than that of Binx, who allows himself to
    be possessed by the anima archetype, as evidenced by his inveter-
    ate moviegoing. Barrett particularly exemplifies the archetype
    of the hero through his participation in the baptism of Jamie
    Vaught. Of the four Percy novels to date, only <u>Love in the Ruins</u>
    is "not primarily a book about archetypal pilgrimage." Percy's
    fourth novel, <u>Lancelot</u>, marks the author's most direct depiction
    of the shadow archetype. By his recognition of the power of the
    shadow archetype in our time, Percy is demonstrating increased
    artistic maturity. But it remains for Percy to "bring his fic-
    tional characters of the future into a profounder relationship
    with the shadow."

28 SWICK, MARLY A. "Romantic Ministers and Phallic Knights: A
    Study of <u>A Month of Sundays</u>, <u>Lancelot</u>, and <u>Falconer</u>." Ph.D.
    dissertation, The American University.
        Like Updike and Cheever, Percy describes the contemporary
    "loss of faith [which] is inevitably accompanied by the loss of
    sexual virility and a fear of impotence."

29 TELOTTE, J.P. "Butting Heads with Faulkner's Soldier." <u>NConL</u>
    9, no. 3 (May):7-8.
        An incident in <u>The Last Gentleman</u> involving Will Barrett
    and a statue of a Confederate soldier echoes the carriage scene
    with Benjy at the end of <u>The Sound and the Fury</u>. Percy seemingly
    renders a conscious analogue to Faulkner in order to indicate the
    necessity of recognizing the hold of the past and of exorcizing
    one's self from its grip, thereby reaching a new awareness of
    individual responsibility in a world no longer informed by the
    tradition which the statue represents.

30 _____. "Walker Percy: A Pragmatic Approach." <u>Southern</u>
    <u>Studies</u> 18, no. 2 (Summer):217-30.
        <u>The Message in the Bottle</u> confirms Percy's indebtedness to
    Charles Sanders Peirce, an influence which has significance in
    relation to the fiction. In attempting to formulate a "unified
    field theory" of language, Percy draws on Peirce, who postulated
    that the act of interpretation forms the third element of a
    triad. Study of Peirce reveals a relationship "between his
    theory of signs and approach to human knowledge," and a thorough
    consideration of this influence on Percy should ultimately focus
    on their common concern with how man "'knows.'" Peirce's theory

of "abduction" serves as a starting point: Percy has discussed
it in linguistic and epistemological terms. In adapting this
theory of abduction, the inferential step--the distinctive human
ability to arrive at correct solutions--Percy suggests connections both with linguistics and with other abductive situations.
While Percy's existential leanings are common knowledge, the "in-
cessant questioning activity" which Peirce outlined can also be
found in Percy's writings. In the novels there is clear evidence;
especially in The Moviegoer such interaction centers on the
"interplay of question and answer." Finally, Percy's heroes become reconciled to their questioning natures; thereby Percy provides models which speak to the American consciousness and offer
assurance.

31   THORNTON, WELDON. "Homo Loquens, Homo Symbolificus, Homo
     Sapiens: Walker Percy on Language." In The Art of Walker
     Percy: Stratagems for Being. Edited by Panthea Reid
     Broughton. Baton Rouge: Louisiana State University Press,
     pp. 169-91.
        In this summary of Percy's essays on language, the author
     presents Percy's basic tenets and examines "certain problematic
     points." Of chief interest is Percy's conviction "that exploring
     the implications of man's unique capacity tor language can be of
     inestimable value in freeing us from our present cultural
     malaise." Percy also reveals a major antinomy in the scientist's
     study of language which fails to account for "what he [the scien-
     tist] is doing when he develops hypotheses, makes assertions, and
     argues about these with his fellow scientists." One problem area
     in Percy's writings about language is his equivocal use of the
     term empiricism: "Percy assumes, apparently unawares, that there
     is a continuity of method between the empiricism of Hume and the
     'genuine' empiricism he calls for." On the whole, "the virtue of
     Percy's essays is . . . they make us aware of how basic the prob-
     lem of meaning is and how inadequately it is handled by linguis-
     tics and psychology."

32   VANDERWERKEN, DAVID L. "The Americanness of The Moviegoer."
     NMW 12, no. 1 (Summer):39-53.
        The Moviegoer shares characteristics of the Jeremiad with
     books by Mailer and Vonnegut; it is a critique of deadness in
     American culture in the fifties. Through characters whom Binx
     presents, various types of living-death are introduced; further
     Binx realizes these characters prefer a death-in-life existence.
     Such characters provide satire about being free and pursuing
     happiness, yet in Percy's view happiness can only occur in an
     unconventional way as it does for Binx. The result of Percy's
     moral judgment forces a reevaluation of American culture.

33   VAUTHIER, SIMONE. "Narrative Triangulation in The Last
     Gentleman." In The Art of Walker Percy: Stratagems for
     Being. Edited by Panthea Reid Broughton. Baton Rouge:
     Louisiana State University Press, pp. 69-95.
         Shifts in the relations of narrator, subject, and narratee
     in The Last Gentleman inform and underscore the novel's structure
     of meaning. At the beginning the configuration can be diagrammed
     "as an equilateral triangle." But as the story progresses, "the
     narratee's apex has receded into the background and narrator and
     subject have come closer," thereby changing the narrative tri-
     angulation. Such shifts can be traced particularly through the
     narrator's names for Will Barrett, through the varieties of means
     used to report discourse, and through the technique of multiple
     points of view. Ultimately, the effect is of a narrator who
     functions not in a realistic way but in a poetic one, of a nar-
     rator who intersubjectively leads the reader "to share in an
     exchange [at Jamie's baptism] which may link him to 'the silent
     Word' beyond the novelist's words."

34   WEBB, MAX. "Binx Bolling's New Orleans: Moviegoing, Southern
     Writing, and Father Abraham." In The Art of Walker Percy:
     Stratagems for Being. Edited by Panthea Reid Broughton.
     Baton Rouge: Louisiana State University Press, pp. 1-23.
         A central paradox informs Binx Bolling's search for meaning
     in The Moviegoer: he recovers the world by detaching himself
     from it. This paradox is underscored by three other paradoxical
     situations in the novel, all of which bear upon "the relationship
     between the fictive Binx and the fiction that contains him."
     First, Binx functions well in his world but does not really feel
     himself to be a part of it; he is in psychological exile. His
     confusion accounts for the multiple beginnings of the novel and
     highlights a major theme: "the necessity of seeing one's life
     as a series of fresh beginnings." Another paradox concerns
     Binx's seemingly solipsistic vision. In actuality, Binx's world
     view is wide, a perception which allows him to see beyond the
     local color of New Orleans and thereby depict it as a microcosm
     of a dying civilization. Finally, the third paradox provides the
     Kierkegaardian framework of the novel. Binx ostensibly searches
     for clues to the mystery of existence but lacks the belief in
     signs of Kierkegaard's knight of faith, the biblical Abraham.
     Binx declares that "Now the only sign is that all the signs in
     the world make no difference." Nevertheless, he makes a leap of
     faith.

35   YAGODA, BEN. "A Lucid, Sympathetic Study of Walker Percy."
     Chronicle of Higher Education 18 (5 March):R11.
         This review of Robert Coles's Walker Percy: An American
     Search welcomes Coles's "treatment of Percy's fiction from a
     broader perspective than the usual literary criticism," but finds
     that the book disappoints in its sparse account of Percy's biog-
     raphy and in its excessive attention to Coles's philosophical

musings and use of "lengthy quotations from his patients and
others." From a critical standpoint, the book also fails: "most
conspicuous is [Coles's] failure to take sufficient account of
Percy's rhetorical complexity."

1980

1   ANON. Review of The Second Coming. Kirkus 48, no. 9 (1 May):
     602.
        Percy's latest novel, The Second Coming, similar in theme
to his others, explores the limited sense of personal identity.
Specifically this takes the form of a satire of the moribund
modern South. Although it lacks an ongoing sense of characterization, Percy is a "cool Dostoevsky . . . more personal than ever
before." This work reveals a better prose than one is likely to
find in most other American writing.

2   ANON. Review of The Second Coming. PW 217, no. 20 (23 May):
     70.
        Regards Percy as "one of the finest novelists of our time."
With The Second Coming, Percy brings hope to modern fiction. His
combination of wit and style brings grace to questions about the
times we live in and the reality of God's existence.

3   ANON. Review of The Second Coming. SatR 7 (August):95.
        Brief mention of the return of Will Barrett. "With a born
storyteller's grace and wit, Percy examines life, its meaning,
its worth."

4   ANON. "Walker Percy." In Contemporary Literary Criticism.
     Vol. 14. Edited by Dedria Bryfonski and Laurie Lanzen Harris.
     Detroit: Gale Research Co., pp. 411-19.
        Introduction states Percy's "fictive concerns are serious
and ambitious: in his work Percy seeks to reconcile the problem
of faith in a secular world." Excerpts are from the following:
Edward J. Cashin (1977.13), Thomas LeClair (1977.35), Robert D.
Daniel (1978.12), and Robert Coles (1978.9).

5   ATCHITY, KENNETH JOHN. "The Fictional Five: Of Life and
     Death, Eloquence and Silence." Los Angeles Times, 9 November,
     sec. 1R, p. 10.
        This brief citation finds The Second Coming "written with a
lyric eloquence that mingles intensity and leisure as it brings
into focus two characters, Will and Allison, who represent between them as much of our own contemporary consciousness as Bloom
represented of Dublin's."

6 ATLAS, JAMES. "Portrait of Mr. Percy." NYTBR, 29 June,
pp. 1, 30-31.
Interview includes biographical data and a brief summary of
Percy's writing career. Parallels are drawn between The Second
Coming and Percy's other novels and also between the novel's protagonists and their creator. Percy classifies The Second Coming
as his "first unalienated novel" because of its happy ending.
Nonetheless, Will Barrett is "a voracious and enraged pilgrim."
Percy acknowledges his own sense of alienation but observes that
it fortuitously coincides with that of twentieth century man, and
so therefore Percy "cultivate[s]" it. He indicates that he also
feels psychologically estranged from his fellow Southerners. The
reviewer observes that "this geographical and spiritual perplexity appears to be widely shared, for Percy has acquired a devoted,
even fanatical following that responds to his work in a very
personal way. . . ."

7 BALLIETT, WHITNEY. "Will and Allison." NY 56 (1 September):
86, 88.
Mostly favorable review of The Second Coming that hails
Percy as "a superb comic social reporter," but complains "the
book falls apart" as Will and Allison fall in love.

8 BATCHELOR, JOHN CALVIN. "The Percy Perplex." Village Voice,
9-15 July, p. 34.
The Second Coming "fails as a romance, fails as a character
novel, fails as a confession, succeeds uncomfortably well as a
stoical groan." Despite these flaws Percy has written another
novel that must be read. Will Barrett, the protagonist of The
Last Gentleman, returns in The Second Coming. His problem is no
longer one of forgetting. Barrett is now a man who remembers too
much--"'If a man cannot forget,' wrote Kierkegaard, 'he will
never amount to much.'" Continuing his search to prove God's
existence, Percy often allows "his relentless God-talk" to get
in the way of character development. Allison, another of Percy's
"wounded-children," is more a "philosophical construct" than a
character. The emotional drama that could evolve is replaced
with melodrama. Despite the novel's weaknesses and the issues
that it sidesteps, "America's gentleman correspondent with the
ghost of Kierkegaard" has written another "brave, mortal book."

9 BATES, RANDOLPH. "Writings about Percy: Reviews." SoQ 18,
no. 3 (Spring):158-63.
This review of Percy criticism concentrates predominantly
on the three book-length studies which preceded Tharpe's: the
works of Martin Luschei and Robert Coles, and the collection of
essays edited by Panthea Broughton. Luschei is commended for the
seminal nature of his work but faulted for his lack of critical
distance, as is Coles to an even greater degree. Given special
mention is Lewis Lawson, "foremost among Percy's readers." Also
noted is the increasing attention being paid to the Christian

emphasis in Percy's work. Broughton's collection is commended
for its range and diversity and for its special attention to the
element of "self-scrutiny" which Percy's work compels. [This
article is not reprinted in Walker Percy: Art and Ethics, edited
by Jac Tharpe. See also 1980.55.]

10   BIGGER, CHARLES P. "Walker Percy and the Resonance of the
     Word." SoQ 18, no. 3 (Spring):43-54.
        Particularly in his manipulation of language, man violates
the mystery of being by approaching the world as a problem to be
solved. "Walker Percy has, with truly remarkable success, set
himself to the task of restoring strangeness to the name and to
ourselves, the users of names." Percy has developed this philosophical perspective despite the prevailing emphasis on posi-
tivism and his own natural predilection for, and training in,
science, with its devotion to the mechanistic model. "Percy saw
that his task in reflecting on the word lay between the space-time
events of naturalism and the alienated realms of spirit." Reprinted: 1980.55.

11   BOLES, PAUL DARCY. "Author-as-God View Flaws Second Coming."
     The Atlanta Journal / The Atlanta Constitution, 27 July,
     sec. F, pp. 4-5.
        The novel is a stacked deck: nothing "is organic, inevi-
table or actually natural. . . . The author plays God personally
or at least acts as if he maintained a pipeline directly to the
Deity. . . ."

12   BRINKMEYER, ROBERT H., Jr. "Percy's Bludgeon: Message and
     Narrative Strategy." SoQ 18, no. 3 (Spring):80-90.
        As a Christian novelist, Walker Percy faces the difficult
task of expounding his message of faith to a post-Christian
audience. In the first two novels the theme of religious redemption as a solution to man's alienation is muted, so low-key as to
be grasped only by readers who recognize their own alienation.
In his second two novels, however, he resorts to shock techniques
to jar self-satisfied readers out of their complacency. Percy
uses this technique throughout Love in the Ruins but even more
jarringly in Lancelot. "Lancelot's tirades are deliberately
grotesque exaggerations designed to electrify the callous sensi-
bilities of the complacent readers." But as a foil to Lancelot
he provides Percival; thus Percy forces the reader into a situation "where he must choose between Lancelot and Percival, but
only after he has revealed the ugliness at the heart of Lancelot's
approach." The last word of the novel is Percival's, and it is
one of affirmation. Reprinted: 1980.55.

13   CHRISTENSEN, JEROME C. "Lancelot: Sign for the Times." SoQ
     18, no. 3 (Spring):107-20.
        Lancelot's madness gives him the advantage of a sharply
circumscribed vision, one that yields a tantalizing fragment of

a message, "Free & Ma B." Speculations about its ultimate implications lend clues to the novel's structure of meaning. Free &
point to Lancelot's freedom from his destructive pattern of
everydayness, a freedom which begins when he discovers in his
daughter's blood type evidence of his wife's infidelity. Lancelot
uses the sexual license, which he seeks and finds, as a barometer
of widespread moral decadence, "starkly legible in the signs of
the times." Ma could refer to his mother's dual function as a
lady and as a whore (the supposedly mutually exclusive categories
to which Lancelot relegates women). ". . . It is his mother's
uncertain fidelity which is the type of that indeterminacy between Lady and Whore that Lancelot aims to extirpate." B, the
last part of the cryptic message, provides the solution to its
meaning because it is the core of existential dilemma. Implicit
in it is the answer which Percival "has been advancing all
along . . . love." Reprinted: 1980.55.

14   CLARK, LINDLEY H., Jr. "A Christmas Potpourri of Books."
      Wall Street Journal, 11 December, p. 26.
         Brief overview of Edmund Fuller's review of The Second
Coming (see 1980.23).

15   CLEMONS, WALTER. "Lay Preacher." NW 96 (7 July):66.
         Review of The Second Coming. This unfavorable review de-
clares that Percy's "worst novel, this one, is still more interesting than most other writers' best shot."

16   DALE, CORINNE. "Lancelot and the Medieval Quests of Sir
      Lancelot and Dante." SoQ 18, no. 3 (Spring):99-106.
         Lancelot deplores modern society, particularly its sexual
excesses, and vows to found a new society, based on ancient
chivalric codes. His auditor, Percival, "endorses Lancelot's
prophecy of a new life in Virginia, but not necessarily the new
life which Lance envisions." His counsel to Lancelot is revealed
in his "yes" at the novel's conclusion, and the implication of
his "answer is available--is, in fact, contained in the structure
of the novel." A significant clue lies in "the structural parallels of Lance's story to the quest of Malory's Sir Lancelot du
Lac. . . . Most significantly, the Grail legend explores the conflict of secular and spiritual love similar to the conflict of
sensual and chivalrous love which torments Lance." The two
accounts diverge noticeably in the attitudes of the two Lancelots
towards love. Because the latter-day Lancelot rejects love, he
chooses a secular life devoted to chivalry, while the Lancelot of
legend renounces secular love for sacred love. But further clues
to Lance's future lie in the similarity of his quest to that of
Dante. Just as Virgil guided Dante to Beatrice to be redeemed by
her love, Percival will be replaced by Anna. Reprinted: 1980.55.

17   DeMOTT, BENJAMIN. "A Thinking Man's Kurt Vonnegut." Atlantic
      246, no. 1 (July):81-84.
          "The Second Coming will probably inspire a further bout of
      brain-cudgeling among linguistic philosophers . . . a number of
      the most striking chapters . . . are those in which Allie Huger,
      whose grasp of the nature of language has become shaky, recovers
      it, bit by bit." However, this is an imaginative work exploring
      a broad range of experiences, from hope and despair to kindness
      and idiocy.

18   DONAVIN, DENISE P. Review of The Second Coming. Booklist 76,
      no. 20 (15 June):1464-65.
          A beautiful, new exploration of Percy's recurrent theme--
      "an individual man's search for the hand of God in the meaning-
      less muddle of contemporary life." Comic relief and sentiment
      are other aspects of this serious novel.

19   EGERTON, JOHN. "Quiet Chaos." Progressive 44, no. 10
      (October):58-59.
          Walker Percy's literary skill is marked by his unsettling
      ability to make his "normal" and "crazy" characters so much
      alike. In The Second Coming, Percy has one such character re-
      turn. Will Barrett's problem is no longer amnesia but "flashes
      of total recall." In The Second Coming--as with all of Percy's
      fiction--there are more questions than answers.

20   EUBANKS, CECIL L. "Walker Percy: Eschatology and the Poli-
      tics of Grace." SoQ 18, no. 3 (Spring):121-36.
          Walker Percy is prominent among current philosophers formu-
      lating a redefinition of man to suit these times of great social
      flux and decay. His particular concern is "to recover the human
      being from the Cartesian split of mind and body which dominates
      much of twentieth century thinking." Furthermore, "his radical
      anthropology has its base in the Kierkegaardian insistence on
      individual sovereignty and choice as well as in the Judeo-
      Christian view of man as the fallen seeker." In Percy's view,
      political reform provides no panacea to the malaise but instead
      exacerbates it; yet his philosophy suffers because of this exclu-
      sion. "The political relationship is a part of the dialectical
      unfolding of consciousness of the self as self and consciousness
      of 'otherness.'" Instead Percy emphasizes "consciousness at the
      expense of experience, on grace as 'Word' and not as 'Word made
      Flesh' [and consequently] does a grave injustice to Christianity
      as well as to the notion of grace." Reprinted: 1980.55.

21   FILIPPIDIS, BARBARA. "Vision and the Journey to Selfhood in
      Walker Percy's The Moviegoer." Renascence 33, no. 1 (Autumn):
      10-23.
          Vision revitalized allows Binx to pierce "the malaise and
      regain access to the essential mystery of existence." Other
      characters in the novel have lost their abilities to see while

Binx, already early in the action, seeks to develop techniques
for fighting the malaise. Moviegoing itself is a metaphor for
learning to watch and wonder "at the mystery of existence." The
trip to Chicago precipitates Binx's realization that he has been
"stripped of his protective lens of irony" and that he and Kate
can help each other; this marks the beginning of a new kind of
vision for him. In the scene on the playground Binx's new way
of seeing is confirmed; through an inner act, an "imaginary vision of apocalypse," he recovers himself and the world.

22   FREMONT-SMITH, ELIOT. "The Trickle-Down Theory of Uplift."
      Village Voice, 31 December-6 January 1981, p. 32.
         Considers the books nominated for the National Book Critics
Circle awards. The Second Coming is a novel of symbols and ideas
in which "satire defines (wars with?) Christian faith in the continuing saga of Will Barrett."

23   FULLER, EDMUND. "Walker Percy's Profoundly Satisfying Novel."
      Wall Street Journal, 23 June, p. 22.
         The Second Coming is the "most life-affirming of all Dr.
Percy's distinguished novels." The counterpoint reflected in the
two main characters, Will and Allie, is an extension of the substance of the book, itself--"the allure of real death and the
multiple seductions of death-in-life." The question that both
characters (must) ultimately face is "'How does one live?'" From
his comments on the treatment of the mentally ill to his exploration of language, Percy gives us a complex comedy of "infinite
possibilities." See also 1980.14.

24   GILDER, JOSHUA. Review of The Second Coming. American
      Spectator 30, no. 10 (October):34-35.
         An unfavorable review, criticizing unfortunate parallels
between The Second Coming and The Moviegoer. In both, Percy
romanticizes insanity by depicting Kate and Allison, not as
clinically ill, but as innocent, perceptive observers of the
world. Percy should be faulted, too, for his stereotypical
presentation of these two characters, "the helpless-child woman"
who must be "saved by the manly hero." Although Percy is described by the critics as a novelist of ideas, he fails in com-
bining the two roles. As a philosopher in The Message in the
Bottle, he is too abstract; as a novelist, his fictional scenes
lack meaning and coherence.

25   GILMAN, RICHARD. Review of The Second Coming. NewR 183
      (5 July):29-31.
         A laudatory review that finds the writing "shrewd, lovely,
wholly original."

26   GRAY, PAUL. "Blues in the New South." Time 116, no. 2
      (14 July):51, 54.
         The "free-floating contemplatives" that have become Walker
   Percy's trademark are again at work in The Second Coming. All of
   his heroes, "unencumbered by the routines and demands of daily
   life," have time to think. Will Barrett must find a reason to go
   on living; and in the process, he must settle his questions about
   the existence of God. The novel's weakness rests in the character flaws of its hero. Percy overcomes this weakness through his
   craftsmanship. In the process of posing questions and searching
   for answers, Walker Percy is able to blend the past with the
   present in an unobtrusive but "meticulously crafted narrative."

27   HARDY, JOHN EDWARD. "Percy and Place: Some Beginnings and
      Endings." SoQ 18, no. 3 (Spring):5-25.
         The beginnings and endings of Percy's first four novels
   reveal the existential situation of the protagonists. The
   "curiously detached" tone and the lack of physical description in
   the first paragraph of The Moviegoer apparently reflect Binx's
   alienation, but the concrete details of setting that he conveys
   in the ensuing paragraphs show Binx's keen sense of place. The
   opening of The Last Gentleman abounds with information related to
   the setting, establishing a "vivid sense of place." Ironically,
   the place is Central Park, "a setting that defies cultural definition as a place." Will Barrett rather remarkably carries
   around with him his "traditional Southern sense of place." While
   containing numerous details of time and place, the opening of
   Love in the Ruins remains confusing about particulars, and "the
   confusion is deliberate." The ending of the novel reveals a
   marked change in Tom More's fate, as he contentedly tends his
   garden in the old slave quarters, having escaped the life-in-
   death of Paradise Estates. Even the imperfections of the place
   and Tom's occasional lapses into drunkenness and lust indicate
   his spiritual rescue; "his final estate . . . leaves him sus-
   ceptible of grace." The opening of Lancelot discloses the protagonist's acceptance of his cell and preferably limited vision,
   indicating "the fanatical egomania which he is further to
   reveal. . . ." The novel concludes with Lancelot planning a new
   Eden in Virginia; thus "Lancelot's madness begins and ends in a
   fundamental disrespect for the reality of the world outside himself." Reprinted: 1980.55.

28   HOBSON, LINDA WHITNEY. "Walker Percy: A Sign of the Apoca-
      lypse." Horizon 23, no. 8 (August):56-61.
         Combines comments made by Percy during an interview, bio-
   graphical material, and a recapitulation of his fictional concerns. Included also is a plot summary of The Second Coming.
   Percy's own sense of "outsidedness," certified for him by his
   readings in existentialism during his illness, led to his prevailing concern for the estrangement of twentieth-century man.
   He feels that he can raise readers' awareness of their own

alienation but that despair can only be ameliorated by an
"'epiphany in ordeal.'" Percy asserts that "writing is the
loneliest goddamn life in the world," but continues because he's
always hoping "to do the really big one." His work in progress
is a book dealing with semiotics, to be entitled Novum Organum.

29   HOLLEY, JOE. "Walker Percy and the Novel of Ultimate Con-
      cern." SWR 65, no. 3 (Summer):225-34.
          Percy's novels reflect his contention that the novelist
should have "an explicit and ultimate concern with the nature of
man and the nature of reality where man finds himself." Each of
his protagonists is at odds with the banal nature of contemporary
American reality. Each attains a measure of authentic selfhood
from insight gained during a search precipitated by catastrophe.

30   KENDALL, ELAINE. "Special Love as a Guide to Renewed Hope."
      Los Angeles Times, 27 July, sec. 1R, p. 4.
          Favorable review of The Second Coming suggests thematic
analogues with George Herbert's 17th-century religious poem, "The
Pulley"; and maintains "the book itself is constructed like a
sophisticated pulley system, composed of separate narrative
strands working smoothly together."

31   KIRKEBY, MARC. "Percy: He Can See Clearly Now." Los Angeles
      Times Calendar, 3 August, p. 52.
          In this interview, Percy registers his pleasure over liter-
ary progressions he sees in The Second Coming: "a victory of
eros over thanatos and life over death"; Barrett's overcoming his
alienation; and the creation of a strong female character,
Allison. Noted also is Allison's creative language as an exem-
plification of Percy's interest in semiotics. Percy relates a
couple of anecdotes concerning the rather eccentric segment of
his readership and includes the story of the publication of A
Confederacy of Dunces.

32   KISOR, HENRY. "Dr. Percy on Signs and Symbols." Critic 39,
      no. 4 (September):2-5.
          This interview traces Percy's interest in semiotics to his
discovery of his daughter's deafness. His preoccupation with
language figures in the characterization of The Second Coming's
Allison, who simultaneously forges for herself a new language and
a new identity. Admitting that all of his protagonists resemble
him to a degree, he maintains that Will Barrett differs from him
in being "a frantic searcher after truth," while Percy feels
secure in his Catholic faith. He reveals that, if starting over,
he might turn to film-making instead of novel writing. Both
media afford a similar broad canvas. The role of the American
novelist, he maintains, is "to question the values of society."

33   KISSEL, SUSAN S. "Voices in the Wilderness: The Prophets of
      O'Connor, Percy, and Powers." SoQ 18, no. 3 (Spring):91-98.
          Percy's Lancelot, Flannery O'Connor's Hazel Motes and
      Tarwater, and J.F. Powers's Father Urban all resemble one another
      in their contempt for the world and ultimate rejection of it.
      "The prophet-protagonists of these three contemporary Catholic
      writers 'die to the world'" in which evil is so pervasive as to
      be commonplace and thus easily tolerated. They cannot find
      solace in the salve of modern Christianity. "The Christianity
      manifest in these protagonists is an abrasive faith which refuses
      to accommodate itself either to modern society or to the modern
      Catholic Church." Reprinted: 1980.55.

34   LAWSON, LEWIS A. "Moviegoing in The Moviegoer." SoQ 18,
      no. 3 (Spring):26-42.
          Binx begins to use moviegoing as an essential part of his
      search when he realizes, after seeing It Happened One Night, that
      his life remains to be lived even though he presumed to have
      deciphered the universe. In that movie he discovers zone-
      crossing, or rotation, as an alternative to his alienated state.
      He thus acknowledges a subject/object split within his being and
      determines that "he will apprehend his world as he views a
      movie. . . . In the novel, then, moviegoing characterizes the
      alienated man's fascinated gaze at a distant reality." During
      his visit at his mother's fishing camp, he sees the movie Fort
      Dobbs, which he especially enjoys because he "wants to live his
      life . . . as if it were a role in a Western movie." As Percy
      discusses in "The Man on the Train," the Western hero remains
      "the locus of pure possibility." As a good actor should, Binx
      "assumes the role expected of him on any occasion." Even after
      he resumes his serious search, he still continues his impersona-
      tions. "He thinks that he can succeed in this performance be-
      cause no one else is involved. . . ." After the sexual debacle
      with Kate, however, she "demonstrates her faith in him as he is;
      and as a consequence Binx is serene in his own identity for once
      in his life." Though the novel contains no Hollywood ending, it
      does conclude with Binx's no longer playacting but pursuing an
      authentic existence. Reprinted: 1980.55.

35   _____. "Walker Percy's Silent Character." MissQ 33, no. 2
      (Spring):123-40.
          Detailed analysis of the temporal structure of Lancelot
      reveals that Lance does not speak in a vacuum; ideas, order, and
      imagery are "at least in part" determined by his awareness of the
      person who visits. The reader is provided with a contrast to
      Lance's rhetoric and thereby develops "an appreciation for gaps
      in the narration." The reader therefore contributes to the char-
      acter growth of the unheard auditor, and raises the visitor to
      his prominence as the one person who has something important to
      say to Lance. This careful reading of the implications of what
      is said, and how Father John conducts himself day by day, is

related to interests of Percy in intersubjectivity where he follows Buber and Marcel and rejects Sartre.

36 _____. "William Alexander Percy, Walker Percy, and the
Apocalypse." Modern Age 24, no. 4 (Fall):396-406.
William Alexander Percy's father, LeRoy, scored impressive
victories against the Ku Klux Klan in Mississippi. Nonetheless,
in his poem "Enzio's Kingdom," the younger Percy, ever the dis-
heartened romanticist, compared his father with the ill-fated
Frederick II of Sicily. Frederick had been hailed by many be-
lievers as the avatar of the millennium predicted by Joachim de
Flora. Though Frederick was defeated, historians such as Eric
Voegelin have demonstrated that millennial thought has persisted
in the European mind with such recent manifestations as Nazism
and Marxism. A four-faceted "aggregate of symbols," consisting
of a sequence of three ages, a leader, a prophet, and a brother-
hood of followers, is an essential component of Joachitic thinking. Such millennial vision appealed to an apocalyptist like
William Alexander Percy and appears in his autobiography as well
as in his poems; but the novels of his adopted son, Walker Percy,
can be viewed as counter-reaction to such thought. Both Binx
Bolling and Will Barrett reject outright such a gnostic attitude,
whereas Tom More and Lancelot Lamar see themselves as the new
savior. Lancelot even creates and survives his own apocalypse.
Indeed, "the initial situation" of Lancelot "bears an uncanny
resemblance to 'Enzio's Kingdom.'" In Lancelot, Percy manifests
"a total rejection of 'Enzio's Kingdom,'" by demonstrating the
dangers of its gnostic conceit.

37 LISCHER, TRACY KENYON. Review of The Second Coming. CC 97
(15 October):979.
Percy believes with Toynbee that all issues are basically
religious and "in times of imminent danger and commensurate hope
the eschatological novelist raises an important voice." Percy's
religious feelings are born in the nature of communication--
"with words the human mind brings beauty out of hiding." His
characters long for a bond between themselves and reality. In
this novel Will Barrett moves "from absolute loneliness to re-
discovery of commitment, from dread of catastrophe to hope of
community." If prophets can't be found, "we sometimes settle for
the quasi-prophet, a serious novelist."

38 LYONS, GENE. "Deep Hidden Meaning." Nat 231 (16 August):
157-58.
A mixed review of The Second Coming, which expresses ad-
miration for the prose in the book's "essentially mimetic passages," but disfavor with the "ceaseless rhetorical questions"
raised.

39   MacKETHAN, LUCINDA. The Dream of Arcady: Place and Time in
     Southern Literature. Baton Rouge: Louisiana State University
     Press, pp. 215-17.
          In the concluding section of this study Percy's The Last
     Gentleman is considered "as an elegy to the Southern dream of
     Arcady." Will Barrett illustrates the problems of "lost com-
     munity and isolation."

40   MERKIN, DAPHNE. "Lost Souls." NL 63 (28 July):15-16.
          A favorable review of The Second Coming. ". . . A very
     wise and very funny novel. . . ."

41   MURRAY, JAMES G. "Fiction in the (very) Low 80s and early
     retrospective with (mostly) regrets for the future." Critic
     39, no. 9 (December):1-8, esp. 6.
          Considers Walker Percy one of "our foremost novelist[s] of
     ideas." His ideas have been viewed in terms of Christian exis-
     tentialism, modernism, and myth and allegory. Percy's thinking
     is neither egocentric nor self-serving. The Second Coming is a
     powerful combination of "uniqueness of voice and realized craft."
     The seriousness of Percy's message can be easily overlooked if
     one focuses attention solely on comic invention and character.
     The integration of Percy's "mind and imagination, perceptive wit
     and moral compassion," gives his fiction a life of its own.

42   MUTHER, ELIZABETH. Review of The Second Coming. CSM,
     20 August, p. 17.
          Recognizes the strong link between Percy's fiction and The
     Message in the Bottle: "The characters in Percy's novels often
     act out problems defined in his essays." Will and Allison ful-
     fill Percy's admonition in the essay, "The Loss of the Creature,"
     to escape the symbol trap in order to experience the world di-
     rectly. In the beginning, even the novel's style seems stiff and
     unrealistic, mirroring Will's and Allison's isolation and self-
     entrapment, but it changes and ripens as the characters' abili-
     ties to communicate improve. The Second Coming is a comic novel
     by a serious Christian writer that satirizes both facile Chris-
     tianity, and the modern clinical view of experience as constrict-
     ing impoverishments of the possibilities of human life.

43   PEARSON, MICHAEL. "Art as Symbolic Action: Walker Percy's
     Aesthetic." SoQ 18, no. 3 (Spring):55-64.
          The centricity of symbol-making to man's thought and action
     undergirds Percy's theories on language and philosophy. In par-
     ticular, Percy stresses the intersubjective nature of symboliza-
     tion as a co-celebration, suggesting "the sacredness of the
     individual and the affirmatory potential of the symbolic ex-
     change." Accordingly, Percy's novels effect a reversal of
     alienation: "reader and author can be co-celebrants in the new
     symbol, the work of art. . . . It is Percy's hope that literature
     can be 'news,' the message that will deliver man from despair."

To spark recognition in his readers' perception, Percy explores
his protagonist's consciousness from a phenomenological stance
and depicts that consciousness primarily through dialogue.
Thereby, "he reminds the reader that consciousness and intersubjectivity are inextricably linked." This relationship is
particularly illustrated in Lancelot, in which "the reader, like
Percival, is a participant in the narrative." Reprinted:
1980.55.

44   REEDY, GERALD. Review of The Second Coming. Commonweal 107
      (29 August):471.
         More than Percy's previous novels, this book accents how
      "human beings may live together with authenticity." Readers will
      find social criticism in this novel, but Percy "has been reluc-
      tant to understand . . . his characters in anything less than a
      fully theological background." These characters "must always
      pass beyond the various clinical helps offered to them" and find
      salvation in another person--a friend or loved one--"whose sub-
      jectivity is eternally and irreducibly hostile to empirical
      analysis." Unlike his other novels, The Second Coming attempts
      to "drown out the discord of twentieth-century America."

45   ROMANO, JOHN. "A Novel of Powerful Pleasures." NYTBR,
      29 June, pp. 1, 28-29.
         This favorable review of The Second Coming especially com-
      mends the novel for conveying ideas of deep theological and
      philosophical impact without sacrificing matters of plot and
      characterization. Minor reservations are registered about
      Percy's "impatience with the quotidian," and seeming implication
      that spiritual transcendence and commitment to others are in-
      compatible. All told, though, the book is "splendid, engrossing"
      and "Percy's best since 'The Moviegoer.'"

46   ROMINE, DANNYE. "Walker Percy Tells How to Write a Good
      Sentence." New Orleans Times-Picayune/States-Item,
      4 September, p. 4.
         Percy is interviewed while vacationing in Highlands, North
      Carolina, after having completed The Second Coming. Much of the
      article recapitulates standard biographical information. Percy
      comments on the relationship between pathology and novel writing:
      "You might say I'm a pathological novelist . . . or a pathologist
      novelist. Novels are really exercises in pathology." He indi-
      cates that if he had stayed in medicine he probably would have
      become a psychiatrist despite his equally strong attraction
      toward a specialty in pathology. He disagrees with Hemingway's
      assertion that a novelist's best writing occurs when the creative
      juices are flowing. His own finest work seems to occur when he
      is most convinced that he cannot write another word: "It's a
      question of being so pitiful God takes pity on you, looks down
      and says, 'He's done for. Let's let him have a couple of good
      sentences.'"

47   SEILER, TIMOTHY LEE. "From Moviegoing to Moviemaking:
      Rhetorical Progression in the Walker Percy Fictive Protago-
      nist." Ph.D. dissertation, Indiana University.
          An analysis of rhetorical and narrative technique in
      Percy's first four novels reveals that "the rising stridency of
      the narrative voice reflects a darkening of Percy's own vision
      and tends in effect to isolate the fictive protagonist from a
      reading audience."

48   SPEARS, MONROE K. "Return of The Last Gentleman." BW,
      20 July, p. 1.
          The Second Coming is Percy's most significant novel, a
      sequel to The Last Gentleman (1966), although it has a sharper
      focus and greater depth. Some readers might sense a lack of
      dramatic activity, but Will Barrett "is explored at greater
      psychological depth than any previous Percy hero." There is
      little existential rhetoric and great precision of detail and,
      indeed, "an unsentimental and unrhetorical affirmation of love
      against death."

49   STUCKEY, W.J. "Walker Percy." In Twentieth Century American
      Literature. Edited by James Vinson. New York: St. Martin's
      Press, pp. 448-49.
          Like T.S. Eliot, Allen Tate, Caroline Gordon, Robert Penn
      Warren, and William Faulkner, Percy is a traditionalist deeply
      disturbed by "the decay of moral standards, the loss of a sense
      of community and of shared values." In his novels, Percy is
      especially concerned with the problem of rampant sexuality and
      the necessity of achieving an equilibrium between sex and love,
      desire and responsibility. He is a realist, a satirist, a
      novelist of manners, but, ultimately, "a religious writer" whose
      style saves him from contrivance and overt didacticism. Stuckey's
      critical essay is preceded by a brief biographical sketch and a
      listing of Percy's works. The only secondary source listed is
      Tony Tanner's City of Words (1971.47).

50   TATE, J.O. "Percy's Reprise." NatR 32, no. 22 (31 October):
      1338-40.
          This mostly favorable review of The Second Coming compli-
      ments Percy for his keen powers of observation and for his abil-
      ity to convey the sense of atrophy of America's spiritual and
      cultural muscle. Fault is found, however, with the presence of
      referential errors, authorial intrusion, and excessive rhetorical
      questioning.

51   TELOTTE, J.P. "Charles Peirce and Walker Percy: From
      Semiotic to Narrative." SoQ 18, no. 3 (Spring):65-79.
          Percy's lingusitic theory, which informs his novels, de-
      rives from the study of semiotics of Charles Sanders Peirce.
      Of particular importance to Percy's philosophy is the signifi-
      cance which Peirce attaches to "the involvement of the human

intellect and thus [to] the <u>meaning</u> which man derives from his use of symbols." Peirce described the triadic nature of the symbol-making function as "a cooperation of <u>three</u> subjects, such as a sign, its object, and its interpretant. . . ." Percy extends this triadic theory to include the intersubjective "function of language as a communication <u>between</u> people. . . ." In Percy's view, alienated man has lost sight of the interconnectedness among self, language, and other people; but with increased awareness he may recover it. As a facilitator of such linguistic renewal, "the novelist initiates a triad with himself as speaker to a listening public, and he functions through the symbolic value of his novel—a symbol writ large—which serves his public as a very vital 'message in the bottle.'" Despite Percy's protestations that his linguistic theories have no bearing on his novels, "the basic act of naming or symbolization . . . is Percy's fundamental truth, that upon which he grounds all of his fictional constructs." Reprinted: 1980.55.

52 ____. "A Symbolic Structure for Walker Percy's Fiction." <u>MFS</u> 26, no. 2 (Summer):227-40.
       Despite Percy's disclaimers that his investigations into language bear little relation to his fiction, he has discussed the way in which his triadic theory of communication obtains in <u>Lancelot</u> (in the interview by Marcus Smith, see 1976.28). Additionally, linguistic structures within <u>Love in the Ruins</u> exemplify theories of symbolization explained in <u>The Message in the Bottle</u>. The narrative structure itself, More's account of events recited into a recorder, is intended by him as a corrective for future generations and, therefore, constitutes an intersubjective act of communication. Dramatized also are contrasts between More's approach to language, in which the naming act is a coupling, or a bonding force, and that of Fedville behaviorists, who view language formation as a stimulus-response activity. The importance of language as a restorative power is particularly illustrated by Mr. Ives's recovery through communication about his "Ocala frieze" discovery, by More's supplication to his sainted ancestor for deliverance from Art Immelmann, and by Father Smith's community prayer at the novel's end "for the unification and regeneration of the United States."

53 THARPE, JAC, ed. Introduction to "Special Issue: Walker Percy." <u>SoQ</u> 18, no. 3 (Spring):1-4.
       Overviews of the essays are given. The collection was generated by wide interest in <u>The Message in the Bottle</u> and <u>Lancelot</u>; so most of the essays focus on those two works.

54 ____. "Special Issue: Walker Percy." <u>SoQ</u> 18, no. 3 (Spring):167 pp.
       Includes essays by John Edward Hardy (1980.27), Lewis A. Lawson (1980.34), Charles P. Bigger (1980.10), Michael Pearson (1980.43), J.P. Telotte (1980.51), Robert H. Brinkmeyer, Jr.

(1980.12), Susan S. Kissel (1980.33), Corinne Dale (1980.16),
Jerome C. Christensen (1980.13), Cecil L. Eubanks (1980.20), Joe
Weixlmann and Daniel H. Gann (1980.58), and Randolph Bates
(1980.9).

55 _____. Walker Percy: Art and Ethics. Jackson: University
of Mississippi Press, 168 pp.
Includes all the essays which originally appeared in The
Southern Quarterly (1980.54) except for the essay by Randolph
Bates (1980.9).

56 TOWERS, ROBERT. "To the Greenhouse." NYRB 27, no. 13
(14 August):39-41.
This mixed review of The Second Coming deems the novel
Percy's best since The Moviegoer ("a minor classic"). Better
related than Will's story is Allison's, particularly in the description of her efforts to use the block-and-tackle. The novel
is ponderously heavy with plot, themes, and symbolism; and some
of the characters and incidents seem mere representations of
ideas.

57 WALTER, J. "Spinning and Spieling: A Trick and a Kick in
Walker Percy's The Moviegoer." SoR 16, no. 3 (July):574-90.
In The Moviegoer, such terms as rotation and repetition
should be interpreted in the light of Binx's use of them, rather
than Kierkegaard's. Binx is at once a searcher, a chronicler of
his experience, and an artist aware of his audience. His method
of artistically abstracting his observations leads him into
stereotyping people and situations. One person whom he and many
critics misread is his mother. She and her bustling family suggest a "harmony with the life in nature," a wholesome contrast
to the cerebral, romantic posturings of the Bolling clan. As a
Bolling, Emily acts "as spokesman for the heroic and for all
values that sustain civilization." But she cannot guide Binx in
the spiritual realm. Binx finally breaks through to a religious
mode of life through his commitment to Kate.

58 WEIXLMANN, JOE, and GANN, DANIEL H. "A Walker Percy Bibliography." SoQ 18, no. 3 (Spring):137-57.
This comprehensive primary and secondary bibliography is
divided into four sections. The initial section lists in order
of publication Percy's first five books with reviews arranged
chronologically. The second section consists of a chronological
list of his essays, articles, and reviews. Presented third is a
list of entries on interviews and panel discussions. The fourth
section entitled "Biography and Criticism" presents "critiques of
each of the five books, general studies, and dissertations and
theses." Entries are listed through 1979. Reprinted: 1980.55.

59   WIEHE, JANET.   Review of The Second Coming.   LJ 105 (July):
      1541-42.
         Brief favorable review: a novel which gives "full rich
      expression" to Percy's ideas, especially about language "reveal-
      ing and concealing."   "Percy's best book yet."

60   WILLIAMS, THOMAS.   "A Walker Percy Novel Puzzles over the
      Farce of Existence."   Chicago Tribune Book World, 29 June,
      sec. 7, p. 1.
         The Second Coming can be puzzling, and even irritating, but
      it is a serious and realistic novel that raises basic questions
      about life.   Percy challenges readers by inviting identification
      with two essentially insane characters, Williston Barrett and
      Allison, daughter of Kitty Vaught Huger.   The Second Coming
      appears to be a sequel to The Last Gentleman, although certain
      episodes and characters in the later novel do not coincide ex-
      actly with the events and people in the earlier work.   The many
      plot twists and surprises lead to a resolution of some purpose-
      fulness for Will, which includes his plan to marry Allison and
      have children.   There is the suggestion by Percy that God may
      somehow figure in Will's future too.

61   WOOD, R.C.   Review of The Second Coming.   Cross Currents 30,
      no. 2 (Summer):206-10.
         Percy's novel seems less artistic than earlier work, "a
      virtual pastiche of his previous work."   As the sequel to The
      Last Gentleman, Percy's idea is ripe with possibility, yet Will
      Barrett is "inexplicably transformed" into the standard Percy
      protagonist--a worldly success, but miserable.   The plot is weak,
      and coincidence allows the characters to fall into place; yet
      Allison is "virtually disincarnate," having no relation to the
      kinds of realities which earlier Percy protagonists must face in
      terms of marriage, family, work, and church.

62   _____.   "Walker Percy as Satirist: Christian and Humanist
      Still in Conflict."   CC 97 (19 November):1122-27.
         Percy's positive satire is based on the premise that God
      accepts and transforms sin into an occasion for mercy; however,
      his recent novels appear to be a decline--characterized by banal
      plots, undeveloped characterization and "slipshod" prose.   All
      Percy's fiction constitutes a denunciation of false humanism
      which implies adjusting to habitat; this is displayed best in The
      Moviegoer and Love in the Ruins.   In Lancelot Percy may mean his
      own affinities lie with Percival, yet the impression given is
      that he "expects the world to be incinerated" by a Lancelot who
      can no longer stomach "spiritual softness."   The Second Coming is
      not guilty of such scorn, but of sentimental romanticism;   Barrett
      seems to care more for freedom than for permanent commitment.
      Alarmingly this is not a new tendency in Percy.   The difference
      between early and late Percy is that in later works there seem to
      be no figures of authentic faith; also missing is a vision of

God's grandeur "charging redemptively through . . . creation."
The conclusion of <u>Love in the Ruins</u> is the true prophetic Percy.

63   YOUNG, THOMAS D. "A New Breed: Walker Percy's Critics'
     Attempts to Place Him." <u>MissQ</u> 33, no. 4 (Fall):489-98.
        Review-essay of books about Percy, including Luschei
     (1972.13), Coles (1978.9), and Broughton (1979.4). The problem
     of "Southerness" is discussed, something not treated by Coles,
     whose most helpful discussion is of Percy's essays. A listing
     of titles from Broughton is provided and Lewis Lawson's essay
     (1979.15) is singled out as a valuable analysis of Southern back-
     ground, scientific interests, and Percy's knowledge of philosophy,
     psychology, and Catholicism.

Master's Theses on Walker Percy

KENT, MARGARET L. "The Novels of Walker Percy." University of North Carolina, Chapel Hill, 1969.

Van CLEAVE, JAMES. "Versions of Percy." University of North Carolina, 1969.

WYCHE, CHARLYNE S. "A Survey of the Southern Legend in the Recent Southern Novel." McNeese State University, 1969.

KILLOUGH, BARBARA C. "The Moviegoer: The Search for an Access to Being." University of Houston, 1971.

MARTIN, LOVICK R., III. "The Theme of Reconciliation and the Novels of Walker Percy." University of North Carolina, Chapel Hill, 1972.

OSINSKI, BARBARA H. "From Malaise to Communion: A Study of Walker Percy's The Moviegoer." Lehigh University, 1972.

STURDIVANT, MARY E. "Christianity in the Novels of Walker Percy." University of North Carolina, Chapel Hill, 1972.

BARNWELL, MARION G. "Walker Percy's American Trilogy." Mississippi State University, 1974.

HOBBS, JANET H. "Alternatives to Alienation in the Novels of Walker Percy." Virginia Polytechnic Institute, 1974.

CARNEY, LINTON. "Nathanael West and Walker Percy: The Moviegoers." University of North Carolina, 1975.

FOLEY, I.M. "The Theory of Language in Walker Percy's The Message in the Bottle." University of New Orleans, 1975.

FOSTER, M. "Pain and Death in James Dickey's Deliverance and the Novels of Walker Percy." University of Houston, 1975.

HALL, CONSTANCE H. "Walker Percy's Women: A Study of the Women in the Novels of Walker Percy." Stephen F. Austin State University, 1975.

JONES, ELINOR B. "The Search as Pilgrimage in the Novels of Walker Percy." University of Georgia, 1975.

WARREN, BRENDA DURHAM. "Existential Christianity in Three Novels by Walker Percy." Middle Tennessee State University, 1976.

PRICE, PATRICIA THIGPEN. "The Search for Order in the Novels of Walker Percy." Georgia Southern College, 1977.

SUTTON, JANE BOYCE. "Kierkegaard's Idea of Possibility/Necessity in the Novels of Walker Percy." University of North Carolina, Chapel Hill, 1977.

MADATHIPARAMPIL, GEORGE J. "Theory and Themes in the Novels of Walker Percy." Indiana State University, 1978.

BOWDEN, PATRICIA DIXON CARROL. "The 'It and the Doing': Sacramental Word and Deed in the Writings of Walker Percy." Georgia State University, 1980.

Peter Taylor

Introduction

Peter Hillsman Taylor was born 8 January 1917, in Trenton,
Tennessee, the son of Matthew Hillsman Taylor and Katherine Baird
(Taylor) Taylor. Although they had the same surnames, his mother and
father were not blood relations, coming as they did from opposite ends
of the state, where each family had contributed its share of prominent
lawyers and politicians. His mother's father, Robert L. Taylor, had
been a famous Tennessee political figure, serving as a United States
Congressman, a three-term governor, and finally a United States Senator. He is most likely the model for the colorful Senator Caswell
in his grandson's play, Tennessee Day in St. Louis, written some
seventy years after the memorable campaign of 1886, which provided
the humorous, but uncomfortable, spectacle of two Taylor brothers,
along with their father, in contention for the office of governor.
Peter Taylor's paternal side of the family was also not without its
political distinctions; his father had been involved extensively in
the political life of the state before assuming the presidency of a
life insurance company in St. Louis. Andrew Lytle, lifetime friend
of the Taylor family, has speculated that the political background
from which Peter Taylor emerged may have influenced his life as a
writer on two levels. The stylistic purity of his short stories is
perhaps a reaction, conscious or unconscious, to his legacy of ora-
torical rhetoric. But it is in the discovery of one of his major
themes that Taylor's relation to his political heritage is most
discernible. For Governor Taylor had believed in the restoration of
family life even during the turmoil of Reconstruction; this prospect
failing, it became the task of Peter Taylor to chronicle the subver-
sion of the family in the modern South by the twin forces of urbaniza-
tion and industrialization.

Just as the South was moving to the city in the 1920s, so the
Taylor family left Trenton, when Peter was only seven, to pursue
business interests in St. Louis and later in Memphis and Nashville.
Taylor's childhood and adolescence allowed him ample opportunity to
observe the life of the upper-middle-class emigré, transplanted from
small Southern town to new urban setting. It may be true, as some
critics suggest, that Trenton was to serve Taylor as the prototype of
the small Southern community/town--his fictional Thornton--which

remained the source of values and beliefs for his characters who have propelled themselves physically to new environments, Southern or Northern.

Taylor's education was to reinforce his early observations, studying as he did with a series of teachers connected in one way or another with the Vanderbilt Agrarian Movement. Beginning his collegiate studies at Vanderbilt, Taylor came under the influence of John Crowe Ransom. When Ransom left for Kenyon, Taylor departed also, studying briefly at Southwestern in Memphis with Allen Tate, who recognized in this young student the makings of a great writer. After a year's separation, Taylor renewed his studies with Ransom at Kenyon, where he also entered into lifelong friendships with Randall Jarrell and Robert Lowell. In the fall of 1940, Taylor enrolled as a graduate student at Louisiana State University. Here, during his brief stay, he was to study with the New Critic, Cleanth Brooks, and with a former member of the Vanderbilt Fugitive-Agrarian Group, who had begun to excell in fiction as well as poetry, Robert Penn Warren.

Warren was to have an immense effect on Taylor's career. He not only published three of Taylor's stories ("A Spinster's Tale," "Skyline," "The Fancy Woman") in the Southern Review, but even more importantly, he wrote the introduction to A Long Fourth and Other Stories (1948.8), announcing the appearance of a new literary talent. In that influential introduction, Warren identifies the milieu of Taylor's stories: "the contemporary, urban, middle-class world of the upper South." He also suggests the major themes of the volume: specifically, the disintegration of family life in the modern world, and, more generally, "the attrition of old loyalties, the breakdown of old patterns, and the collapse of old values"; and he classifies Taylor's sensibility as ironic, not an easy irony, but one that discovers extraordinary significance in "the small collisions" of everyday life. The critics agreed unanimously with Warren that A Long Fourth was a brilliant first work by an obviously gifted writer. But, in addition to introducing Taylor to the world of letters, Warren's preface was of considerably greater importance in that it set the general tone and mode of inquiry for much of the subsequent criticism.

Taylor's second book, A Woman of Means (1950), however, did not meet with the same universal acclaim accorded to A Long Fourth. The thirty-thousand-word narrative, referred to by Taylor on different occasions as a novel and a novella, traces an adolescent boy's growing awareness of the disintegration of his father's second marriage and the descent of his stepmother into madness. For most critics, this work remained an extended short story, lacking the structure and complexity essential to a novel, but there were readers who reacted favorably to the author's brilliant use of irony and his successful characterizations. Two of the most sympathetic and perceptive responses to the novel have been Thomas Wilcox's "A Novelist of Means" (1951.1), and James Penny Smith's "Narration and Theme in Taylor's A Woman of Means (1967.5).

Introduction

In Taylor's next published work, The Widows of Thornton (1954), the eight short stories and one short play are unified by two recurring themes. The first of these had figured in his earlier stories but is given special emphasis in this volume: families or individuals who have migrated from a country town (Thornton, Tennessee) to various cities of the South or Midwest, but whose values and behavior are, nonetheless, determined by the old provincial patterns. The second leit motif, the theme of widowhood, must be understood in more than the usual sense of the word. Most of the women in these stories have been widowed, not by the literal deaths of their husbands, but rather by the male's desertion of the old shared life of domesticity for the competitive, masculine world of business and commerce. In this notion of widowhood, Taylor appears to be rediscovering a more general theme which has always lain just beneath the surface of his stories--betrayal and victimization of self and others. For the critics, this new volume provided proof positive of Taylor's mastery of the short story and of his emergence as a master of the form.

The Death of a Kinsman, the short play that appeared in The Widows of Thornton, was Taylor's first dramatic venture. It was followed by Tennessee Day in St. Louis: A Comedy (1957), A Stand in the Mountains (Kenyon Review, March 1968), and Presences (1973), a collection of one-act "ghost plays." Taylor's devotion to the theater is genuine, and citing the examples of Chekhov and Pirandello and the short story's inherent dramatic quality, he claims the play rather than the novel as the short fiction writer's natural domain. Although some of the plays have been produced successfully at Kenyon and other places, they are for the most part closet dramas. While critics such as Brainard Cheney (1962.3) and Albert J. Griffith (1970.3; 1977.19) have been interested by and responsive to Taylor's plays, noting thematic and stylistic similarities between them and his fiction, they have generally considered these dramatic pieces as artistically inferior to the fiction.

With the appearance of Happy Families Are All Alike (1959) and Miss Leonora When Last Seen (1963), Taylor's reputation as a writer of short fiction continued to soar. Two of the best stories he has ever written, both in his estimation and that of the critics, appear here: "Venus, Cupid, Folly and Time" and "Miss Leonora When Last Seen," the former winning an O. Henry Awards first prize.

The publication of Taylor's last two works of fiction, The Collected Stories of Peter Taylor (1969) and In the Miro District (1977), allowed the critics an opportunity for a reevaluation of an author who had previously been described as the finest living short-story writer in America. Generally, the reviews remained consistent in their praise although there was some dissent, an inevitable reaction to a writer who had begun to command national attention. Some critics, for example, were puzzled by the verse narratives in In the Miro District, finding no good reason for abandoning prose as the narrative mode. Others praised certain stories, but found Taylor's overall production uneven or monotonous.

The Collected Stories prompted a particularly spirited debate
between Barbara Raskin and Jonathan Yardley in the New Republic
(1969.12-13, 18). In a scathing review, Raskin accuses Taylor of
producing black stereotypes, particularly in such stories as "What
You Hear From 'Em?", of being insensitive to social and racial issues, and of repeating themes and characters already exhausted by
other Southern writers. Yardley, replying that Miss Raskin's review
reveals more about her own political prejudices than about the
author's work, vigorously defends Taylor's subject matter and manner
of characterization as revealing both his originality and universality.

In reviewing the criticism of Taylor's work, four general approaches can be detected. The first and earliest approach, explored
by such critics as Warren, Lytle, Ashley Brown, Barbara Schuler, and
others, emphasized what they believed was Taylor's essential theme:
the dissolution of the family and the community in the contemporary
world and the evils that ensue from this loss. This particular
avenue of criticism inevitably produced its dialectical opposition
in such critics as Glendy Culligan (1964.4) and Jan Pinkerton
(1970.8) who discern in Taylor's irony an implied attack not only on
family and community, but also on veneration of the past and respect
for traditions. The title of Pinkerton's essay, "The Non-Regionalism
of Peter Taylor," indicates her general understanding of Taylor,
whose message for her is "keep moving, be open to new experiences."
A third attempt at an overview is the synthesis most recently sug-
gested by Jane Barnes Casey (1978.2) and Alan Williamson (1978.6),
both of whom are following similar approaches. For Casey, the tension between order and disorder, and "the great modern problem of how
to incorporate the most vital but also the most archaic urges into
civilized life," constitute the real subject of Taylor's fiction; it
is only in the stories in the last volume, In the Miro District, that
a proper equilibrium between these forces has been struck. Williamson's position differs from Casey's in that he sees the opposing
forces seeking resolution as "the wider eros," which directs us outward to achieve social, ethical, and even transcendent, relationships, and the narrow "self-love," which constrains our sympathies
and emotional involvements. Refraining from seeking synthesis or an
overview of Taylor's work, a fourth group of critics, represented at
their best by Morgan Blum (1962.1) and Kenneth Cathey (1953.1;
1974.2), has contented itself with the formalistic approach. Examining structure, texture, point of view, irony, and symbolism in
various stories or groups of stories, these critics have contributed
valuable insights into Taylor's fictional devices and techniques.

Peter Taylor has been fortunate in the individuals and the journals that have given critical support to his work. The Sewanee
Review, usually through the influence and inspiration of Andrew
Lytle, has on various occasions carried critical articles and reviews examining Taylor's fiction and plays. In 1967, Critique
(1967.2, 4-5) presented, in addition to articles on his fiction, a

Introduction

Peter Taylor checklist compiled by James Penny Smith (1967.6), representing the first systematic attempt to produce a complete listing of Taylor's work and the critical responses. Ten years later, Shenandoah (1977.7) would celebrate Taylor's sixtieth birthday by devoting the entire issue to essays and reminiscences by the author's friends, associates, and former students. Taylor's reputation was enhanced also by Albert J. Griffith's Peter Taylor (1970.3), the only book-length study, to date, of the author's work. In addition to an intelligent and judicious interpretation of each of Taylor's individual works, Griffith provides a scholarly, penetrating investigation of Taylor's most characteristic narrative habits: his digressive-progressive development of the memoir story, his masterful employment of the unreliable narrator, and his ironic qualifications, intended to reflect the complexity and duality of human experience.

But what can we expect from Taylor in the future, and from the accompanying criticism of his work? Will the growth of his reading audience continue, as in the past, slow but certain, as his stories make their periodic appearances in the New Yorker? Or will he draw sudden and dramatic attention to his short stories by writing a successful novel, as was the case with Katherine Anne Porter, a writer to whom he is sometimes compared? One thing appears certain. He will not abandon the story. As recently as 1973, in an interview in Shenandoah (Winter), Taylor indicated that he would be turning his attention to plays and novels. Since that time, however, In the Miro District (1977), considered by many critics Taylor's best collection of short stories, has appeared, and in 1979, "The Old Forest" (New Yorker, 14 May), a long story of some twenty thousand words.

As to the critics who continue to write about Taylor, they are reminded of their work yet to be done by Griffith's observation that even though Taylor's opus is small, his stories frequently have the complexity, the density, and the scope of novels. There is the attractive challenge, too, of trying to sum up the ever-elusive Taylor, who in each story appears to examine an old problem from a new perspective. For example, in his most recently published story, "The Gift of the Prodigal" (New Yorker, 1 June 1981), he returns to a former theme but in a different posture. The necessity to live imaginatively upon the lives of those around us is no longer seen as healthy and productive ("Daphne's Lover"), but now as an almost pathetic, perhaps even pathological, compulsion. The fascination of Taylor will continue to intrigue critics and attract readers, who will respond appreciatively to his comic spirit, but will remember him best for the terrible things he tells us about ourselves in the most gentle and genteel of voices.

C.H.G.

Writings by Peter Taylor

A Long Fourth and Other Stories. Introduction by Robert Penn Warren.
    New York: Harcourt, Brace & Co., 1948.

A Woman of Means. Illustrated by Margaret Bloy Graham. New York:
    Harcourt, Brace & Co., 1950.

The Widows of Thornton. New York: Harcourt, Brace & Co., 1954.

Tennessee Day in St. Louis. New York: Random House, 1957.

Happy Families Are All Alike: A Collection of Stories. New York:
    McDowell, Obolensky, 1959.

Miss Leonora When Last Seen and Fifteen Other Stories. New York:
    Ivan Obolensky, 1963.

Randall Jarrell, 1914–1965. Edited by Robert Lowell; Peter Taylor;
    and Robert Penn Warren. New York: Farrar, Straus & Giroux,
    1967.

The Collected Stories of Peter Taylor. New York: Farrar, Straus &
    Giroux, 1969. Reprints. New York: Farrar, Straus & Giroux,
    1971, 1979.

Presences: Seven Dramatic Pieces. Boston: Houghton Mifflin, 1973.

In the Miro District and Other Stories. New York: Knopf, 1977.
    Reprint. New York: Knopf, 1977.

Writings about Peter Taylor,
1948-1980

1948

1   ANON. Review of A Long Fourth and Other Stories. Booklist
     44 (1 May):299.
          "First volume . . . by a promising young Tennessee writer."

2   ANON. Review of A Long Fourth and Other Stories. NY 24
     (13 March):124.
          The book is considered an "excellent collection," notable
     for its humor and lack of the usual Southern writer's regional
     chauvinism.

3   BRACE, MARJORIE. "Southern Incidents." SatR 31 (27 March):
     17-18.
          Cites Taylor's unpretentious and original talent in A Long
     Fourth, which approaches reality through "considered and question-
     ing rearrangement," and which inquires into "relations through
     which things take on their meaning," thereby shaking readers into
     "emotional insecurity."

4   CREEKMORE, HUBERT. Review of A Long Fourth and Other Stories.
     NYTBR, 21 March, p. 6.
          In contrast to the extremes of violence and degeneration
     that some authors portray, Taylor's emphasis upon characters who
     are balanced between strength and weakness provides "a humanness
     and fascination." With a traditional but "rewarding" style,
     Taylor provides stories about family mores with ironic effects.
     His concern for the "quotidian" and his rendering of characters
     strengthen the stories.

5   FARRELLY, JOHN. Review of A Long Fourth and Other Stories.
     NewR 118 (8 March):25-26.
          Reviews A Long Fourth as a book of "unusually fine" stories
     with a variety of characters and incidents, and a unity of "well-
     rendered background."

6 POWERS, J.F. Review of A Long Fourth and Other Stories.
Commonweal 48 (25 June):262-63.
Notes Taylor's "poet's gift" for letting characters speak
the "clichés of a nation" so naturally that they almost convince
us that they are true. Powers believes that these stories, several of which he refers to individually, present the truth, sub-
tly and disquietingly; they will cause "the shock of recognition"
and are something new about the South.

7 ROSENBERGER, COLEMAN. "An Island of Excellence in Short
Stories." Books 24, no. 30 (14 March):5.
Written over a ten-year period these stories have "the
qualities of permanence." Taylor's concern is not with legend,
but with "its attenuation in the present." Insightful comments
about several of the stories suggest their complexity.

8 WARREN, ROBERT PENN. Introduction to A Long Fourth and Other
Stories. New York: Harcourt, Brace & Co., pp. vii-x.
In a significant introductory essay, which was to influence
much future criticism of Taylor's work, Warren identifies Taylor's
subject matter as "the contemporary, urban, middle-class world of
the upper-South" where "the old-fashioned structure of family
still persists, disintegrating slowly under the pressure of
modernity." Such a world subject to "the attrition of old loyalties, the breakdown of old patterns, and the collapse of old
values" should invite satirical presentation, but Taylor assumes
instead an ironical stance, "blended of comedy and sympathetic
understanding." Violence is eschewed for the smaller dilemmas of
life, which are narrated in a natural style "based on conversation and the family tale," a style that radiates from the center
of the story itself and is not imposed by the author. Fortunately, Warren also provides interesting biographical information
about Taylor, including the fact that as editor of The Southern
Review, he made the mistake of rejecting two of Taylor's stories,
which later appeared elsewhere. Warren's essay focuses on an
author who "has a disenchanted mind, but a mind that nevertheless
understands and values enchantment."

1950

1 ANON. "As a Boy Grows Older." Time 55 (15 May):110.
Review of A Woman of Means: a "good, if not a major
novel." Considers the inadequate preparation for the stepmother's crackup a flaw, but finds Quint "one of the most vivid
children of the year's fiction."

2 ANON. "Briefly Noted." NY 26 (20 May):117.
Review of A Woman of Means. Taylor does not break the
reader's heart since he "attempted too little rather than too
much." Mood and locale are reminiscent of Cather.

3   ANON. Review of A Woman of Means. Booklist 46 (1 June):304.
    "The characterization is good, the analysis of the boy's
reactions excellent."

4   ANON. Review of A Woman of Means. Bookmark 9 (July):244.
    Brief review: "restrained, yet forceful," story told by a
twelve year old as he adjusts and becomes aware of "hidden motives
in his father's remarriage."

5   ANON. Review of A Woman of Means. Kirkus 18, no. 9 (1 May):
    267.
    An extension of the short story medium which reveals "a
fine-drawn talent." "Impressionistic, indirect."

6   ANON. Review of A Woman of Means. US Quarterly Booklist 6
    (September):285.
    Fairly successful interweaving of bildungsroman. The story
of Quintus Dudley's rural background, and relationships with his
family; also a novel of the marriage of Mrs. Lauterbach, who is
drawn sympathetically. Taylor's well-disciplined artistry is at
work here "upon a problem somewhat too complex, perhaps" at this
stage in his career.

7   EATON, EVELYN. "Stepmomism." SatR 33 (June):13.
    Compared to David Westheimer's "The Magic Fallacy,"
Taylor's novella, A Woman of Means, is believable, but "there is
a dim mistiness about [the characterization] which makes their
tragedy of no particular impart." The novella does not have the
impact of Taylor's "fine stories."

8   ENGLE, PAUL. Review of A Woman of Means. Chicago Sunday
    Tribune Magazine of Books, 14 May, p. 7.
    Taylor's A Woman of Means is so brilliantly crafted
sentence by sentence, page by page, that the reader is amazed to
discover at the conclusion how far his own imaginative horizons
have been expanded. The glory of the book lies in the way it is
poised between ironies: How little or how much does money matter
in the decision by Quint's father to marry? Conversely, how
important or unimportant a part does Anna's desire to acquire a
son play in her decision to marry Quint's father? In the balance
of these ironies hangs Anna's sanity. There is only one reserva-
tion about the novel's resolution, Anna's descent into madness.
Does the decline occur too rapidly? Is the "authenticity" of
the novel damaged by Anna's too sudden transition from spirited
grande dame to dangerous lunatic?

9   KEE, ROBERT. "New Novels." New Statesman 40 (2 December):
    566.
    Review of A Woman of Means. In an anecdotal sort of way
Taylor conveys a sense of an eccentric household in St. Louis of
the early twenties, yet while his prose is quite good, there is

a "static" quality about the book which makes one impatient with
its merits. What development does take place seems "a little
awkward."

10   MILES, GEORGE. Review of A Woman of Means. Commonweal 52
      (23 June):275.
          Incidents in the novel are "natural, limited, and plausi-
      ble"; however, most of them are introductory scenes for the
      "final, tragic moments" and form an expanded short story rather
      than a novel. The "general merit" of the work is not lessened by
      its quick resolution.

11   PICKREL, PAUL. "Outstanding Novels." YR, n.s. 39, no. 4
      (Summer):768.
          Review of A Woman of Means. Unfavorable comment: "slight
      but pleasant series of recollections," which toward the end
      Taylor asks us to take more seriously.

12   ROSENBERGER, COLEMAN. "Family in Flux." Books 26, no. 40
      (21 May):10.
          A "perceptive account" of the "splintered parts of two
      families," and a novel which suggests a whole society in flux.
      The "slightness" of this novella is deceptive for it is a solid
      work of "very solid merit," yet not a "fully realized novel."

13   STERN, JAMES. "The Power of Charm." NewR 122 (26 June):20.
          Review of A Woman of Means that is complimentary of
      Taylor's "audacity" in creating a woman whose charm is success-
      fully conveyed through the first person narrative of a twelve
      year old. Except for reservations about the suddenness of the
      disintegration of Mrs. Lauterbach, the novel comes close "to be-
      ing a complete success."

14   WARREN, ROBERT PENN. Review of A Woman of Means. NYTBR,
      11 June, p. 8.
          While relatively short, Taylor's narrative gives the effect
      of a "full-bodied narrative." The action is summarized; however,
      because Taylor's method intersperses "flashes, to break the ordi-
      nary texture" and quickly returns to the narrative before the
      "full significance of what lies beyond the curtain" is apparent,
      the effect is beyond ordinary realism. In strong control of his
      materials, Taylor gives the illusion for the reader of making the
      interpretation.

                              1951

1   WILCOX, THOMAS. "A Novelist of Means." SR 59, no. 1
      (Winter):151-54.
          Taylor's A Woman of Means "is short, it is not small," and
      the aesthetic activity it inspires for the reader is great. In

its closeness to life, the novel does not provide answers or
simple solutions but rather reflects the ambiguities and ironies
of real experience. No one in the book, including the narrator,
fully understands the motivations of other characters or why
things happen as they do. The only true explanations are to be
found in "the full statement the novel makes," which is like the
activity of life itself. Taylor is to be commended for consis-
tency of tone, choice of details, sense of timing, and his direct
and straightforward presentation. The characters' lives are af-
fected by their social positions so that the book is a real contribution toward understanding "American cultural history."

1952

*1   ANON. [Joint Committee of the North Carolina English Teachers
      Association and the North Carolina Library Association.]
      "Peter Taylor." In North Carolina Authors: A Selective
      Handbook. Chapel Hill: University of North Carolina Library
      (Extension Publication, 18, no. 1).
           First-person capsule biography of about 175 words. Source:
      1970.3, p. 171.

2   WEST, RAY B., Jr. "The Short Story in the Forties." In The
      Short Story in America. Chicago: Henry Regnery Co.,
      pp. 103-22, esp. 105-11.
           Taylor is listed as one of those American writers who is
      important in the 1940s and shows even greater promise for the
      future. The pattern of Taylor's work is "less complete," but not
      unlike that of Eudora Welty's. Taylor continues to publish in-
      dividual stories in The New Yorker, but his only published volume
      since 1948 is A Woman of Means, "a well-constructed but slight
      novel."

1953

1   CATHEY, KENNETH CLAY. "Peter Taylor: An Evaluation." WR 18,
      no. 4 (Autumn):9-19.
           Although he has narrow limits, Taylor has extraordinary
      success within them and is certainly one of the most promising
      new writers. He reveals "a sensitive perception, a keen observa-
      tion, and a remarkable ability to control his materials." A sig-
      nificant critical approach would be to compare the "structural
      variations" in his early work to those in his later pieces. The
      dominant characteristic is improvement in technique and content.
      With technical problems resolved, "it becomes most strongly
      apparent what Taylor had been striving to accomplish since the
      beginning of his career. . . ."

1954

1   ANON. Review of The Widows of Thornton. Booklist 50 (1 June):
    381.
        "Subdued but perceptive series of character studies."

2   ANON. Review of The Widows of Thornton. Kirkus 22, no. 4
    (15 February):133.
        "Series of vignettes affirms once again a fresh, individ-
    ualistic talent." Stories are part of a regional revival "which
    feeds on the attrition of the past of the country from which it
    derives."

3   ENGLE, PAUL. "Finely Poised Stories of Southern Family Life."
    Chicago Sunday Tribune Magazine of Books, 30 May, p. 4.
        The truly remarkable thing about the stories in The Widows
    of Thornton is their insightful revelations of human sentiments
    without sentimentality. In "What You Hear from 'Em?" Taylor, in
    his restraint, presents a character who is neither sentimentalized
    nor trivialized. In "Their Losses," he reveals the lives of
    three women with such calm understatement that their pasts and
    futures are vividly implied. The handling of physical and social
    details, especially accurate dialogue, contributes to the stories'
    realism, but it is the authentic characterizations which give the
    stories their greatest distinction.

4   HAYES, RICHARD. "Pain, Knowledge, and Ceremony." Commonweal
    61 (17 December):317.
        Taylor achieves a "portrait of a complex society held in
    the most fastidious dramatic suspension" in The Widows of
    Thornton, and his form is variations on a theme "of the pre-
    carious individual consciousness assaulted by a tide of ances-
    tral . . . pieties." Taylor uses but does not exploit the themes
    of Southern literature, and the result is that "no single place"
    claims him; Turgenev and Chekhov would approve.

5   LYELL, FRANK H. Review of The Widows of Thornton. NYTBR,
    2 May, p. 5.
        This volume fulfills earlier predictions of Taylor's skill.
    Forming a homogeneous group, the nine stories are unified in
    place, subject-matter, and themes. Taylor is especially skillful
    in showing how the beauty of family life "vanishes in the absence
    of a free interchange." The Negro characters are superb; the
    stories--outwardly simple--"are psychologically complex and
    powerful."

6   McDANIEL, D.R. Review of The Widows of Thornton. San
    Francisco Chronicle, 13 May, p. 19.
        Hails Taylor as "a new major writer of American fiction."
    The main characters in these stories are Southerners who have
    migrated northward or from Southern community to Southern city.

Despite the geographical transitions, "the patterns of life and
manners bred into them through generations of Southern ways remain to color their new lives and dictate their actions." "The
Dark Walk"; "Two Ladies in Retirement"; "Cookie"; and "Bad
Dreams" are singled out for brief discussion.

7   MORRISS, MACK. "South in the Sun." SatR 37 (8 May):14.
        Review of The Widows of Thornton. Taylor's work might be
compared to the fragrance of an old kitchen pantry safe: these
stories, "free of ugliness," create a "wistful, clinging, but
utterly non-depraved image of the Deep South" so different from
Capote and Tennessee Williams. This volume "confirms the talents"
of a very fine Southern writer.

8   WALBRIDGE, E.F. Review of The Widows of Thornton. LJ 79,
        no. 11 (1 June):1058.
        A very good collection "chiefly about relations between
upper-middle-class families and their colored retainers."

9   WICKENDEN, DAN. "A Fine Novel of the South." Books 30,
        no. 38 (2 May):4.
        The Widows of Thornton is unified by a mood which is
"elegiac, ironic, affectionate." The concluding novella makes
the title's full significance clear. Taylor promises, since this
book is "more substantial" than A Woman of Means, to be a major
writer of novels. Impossible that any American work more distinguished will appear this year.

                              1958

1   LYTLE, ANDREW N. "The Displaced Family." SR 66, no. 1
        (Winter):115-20.
        Review of Tennessee Day in St. Louis. Taylor is the only
American author whose subject is "the dislocation and slow destruction of the family as an institution." As a southern writer,
he has a distinct advantage in analyzing the family, which is
"the institution of Southern life." The military defeat of the
South resulted in a slow but continuing disintegration of this
most Southern of institutions. Taylor is aware of this decline,
and "exiled at home" might best describe the implications of A
Long Fourth, while this exile has become actual in The Widows of
Thornton and Tennessee Day in St. Louis. In Taylor's play, self-
indulgence, self-interest, and "a competition between the public
and private things" work to the detriment of family life. Each
family member, aware of the failures of others but blind to his
own shortcomings, exists in isolation, but frantically struggles
to keep up "the appearance" of a harmonious, communal family.

<u>1959</u>

1   ANON. Review of <u>Happy Families Are All Alike</u>. <u>Kirkus</u> 27,
    no. 20 (15 October):796.
        One characteristic unites these stories, "a narrative atti-
    tude of a certain maturity, if not wisdom, which has been gained
    in looking back."

2   BARO, GENE. "A True Short Story Artist." <u>Books</u> 36, no. 18
    (6 December):9.
        Review of <u>Happy Families Are All Alike</u>: "distinguished
    stories." Taylor is not concerned with "psychological nuance for
    its own sake"; rather it is a matter of understanding characters
    through "understanding the social context of their lives." The
    stories are "remarkably skillful" and "within their scope,"
    valuable statements about our society and times.

3   BLACKMAN, RUTH. "Complex Stories of Family and Community."
    <u>CSM</u>, 24 December, p. 11.
        Review of <u>Happy Families Are All Alike</u>. Taylor's title for
    this complex set of stories about family life is taken from the
    opening lines of Tolstoy's novel, <u>Anna Karenina</u>. A common theme
    among the stories is "the interlocking claim" which exists among
    members of the same family. "The Little Cousins"; "A Friend and
    a Protector"; and "Venus, Cupid, Folly and Time" are briefly dis-
    cussed in light of their common theme. In method, Taylor uses
    the device of the detective-story writer: he loads his stories
    with details, some of which are important to solving the mystery.
    This method fails in one or two stories which have themes so
    banal that the excessive details seem unnecessary baggage.

4   LYELL, FRANK H. Review of <u>Happy Families Are All Alike</u>.
    <u>NYTBR</u>, 22 November, p. 4.
        "American short story writing at its best"; Taylor's "in-
    telligence, taste and instinctive refinement are, once again, as
    much in evidence as technical skill." Impressive alone, together
    these stories provide a "unified, sensitive, balanced" view of
    life. Each of the stories is essentially a family portrait when
    the tranquil surface of life is ruffled. Taylor uses the sim-
    plest everyday events to create suspense, to suggest complex
    relationships, and to provide a "timeless" quality.

5   MORGAN, CHARLES. Review of <u>Happy Families Are All Alike</u>.
    <u>San Francisco Chronicle This World Magazine</u>, 6 December,
    p. 39.
        Praises "Venus, Cupid, Folly and Time"; "A Friend and Pro-
    tector"; "A Walled Garden"; and "The Other Times." The location
    of the stories, "geographically Northern and culturally Southern,"
    would challenge any author in meeting the rigorous demands of the
    short story for resolution and change. Sometimes these demands

are not met, and there are some pieces "which don't come off."
The failures may not be the author's, but "the reader's lazy
failure to establish empathy."

6   PEDEN, WILLIAM. "Assessments of the Finely Aware." SatR 42
     (28 November):33.
          Review of Happy Families Are All Alike: sees Taylor's
     origin in Henry James and James's "fine awareness." The book
     reveals the changing society of the American South and Midwest.
     Examines characters' lives in terms of conflicts caused by
     heredity, environment, past versus present, urban versus rural,
     and intellect versus emotion. Stories succeed because the world
     represented is moving and convincing.

7   SULLIVAN, RICHARD. "Quiet Intensity Marks Collection of 10
     Stories." Chicago Sunday Tribune Magazine of Books,
     6 December, p. 12.
          Review of Happy Families Are All Alike. Whether children,
     adolescents, married couples, or elderly men and women, Taylor's
     characters, wherever they may wander, still remain essentially
     the products of their Southern, small-town backgrounds. Because
     of Taylor's fine, restrained craftsmanship, his stories seem "not
     so much written as remembered out into words." They meander,
     pause for asides, build slowly in intensity, until suddenly all
     elements combine to evoke the "bright quick total illumination."

                              1960

1   ANON. "Happy Families Are All Alike." In Masterplots 1960
     Annual. Edited by Frank N. Magill. New York: Salem Press,
     pp. 80-82.
          Tolstoy's phrase "Happy Families . . ." suggests the major
     themes: happiness, which may resemble Taylor's own family, and
     the "growing up" experience of children learning about life. In
     "1939" a later stage in the maturing process is shown. The first
     three stories are set in the fictional city of Chatham in the
     1930s; the others have varied locales. Taylor experiments with
     point of view; his stories differ greatly from Faulkner or Welty.
     He has little interest in rural areas, but he is interested in
     the contrast between urban and rural characters. Taylor's art
     allows him to present scenes from life, but with aesthetic re-
     arrangement because of a subtlety of presentation. The style (no
     Faulknerian tricks, no Caldwellian repetitiveness) is urbane and
     suited to the subject.

2   ANON. Review of Happy Families Are All Alike. Booklist 56
     (15 January):296.
          Brief review: "sophisticated . . . stories . . . skill-
     fully portray a variety of complex family situations."

3   ANON. Review of <u>Happy Families Are All Alike</u>. <u>KR</u> 22, no. 1
     (Winter):167.
     Taylor has found his own exclusive short-story style, a
carefully camouflaged technique, an "uncanny ability" to present
the concealed motives of his characters.

4   ANON. Review of <u>Happy Families Are All Alike</u>. <u>TLS</u>,
     19 August, p. 525.
     Notes Taylor's concern with the "emergence of moods and the
developments of human situations"; respects his cautious approach
and intellectual respect for his characters.

5   ANON. Review of <u>Happy Families Are All Alike</u>. <u>VQR</u> 36, no. 2
     (Spring):xl.
     This book reaffirms Taylor's "enormous potentialities as a
creative writer," though the reviewer laments the nonappearance
of "that major work." Considers Taylor is at his best in projecting character in his specific Tennessee urban milieu.

6   BROOKS, JEREMY. "New Short Stories." <u>New Statesman</u> 60,
     no. 1534 (6 August):192.
     Review of <u>Happy Families Are All Alike</u>. These stories are
so good "that it would be hazardous to guess openly whether . . .
Taylor imagines he is writing about happy families or unhappy
ones." Taylor may suggest Sinclair Lewis, but that is a "false
echo" for he is after the "reality that lies behind the seeming-
reality."

7   COSMAN, MAX. "The Enchantment of Veracity." <u>Commonweal</u> 71
     (1 January):401-2.
     Review of <u>Happy Families Are All Alike</u>. Taylor's new vol-
ume "should heighten the repute" he has achieved. "Elegiacal
without being mawkish" and "potent as ever," these stories exhibit his continuing concern with "truthful social analysis."
Taylor's work is of importance because he makes us aware of a
"world that tells us things about ourselves."

8   DuBOIS, WILLIAM. Review of <u>Happy Families Are All Alike</u>.
     <u>New York Times</u>, 12 January, p. 45.
     "A literary event of first importance." The first story,
"The Other Times," is representative of his oblique but stimulating style, requiring the "closest collaboration between reader
and author." Each story "centers on a moment of controlled crisis that is the hallmark of any effective work of fiction." Mr.
Taylor develops his stories with careful understatement rather
than "on the spot involvement." Although his critical success is
substantial, he will remain with a small audience unless he
"steps down . . . and raises his voice in anger."

9   PARKER, DOROTHY. Review of Happy Families Are All Alike.
    Esquire 53, no. 3 (March):60.
        A brief mention of Happy Families: about quiet people in
    quiet surroundings, but a book not likely to leave the reader
    quiet.

10 STUCKEY, WILLIAM. "Some Recent Fiction." The Minnesota
    Review 1, no. 1 (Fall):115-17.
        The stories in Happy Families Are All Alike are not as in-
    teresting or successful as those in A Long Fourth. The limita-
    tions in Happy Families occur because the author is unable "to
    engage the reader's feelings and emotions directly." Thus, there
    is a resulting lack of intensity, except in those stories which
    have narrators closely resembling Taylor. The other tales,
    further removed from Taylor's own experience, fail because they
    have not been imagined "subtly or powerfully enough." Such a
    story, "Venus, Cupid, Folly and Time"--"a melodramatic allegory"
    --presents a standard Southern theme, the passing of a ruling
    order and the insanity arising from resistance to this inevitable
    social mutability. "Guests," a story dealing with the contrast
    between city and country, is closer to the center of Taylor's
    experience and is the best story in the collection.

                                1961

*1 MERIWETHER, JAMES B. "A Peter Taylor Checklist." In South:
    Modern Southern Literature in Its Cultural Setting. Edited by
    Louis D. Rubin, Jr. and Robert D. Jacobs. Garden City, N.Y.:
    Doubleday & Co., 433 pp.
        Reprinted: 1974.2.

*2 SULLIVAN, WALTER. "The Continuing Renascence: Southern Fic-
    tion in the Fifties." In South: Modern Southern Literature
    in Its Cultural Setting. Edited by Louis D. Rubin, Jr. and
    Robert D. Jacobs. Garden City, N.Y.: Doubleday & Co.,
    433 pp.
        Reprinted: 1974.4.

                                1962

1   BLUM, MORGAN. "Peter Taylor: Self-Limitation in Fiction."
    SR 70 (Autumn):559-78.
        In his best work, Taylor "by neglecting some things, . . .
    has been able to do others extremely well." By avoiding extremes
    in action and violence, he creates characters who mirror their
    history and families, like those of Tolstoy, involved in credible
    scenes of domestic life. His greatest self-limitation, an in-
    sistence on working from first-hand observation, does not inter-
    fere with his creating characters and experiences quite different

from his own. He is saved from mere autobiography by "an eye
that looks and an imagination that builds." His self-imposed
limitations have resulted in stories and plays with endings which
"seem inevitable, but hardly predictable."

2   BROWN, ASHLEY. "The Early Fiction of Peter Taylor." SR 70
      (Autumn):588–602.
        By 1962 Mr. Taylor had written a small but important body
of work. He could no longer be considered just a young Southern
writer, but one who demanded a critical presentation. "'Sky Line'
(1939) is an example of his skills at an early stage of his
career. . . . Taylor's later and more characteristic work . . .
is essentially social comedy." He has an unusual insight into
how our society reveals itself.

3   CHENEY, BRAINARD. "Peter Taylor's Plays." SR 70 (Autumn):
      579–87.
        Why does an established fiction writer of Mr. Taylor's
calibre turn his attention to playwriting? The most likely
answer is that Taylor's subject matter, the family as a decaying
institution, insists upon the ritualistic presentation of the
drama. In addition, Taylor's "intuition for dramatic dialogue"
and his highly developed sense of humor impel him toward the
theater. "But it is a drama best suited for fiction." And although his scenes are dramatically successful, Taylor has not yet
"been willing to limit himself to the dimensions of the stage."

1963

1   BRADBURY, JOHN M. Renaissance in the South: A Critical His-
      tory of the Literature, 1920-1960. Chapel Hill: University
      of North Carolina Press, pp. 16, 74, 117, 120.
        Taylor's gifts reveal another example of "the New Tradi-
tion's later mastery of form and feeling." In his mastery of the
short-story form, he can be compared only to Katherine Anne
Porter and Eudora Welty, yet he differs significantly, avoiding
Porter's concern with social issues and Welty's overt use of
irony and violence. In A Long Fourth, The Widows of Thornton,
and Happy Families Are All Alike, he demonstrates Southern interests and themes, but he is probably "the least chauvinistic" of
regional authors. His novel, A Woman of Means, does, however,
reveal, in a way his stories do not, a basic sympathy with the
principles of agrarianism.

2   EISINGER, CHESTER. "The Conservative Imagination." In
      Fiction of the Forties. Chicago: University of Chicago
      Press, pp. 193–96.
        Taylor resembles Gordon and Lytle, yet he is more a product
of the New Criticism "than a peer of those who made it." Short
stories in A Long Fourth show much of the pessimism that marks

Gordon's treatment of crumbling culture. A Woman of Means examines problems in a modern economic and moral context, yet Taylor is essentially an elegist for what has passed.

3   RICKETTS, A.S.   Review of Miss Leonora When Last Seen and Fifteen Other Stories. LJ 88, no. 21 (1 December):4666.
         Favorable review: "Throughout . . . Taylor exhibits a formidable talent for menacing understatement and evocation of mood and place."

1964

1   ANON.   "Ghosts in the Closet." Time 83 (13 March):107-8.
         Review of Miss Leonora When Last Seen and Fifteen Other Stories. Taylor, unlike writers who "drop a pebble" and write about the splash "waits, and from the vantage point of memory, recalls the ever-widening rings of ripples that slowly subside." While he may not be suitable for everyone's taste, because he does not "point," or "posture," or "underscore," he does conjure up ghosts that will stay with the reader's imagination.

2   ANON.   Review of Miss Leonora When Last Seen and Fifteen Other Stories. VQR 40, no. 3 (Summer):civ.
         Briefly noted: with each new story Taylor's "pre-eminence" achieves affirmation. Because all of the stories in this volume are reprinted, readers who wish for new Taylor stories must take consolation "in these familiar, almost perfect pages."

3   BARO, GENE.   Review of Miss Leonora When Last Seen and Fifteen Other Stories. NYTBR, 29 March, pp. 4, 30.
         The quality of "transcending the literal, the limited or the everyday circumstance" is characteristic of "really fine stories," and this is a characteristic of Taylor's work. The solidity of his works accomplished, and these new stories, allow one to see his "dominating and developing" concerns; Taylor's art renders the environment observed, but his real concern is with how time changes things. "Firm detail" strenthens the fiction; his themes "have enduring interest."

4   CULLIGAN, G.   Review of Miss Leonora When Last Seen and Fifteen Other Stories. Books 1, no. 26 (8 March):11.
         Newest volume of short stories provides the occasion for viewing the continuity in all of Taylor's work, such as the recurrent theme of "the failure of intimacy." His preoccupation with "the family framework of emotions," a legacy from Tolstoy and his own Southern background, has resulted in the depiction of characters in their covert and unsuccessful attempts to escape family and community. For Taylor, "togetherness" can be "a constant, dangerous undertow." In a Taylor story, violence and strong emotions are suggested rather than presented. "Up to

a point, this ironic contrast between bland surface and the vol-
canic subsoil provides some of Taylor's strongest effects. . . ."
His development of a personal, colloquial style also heightens
this irony and contributes to "meticulous particularization," but
at the risk of losing some dramatic tension. His willingness to
take such a risk suggests that Taylor may be moving in the direction of the novel.

5   LEARY, LEWIS. "Winning But Not Winners." SatR 47 (16 May):
     45-46.
        Miss Leonora When Last Seen and Fifteen Other Stories
possesses characters who are strong, yet Taylor manages his interest in such characters "better than most" writers, perhaps
because he seems to know "more about more different kinds of
people" than Welty, Capote, McCullers or even Sherwood Anderson.
The principal reason for Taylor's superiority is that he writes
with "such unobtrusive artistry."

6   MEEKER, RICHARD K. "The Youngest Generation of Southern
     Fiction Writers." In Southern Writers, Appraisals in Our
     Time. Edited by R.C. Simonini, Jr. Charlottesville:
     University of Virginia Press, pp. 173-74.
        Taylor is briefly discussed as an analyst of the decay of
the Southern family; "A Long Fourth" is described as the most
ambitious story of the first volume, and The Widows of Thornton
also "chronicles family dissolution."

7   SCHULER, SISTER COR MARIAE, R.S.H.M. "The House of Peter
     Taylor: Vision and Structure." Ph.D. dissertation, Univer-
     sity of Notre Dame.
        Exploration of Taylor's fiction as well as two plays.
Setting creates and supports the characters often recently up-
rooted from agrarian backgrounds; and physical fact is raised to
a symbolic level, as in his frequent use of houses. In most of
his works, Taylor's concern is with family and how his characters
struggle to maintain old structures as they are changing. Thematically Taylor's focus is on conflicts between past and present. His technique--language, point of view, irony--elicits
comparisons with Ivan Turgenev and Henry James. (Appendix lists
stories chronologically.) See also 1967.4.

8   SULLIVAN, RICHARD. Review of Miss Leonora When Last Seen and
     Fifteen Other Stories. Chicago Sunday Tribune Books Today,
     5 April, p. 4.
        Taylor would satisfy Willa Cather's insistence that a good
writer have both "a technique and a birthright." Although ten
of the stories in Miss Leonora When Last Seen are reprinted from
two earlier volumes, it is impossible to tell the new work from
the old, for "the same quiet intensity permeates it all."
Taylor's integrity and scrupulous craftsmanship guarantee an
absolute fidelity to his material and its imaginative

reproduction. The insight most frequently gained from these stories is an awareness of "social, regional continuity, broken into by time and change." This volume confirms Taylor's deserved reputation as an important American artist.

9   THOMPSON, JOHN. "The Stories of Peter Taylor." NYRB 2, no. 9 (11 June):11-12.
    By making thoughtful connections with other writers who focus on the middle class in the middle west, the reviewer analyzes how Taylor's work, which seems to share the fate of that class, is "even more complex and elusive than the subject[s]" of stories by Katherine Anne Porter "that were so admired for their art." Taylor's "uninsistent" art tells us what it is like to be part of this changing middle class, and what it is to be human.

1965

1   BAUMBACH, JONATHAN. "Miss Leonora When Last Seen." In Masterplots 1965 Annual. Edited by Frank N. Magill and Dayton Kohler. Englewood Cliffs, N.J.: Salem Press, pp. 202-4.
    Taylor presents a fictional world that is "haunted by memories of the past" with no easy resolutions. Like Chekhov and Joyce, his stories seem deceptively "casual, anecdotal, and unplotted." His work is as serious and as skilled as any writer of our time. His accomplishments have not received proper recognition, due in part to the medium in which he works, his preference for refusing to accommodate modernism, and his ability to make his stories natural occurrences. The dissolution of a society and the loss of a civilization are revealed by Taylor's characters, one of whom says, "'In mourning my family, I mourn the world's disappearance'"; and the impact and comprehension of the imbalance of such disorder on "its dispossessed survivors" is the subject of Miss Leonora When Last Seen. Includes a summary/analysis of "Their Losses"; "Miss Leonora When Last Seen"; "At the Drugstore"; "Bad Dreams"; "Two Pilgrims"; "A Strange Story"; "A Wife of Nashville"; and "Sky Line."

2   HANZO, T.A. "The Two Faces of Matt Donelson." SR 73, no. 1 (Winter):106-19.
    A complex analysis of Miss Leonora When Last Seen and Fifteen Other Stories. "At the Drugstore" is especially emblematic of Taylor's theme of "a past recovered or confronted without ascertainable meaning," and demonstration of his "subtle and intimate manner." Other stories are analyzed and compared with writers, such as John Hawkes, to demonstrate Taylor's skill as observer of the contemporary scene. "Never parochial," Taylor's art shows how ordinary experience allows a way for the hero "to go down into the past"--true heroism.

<u>1967</u>

1   ANON. "A Poet Who Was There." <u>Time</u> 90 (15 September):102.
       Review of <u>Randall Jarrell, 1914-1965</u>. Cites remarks of
    some contributors; Taylor is not mentioned except as editor.

2   KORGES, JAMES, ed. "Symposium of Taylor." <u>Crit</u> 9, no. 3:
       6-36.
       Includes works by Barbara Schuler (1967.4) and James Penny
    Smith (1967.5-6).

3   MOYNAHAN, JULIAN. Review of <u>Randall Jarrell, 1914-1964</u>.
       <u>NYTBR</u>, 3 September, p. 4.
       Background about Jarrell; book described as "arranged
    alphabetically and designed to draw the portrait of a literary
    genius." The editors "wisely . . . attempt no final assessment."

4   SCHULER, BARBARA. "The House of Peter Taylor." <u>Crit</u> 9,
       no. 3:6-18.
       Taylor, a member of the Southern Renascence, has as his
    central theme "the disintegration of the family in the New
    South," whose characters are "vulnerable before the ethically
    deteriorating influences of urbanization." His finest image of
    modernization is the train depot in "At the Drugstore," where,
    "the physical alteration of the station is a startlingly vivid
    projection of the corresponding change in the social structure."
    Although Taylor supplies no answers to the human condition, the
    "'house'" of his fiction is supported by fine craftsmanship and
    universality. . . ." See also 1964.7. See 1967.2.

5   SMITH, JAMES PENNY. "Narration and Theme in Taylor's <u>A Woman</u>
       <u>of Means</u>." <u>Crit</u> 9, no. 3:19-30.
       Quint Dudley is the narrator "whose usually reliable nar-
    ration is given support or correction through the opinions of the
    adults among whom he lived, but from whom he is separated by age
    and, therefore, moral and intellectual differences." Although
    the novel reveals Quint's growing awareness of himself, its
    theme is more properly the imperfect identification of one's self
    and the problems emerging from this faulty identification. See
    1967.2.

6   _____. "A Peter Taylor Checklist." <u>Crit</u> 9, no. 3:31-36.
       Listing of primary works, reviews, significant reprints and
    textbook inclusions as well as listing of uncollected work, work
    in progress, and general studies on Taylor's writing. See 1967.2.

7   TAYLOR, PETER HILLSMAN. "Randall Jarrell." In <u>Randall</u>
       <u>Jarrell, 1914-1965</u>. Edited by Robert Lowell; Peter Taylor;
    and Robert Penn Warren. New York: Farrar, Straus & Giroux,
    pp. 241-52.
       A personal reminiscence, beginning with the literary stu-
    dents at Vanderbilt and their two parties, one led by George

Marion O'Donnell and the other by Randall Jarrell, continuing
through Jarrell's teaching period and Taylor's student work at
Kenyon College. After the Kenyon period and World War II, Taylor
and Jarrell were together intermittently over a period of twenty
years, although "once you were a student of Randall's, once you
were a friend of Randall's, it was for life." The most important
part of the friendship, however, was that Jarrell cared about
one's writing and "there is no better friend than that."

8   WHITTEMORE, REED. "Brothers in Loss." <u>SatR</u> 50 (2 September):
     26.
         Review of <u>Randall Jarrell, 1914-1965</u>. Refers to the con-
     tributors as members of a "tight little community or club," all
     of them more or less tense about the club's existence; then re-
     fers to the relations of various "members" to Jarrell and each
     other. Taylor is not mentioned by name.

                         <u>1968</u>

1   ANON. "The Short Stories of Peter Taylor." In <u>Masterpieces</u>
     <u>of World Literature in Digest Form</u>. Edited by Frank N.
     Magill. 4th ser. New York, Evanston, and London: Harper &
     Row, Publishers, pp. 1145-48.
         Commentary about the first four collections of stories:
     outlines the "flawless technique" and Taylor's concern for
     family. An island "risen out of Faulknerian seas," Taylor's
     world is ironic, less "impassioned grief than melancholy." His
     style is almost a studied avoidance of style (one cannot imagine
     him parodied like Hemingway or Salinger), yet that style is like
     a clean window. Implication gives power to Taylor's fiction. He
     selects details unerringly. Reprinted: 1976.1.

2   BAUMBACH, JONATHAN. "Peter Taylor." In <u>Moderns and Contempo-</u>
     <u>raries: Nine Masters of the Short Story</u>. Edited by Jonathan
     Baumbach and Arthur Edelstein. New York: Random House,
     pp. 343-44.
         Taylor's stories, set for the most part in the middle-
     South, are concerned with the effects of a lost history upon a
     society unsure of its present direction, and uncertain of the
     reality of its past. The violence and horror, latent in the
     work, is both muted and intensified by the genteel voices of the
     narrators. Taylor's style, like D.H. Lawrence's, is heavily de-
     pendent upon a rhythm which evokes the lives of the narrator and
     the characters. Always his style is subtle but precise, and
     there is great pleasure to be derived from the savoring of a
     single paragraph.

3   HALIO, JAY L. Review of <u>Miss Leonora When Last Seen and Fifteen Other Stories</u>. <u>SoR</u>, n.s. 4, no. 1 (Winter):236-47.
     The stories treat a dominant and recurring theme: an old
order passing and the coming of a new. Something is lost and
"what is lost is something quite irretrievable. . . ." The characters retain their dignity and courage as Faulkner's characters
do. Taylor, indeed, should be compared with Faulkner, even
though there are significant differences.

4   LEVENSON, J.C. Review of <u>Randall Jarrell, 1914-1965</u>. <u>VQR</u> 44,
no. 2 (Spring):318-23.
     While the real "memorial volume" will be the "Complete
Poems," this book put together by friends will "help the public
come into its inheritance." "The exquisite loveliness of the
commonplace" was Jarrell's special subject.

5   WALSH, CHAD. Review of <u>Randall Jarrell, 1914-1965</u>. <u>BW</u>,
3 March, pp. 4-5.
     A varied collection of pieces, including one by Peter
Taylor, that is "for the most part a cozy conversation among
poets and critics who know what each will say or write before he
says or writes it." Essays by Mrs. Jarrell and Karl Shapiro are
favorably discussed.

1969

1   ANON. "1969--A Rich Year for the Novel." <u>NW</u> 74 (22 December):
98.
     Brief mention of <u>Collected Stories</u>: Taylor works in the
tradition of Chekhov and James, and while his situations may seem
commonplace, as they unfold the reader is drawn into "menacing
complications." Collection provides opportunity for a long over-
due reassessment.

2   ANON. Review of <u>The Collected Stories of Peter Taylor</u>.
<u>Booklist</u> 66 (15 December):497.
     Brief notice: "short stories masterfully fashioned";
Southern locale, but "universal application."

3   ANON. Review of <u>The Collected Stories of Peter Taylor</u>.
<u>Kirkus</u> 37, no. 15 (1 August):804.
     Favorable review of <u>Collected Stories</u>: "masterworks of a
cool and tidy elegance."

4   ANON. Review of <u>The Collected Stories of Peter Taylor</u>. <u>PW</u>
196 (4 August):42.
     "High quality" stories which concern changing ways of life
as the old order gives way to the new. Taylor's talent is
"formidable."

*5   BROOKS, CLEANTH. "The Southern Temper." <u>Archives</u> 206 (May):
       1-15.
           Reprinted: 1971.2.

6   CASSILL, R.V. "The Departure of Proserpine." <u>BW</u>, 12 October,
       p. 6.
           <u>Collected Stories</u> proves that a Golden Age for the American
       short story began shortly after World War II. Because many of
       these writers were influenced by Ransom, they "brought into prose
       fiction the hard cunning and resource of poetry without being
       tempted to write . . . poetic prose." Furthermore, Taylor's fine
       prose encompasses a large world. In the best stories, regional-
       ism and local color give way to "how the world spins out from
       Tennessee and closes its vast circles there."

7   HAMLIN, WILLIAM C. Review of <u>The Collected Stories of Peter
       Taylor</u>. <u>SatR</u> 52 (18 October):40.
           Discusses the "basic thematic formula" which seems to be
       that change of any sort results in alienation. "Like Faulkner he
       laments the passing of whatever seemed worth saving, but he never
       sentimentalizes its going."

8   HOWARD, RICHARD. Review of <u>The Collected Stories of Peter
       Taylor</u>. <u>NYTBR</u>, 19 October, pp. 4, 26.
           Taylor, "one of the best writers America has produced," has
       winnowed and pruned to shape a "monument to show his meaning."
       Omitting seventeen from the final canon, these stories are "per-
       suasive . . . never hurrying, steadily gaining ground." The true
       "burden" of Taylor's stories is "Happy Families," and the success
       of his art derives from the fact that the "central outrage" of
       his stories rests on a provocative neutrality of "structure, tone,
       and circumstance." Taylor's subjects--"politics, love, family
       life" are "great chords that sound together . . . of a region
       discovering that without a past," man has but a "nameless
       future."

9   LASK, THOMAS. "Brief Lives." <u>New York Times</u>, 11 October,
       p. 35.
           Review of <u>The Collected Stories</u>. His greatest success
       comes when "he does not work from the inside of his characters,
       when he does not interpret them to us, but when he describes them
       empirically in their relationship to others, to their situation,
       to the past." They find solace only when the bonds of family are
       strong, but if "home is a refuge, his characters are seldom in
       it." Specific examples of his craftsmanship are "Their Losses"
       and "Venus, Cupid, Folly and Time."

10   MORRIS, ROBERT K. "Repressed Consciousness." Nat 209,
      no. 13 (20 October):418-19.
          Review of The Collected Stories. "If there is a unifying
      thread [in] these unflawed pieces," it is "how human fallibility
      is mirrored in the breakup of the old genteel order," which has
      fallen apart in the South. Taylor avoids the extremes of Welty,
      Capote, or O'Connor, and shows "charity, warmth, patience" for
      characters who fall back on what can no longer be real "in order
      to avoid confronting what is." He is not pessimistic; rather
      understanding brings his characters to "their first real hope."

11   NELSON, BARBARA. Review of The Collected Stories of Peter
      Taylor. LJ 94, no. 19 (1 November):4028.
          Favorable review: "craftsmanship and meticulous care are
      abundantly evident."

12   RASKIN, BARBARA. "In Reply" [Rejoinder]. NewR 161
      (22 November):29.
          While the "Southern world view still has a universal valid-
      ity," that world view is not shown in the contrasts which Taylor
      provides. See 1969.13, 18.

13   _____. "Southern Fried." NewR 161 (18 October):29-30.
          Taylor's stories, "careful, craftsmanlike," are ultimately
      "mind-deadening." We have had enough of his subjects, and while
      one "wonders whether these stories" of white women surprised by
      black servants "are really clever, underspoken put-downs,"
      finally Taylor's return to the same kind of situation "implicates
      and indicts the author as much as the work." His best stories
      deal with young people, for the most part ex-Southerners. See
      1969.12, 18.

14   SALE, ROGER. "Its Discontent." HudR 22, no. 4 (Winter):
      709-10.
          Review of Collected Stories. While substantial in some
      ways, Taylor's stories sometimes seem to be about a world of
      people who "seem almost never to have lived." It would be hard
      to arrange these stories chronologically, yet they were produced
      over a thirty-year period. Such slightness of incident, accom-
      panied by a stability of social structure and attitude, can have
      the effect of rendering events "close to irrelevant."

15   STILWELL, ROBERT L. Review of Randall Jarrell, 1914-1965.
      Books Abroad 43, no. 1 (Winter):115.
          Secondary material in abundance can be found in this "ex-
      cellent commemorative volume," a "fine gathering."

16   THOMPSON, JOHN. "The Clever, the True and the Marvelous:
      Three Fiction Writers." Harper's 239, no. 1434 (November):
      130, 134.

Collected Stories reviewed with The Waterfall by Margaret
Drabble and A Special Providence by Richard Yates; the first
"literary"; the second "straight-forward"; while Taylor's demonstrates that he "belongs . . . near the top . . . of major American writers." Taylor's chronicle of our culture carries in its
very texture the understanding that these fragile contrivances
are the only things we have which stand between us and "the
essential horror of our animal condition."

17   WOLFF, GEOFFREY. "Master of Hidden Drama." NW 73
      (20 October):121-22.
      The Collected Stories "shows an artist of the very first
rank." Taylor should be added to the list of James, Hawthorne,
and Faulkner as an artist who can fashion narrative without
"resorting to overheard conversations." Generally these stories
grow of a "seemingly inconsequential crisis." One of the reasons
Taylor writes so well is that he is "wary of literature, but re-
spectful of life."

18   YARDLEY, JONATHAN. Correspondence in reply to Barbara
      Raskin's review of Collected Stories. NewR 161 (18 October):
      27-29.
      Raskin's review "is a savage and self-indulgent exercise in
sophistry," and ultimately says a good deal more about her, than
about Taylor's work. Objecting to comments about Taylor being
"'Faulknerian,'" that his characters are "'reminiscent'" of
Williams or Capote, Yardley points out that Raskin's review is
based on the untenable premise "that all Southern fiction is
alike." See 1969.12-13.

                              1970

1   ANON. Review of The Collected Stories. Choice 7, no. 3
     (May):388.
     Taylor's clear informal prose shapes a "Southern world with
well-known characters and familiar themes." This collection re-
inforces the claim of many that he is the "finest living American
writer" of short stories.

2   GOODWIN, STEPHEN. "Life Studies." Shenandoah 21, no. 2
     (Winter):100-102.
     "The triumph of his storytelling is that he has managed to
enclose so much experience in the confines of the form he has
chosen." His best stories seem as complete as novels, for he
carries his reader "beyond the fiction of permanence," yet "never
encourages our hope that these emotions and discoveries may be
lasting." Because of his art, Taylor begins each story anew and
thereby assures us that even the most "radical insight" need
"not cause despair."

3   GRIFFITH, ALBERT J. Peter Taylor. TUSAS 168. New York:
    Twayne, 183 pp.
        The only book-length treatment of Taylor's work. The first
    chapter, a brief but thorough biographical introduction, is suc-
    ceeded by individual chapters devoted to Taylor's books, their
    content and form discussed in considerable detail. In addition
    to Taylor's novella, A Woman of Means, and the volumes of pub-
    lished short stories (In the Miro District had not yet appeared),
    Griffith surveys and evaluates the then published plays, The
    Death of a Kinsman, Tennessee Day in St. Louis, A Stand in the
    Mountains, as well as the uncollected short stories. He defines
    precisely and clearly "the memoir story," and takes the position
    that this "Sterne-like digressive-progressive form" is far more
    typical of Taylor than the grotesque, surrealistic approach taken
    in the O. Henry Prize winner, "Venus, Cupid, Folly and Time."
        In the final chapter, Griffith assesses Taylor's achievements
    in fiction and relates his work to the body of Southern litera-
    ture produced since 1920. Although clearly a Southern writer,
    Taylor shares as many differences as similarities with this
    school of writers. Unlike many of his contemporaries, he gen-
    erally eschews the violent and the grotesque as well as a flam-
    boyant prose style, his own being "cool, classically simple,
    urbane." Even his sense of place is unique in that the country
    town serves as the remembered background of his characters rather
    than as the actual setting of the action. His settings frequently
    present and explore, as few other Southern writers have chosen to
    do, the urban centers of the New South or the expatriate communi-
    ties of Southerners now living in the North or Midwest. Although
    his work is certainly concerned with history, tradition, change,
    and the erosion of institutional values in the modern world, his
    ubiquitous irony qualifies these concerns. Even the family it-
    self "is not treated as an institution but as one part of a com-
    plex background for personal discoveries and developments." This
    pervasive ironic tone, coupled with a self-imposed limitation as
    to themes and subject matter, has produced a writer like Chekhov,
    more concerned with asking the proper questions than providing
    definitive answers. Taylor's greatest accomplishment as a writer,
    however, is his ability to create, within the short-fiction form,
    characters of the depth and complexity usually encountered only
    in the novel.
        Griffith's book is prefaced by a chronological listing of
    Taylor's life, and concludes with a selected bibliography of
    primary sources and an annotated bibliography of secondary
    sources.

4   _____. Review of The Collected Stories of Peter Taylor.
    Commonweal 91 (6 February):516.
        Volume shows the "incredible skill" of a master craftsman
    and notes characteristics both of Taylor's style and subject
    matter. Non-exploitable, timeless, the stories deserve wider
    recognition.

5   OPDAHL, KEITH M. "His Stories Lay Quiet Siege." CSM,
     22 January, p. 11.
          Review of The Collected Stories. Taylor is a fine writer
     who has yet to receive his deserved recognition. Although defi-
     nitely linked to the Southern school, Taylor's real subject is
     "mid-America, heightened by a Southern accent." He does give us,
     however, "a final leisurely look at those old folks, who are just
     about gone, lingering shadows, the grandfathers and country rela-
     tives, and founding families, and yes, elderly, loving, cranky
     Negroes." In comparison with Hemingway, Taylor appears "to be
     pleasant rather than powerful." But what Hemingway lacks in his
     stories, Taylor's possess in abundance: "the groping, the re-
     serve, the infinite need, the endless guessing of another's mind."
     At his best, Taylor may be writing our social history by telling
     us "exactly what it is we're living."

6   [P., J.]. Review of The Collected Stories. Malahat Review
     no. 15 (July):115-16.
          It is misleading to compare Taylor to Chekhov for he is
     "nostalgic" in a quite un-Russian way and his conception of char-
     acter is also unlike Chekhov. Further, Taylor's sensitivity to
     the role of narrator makes his stories distinctive, yet unlike
     most raconteurs he never obtrudes. Reading these stories care-
     fully reveals a skillful writer who requires a good deal of his
     reader.

7   PEDEN, WILLIAM. "A Hard and Admirable Toughness: The Stories
     of Peter Taylor." HC 7, no. 1 (February):1-9.
          Taylor's Collected Stories are deceptive because they seem
     to suggest that time has stopped, yet his fiction is always con-
     cerned with the difficult changes in American society during the
     past several decades. Upon close examination it is clear his
     vision is austere; he reveals how many levels of society are all
     implicated in changes. Specifics in "A Friend and Protector";
     "At the Drugstore"; and "Cookie" illustrate the complexity of
     characterization. What is most significant is the internal drama
     of these characters. While Taylor has been called a "gentle
     writer," his vision is essentially one which admires decency and
     decorum. See also 1971.5.

8   PINKERTON, JAN. "The Non-Regionalism of Peter Taylor: An
     Essay Review." GaR 24, no. 4 (Winter):432-40.
          Taylor's The Collected Stories have often been wrongly read
     as stereotypes, but closer examination reveals that he is a
     Southern writer who distrusts the past and a conservative writer
     who believes in change. His treatment of "Southern themes" is
     often controversial. Some critics, such as Barbara Raskin, have
     failed to distinguish between the characters and Taylor, and,
     also that, characters who mourn the loss of the past are not
     peculiar to just one region. Examination of themes such as the
     fascination with role-playing by his characters reveals that his

attitude may be a "heretical espousal" of transience, "even of uprootedness." In a number of the stories he indicates that the problem is not change, but the failure to initiate or respond to it.

9   RICKS, CHRISTOPHER. "The Unignorable Real." NYRB 14, no. 3
     (12 February):22-24.
         Unfavorable review of The Collected Stories; categorized as
     fiction "almost . . . asking to be taken as photographs," and
     labeled as "liberal literature." "The anxieties of the liberal
     conscience steal the show." Taylor's best stories are a "train-
     ing in vigilance, but the vigilance then damages the less than
     best."

                              1971

1   ANON. Review of The Collected Stories of Peter Taylor. VQR
     47, no. 1 (Winter):xii.
         "Surely a significant publishing event"; as the reader con-
     fronts the "whole talent," the finish of these stories stands out,
     but more importantly, it is possible to see that the later work
     is more crafted. Indirection and irony are refined. These sto-
     ries "offer something to every reader," without descending to a
     "mediocre level of technique or interest."

2   BROOKS, CLEANTH. "The Southern Temper." In A Shaping Joy:
     Studies in the Writer's Craft. New York: Harcourt Brace
     Jovanovich, pp. 198-214.
         Using the fictional character of a middle-aged spinster as
     representative of the Southern temper which symbolizes cultural
     aspirations, Brooks approaches the subject in an analytical man-
     ner by analysis of "Miss Leonora When Last Seen." Through com-
     parisons with Faulkner, James, Sinclair Lewis, and Katherine Anne
     Porter's characters, Taylor's Miss Leonora is examined as a com-
     plex character who possesses a mixture of admirable and not so
     admirable traits. The narrator, although not fully aware of it,
     does not want her to surrender to conformity and modernity.
     Taylor's portrait is successful because it is a mixture, and he
     takes delight in contemplating aspects of human nature which are
     numinous. Reprint of 1969.5.

3   OATES, JOYCE C. "Realism of Distance, Realism of Immediacy."
     SoR 7, no. 1 (Winter):295-313, esp. 299-302.
         Review-essay in which parallels between Flannery O'Connor's
     work and Taylor's are elaborated; in Taylor occasionally "the
     grotesque shows through." His stories are like dreams: events
     are brought into focus, then a mysterious "'point'" is reached, a
     "point of surrender and the story is completed." What is sur-
     prising is that these are moments of terror in the lives Taylor
     imagines. While he is "Chekhovian" or "Jamesian," he is more

importantly himself. No one writes "more beautifully" of tension
in the love of tradition.

4 PHILLIPS, ROBERT. Review of The Collected Stories of Peter
   Taylor. SSF 8, no. 3 (Summer):487-89.
        While the title is misleading because the book really is
   "new and selected stories," it provides an occasion to review
   solid achievement. His primary concern the family, Taylor uses
   the home as focal point. His finest stories "capture characters"
   at moments when sacrifice is crucial. The weakest stories are
   chronologically the latest.

5 PINKERTON, JAN. "A Critical Distortion of Peter Taylor's 'At
   the Drugstore.'" NConL 1, no. 4 (September):6-7.
        In reply to William Peden's discussion of the protagonist
   of "At the Drugstore" wherein he argues that Matt Donelson is
   Taylor's "'least admirable character,'" it is demonstrated that
   the quotation used to support Peden's assertion is in error.
   Matt is a significant vehicle for Taylor's examination of the
   compulsion to return to the past, but not the aggressor as Peden
   assumes. See 1970.7.

6 SCRIVNER, SUSAN JOHNSON. "The Short Stories of Peter Taylor:
   A Critical Study." Ph.D. dissertation, Florida State University.
        Study of the short stories with reference to the novel and
   plays. The conflict between past and present is first investigated. Themes such as growing up, alienation, and vicarious
   living are examined. Recurrent character types, such as the
   strong dominating woman, are studied. Systematic investigation
   of the Tollivers, a family which appears in several stories, the
   use of myth, and techniques of structuring are examined. Taylor's
   work forms a unified body.

7 WORKMAN, CHARLES. "The Collected Stories of Peter Taylor."
   In Masterplots 1971 Annual. Edited by Frank N. Magill.
   Englewood Cliffs, N.J.: Salem Press, pp. 46-51.
        For Taylor the past survives, but often grotesquely. These
   stories can be classified according to how characters relate to
   time: some are "lost to the past, others in the past, and still
   others from the past." Analysis of "What You Hear from 'Em?";
   "Reservations"; and "Dean of Men" illustrate these points. Other
   stories are also discussed, usually in relation to narrators and
   themes having to do with the past. Taylor's fiction has affini-
   ties with the "divided worlds of Arnold, Lawrence, Conrad," and
   with the "disparate worlds of James." His art is "quiet and unobtrusive." Some of his stories are in the Gothic tradition of
   Hawthorne and Flannery O'Connor, and the stories will always
   appeal to those who have "old memories or a sense of discon-
   tinuity."

1972

1   KESTERSON, DAVID B.   Review of Peter Taylor, by Albert J.
    Griffith.   SSF 9, no. 1 (Winter):113-14.
        Laudatory review: "an unusually objective study." Because
    Griffith isolates Taylor's strengths and judges his failures he
    has performed "an admirable job of assessment." Griffith sees
    Taylor "more as an individualist than as a regionalist."

2   SULLIVAN, WALTER.   "The Decline of Southern Fiction." In
    Death by Melancholy: Essays on Modern Southern Fiction.
    Baton Rouge: Louisiana State University Press, p. 89.
        In a list of writers cited in relation to their loss of
    creative power, Taylor is included as someone who "no longer
    shows us much that is new."

3   WELKER, ROBERT L.   "Peter Taylor." In Contemporary Novelists.
    Edited by James Vinson. New York: St. Martin's Press,
    pp. 1125-27.
        A brief but highly factual biographical sketch precedes the
    article. Concerned with the concept of "role playing" as an
    essential ingredient in Taylor's fiction. In static societies,
    men develop roles for identity and stability, and "life becomes
    ceremonies, rituals, traditions, manners. . . ." Taylor, like
    his mentor Henry James, provides the reader brilliant portraits
    of men and women in the modern world who have discovered that
    they have outlived the roles that society once expected of them.
    Does one change to meet the times or remain loyal to the old role
    no longer understood or tolerated by the world: "betray or be
    betrayed"? Such is the dilemma for some of Taylor's most fasci-
    nating characters, Miss Leonora and Aunt Munsie being two of the
    most obvious.

1973

1   ANON.   "Notes on Current Books." VQR 49, no. 2 (Spring):cxii.
        Review of Presences: Seven Dramatic Pieces. Taylor,
    "adroit at depicting character relationships through dialogue
    . . . lacks still the visibility of dramatic action." Read as
    literary efforts without a narrator these pieces are fine; as
    drama, they are "thin as ghosts."

2   ANON.   "Peter Taylor." In Contemporary Literary Criticism.
    Vol. 1. Edited by Carolyn Riley. Detroit: Gale Research,
    pp. 333-35.
        Taylor, Peter. "A Southern American short story writer
    and novelist, Taylor is the author of Happy Families Are All
    Alike." Excerpts from the following: Barbara Schuler (1967.4),
    Jonathan Baumbach (1968.2), Jan Pinkerton (1970.8), Stephen
    Goodwin (1970.2), Albert J. Griffith (1970.3), and Joyce Carol
    Oates (1971.3).

3   ANON. Review of <u>Presences: Seven Dramatic Pieces</u>. <u>AR</u> 32,
     no. 4 (November):700.
          As in his stories, Taylor's plays are "heavily concerned
     with <u>family</u> and <u>place</u>." Objects to some of Taylor's choices of
     contemporary themes; nevertheless, his success is that he has
     found a fresh way to dramatize everyday events and the agonies
     that "boil insistently" at the edge of life while seldom
     erupting.

4   ANON. Review of <u>Presences: Seven Dramatic Pieces</u>. <u>Booklist</u>
     69 (15 June):969.
          "Masterful crafting" of techniques in <u>The Collected Stories</u>
     "applied on a new form." Private perceptions and imperfect vi-
     sions become ghostly presences.

5   ANON. Review of <u>Presences: Seven Dramatic Pieces</u>. <u>PW</u> 202
     (4 December):59.
          Taylor's reputation as story-teller is enhanced by this
     collection of plays. He has been compared to Chekhov and these
     "one-act gems" enhance that comparison.

6   GOODWIN, STEPHEN. "An Interview with Peter Taylor."
     <u>Shenandoah</u> 24, no. 2 (Winter):3-20.
          Mr. Taylor reveals the poets at Kenyon College, including
     Ransom and Jarrell, had a strong effect on him, particularly
     their concern about technical problems. This was responsible for
     him becoming a writer of short stories rather than a novelist.
     Additionally, his family manifested a Southern tradition of story
     telling and of constant conversations about the past. Taylor be-
     lieves, however, that he will not write many more short stories;
     he would rather spend his time writing plays, particularly those
     which can be read as well as produced. "I feel that I've done
     what I want to do as a short-story writer."

7   HEYMAN, HARRIET. "Books in Brief: Current Books in Short
     Compass." <u>World</u> 2, no. 4 (13 February):52.
          In the manner of Peter Taylor's short stories, the seven
     dramas that comprise <u>Presences</u> are clear and succinct. The rela-
     tionships revealed through dialogue, devoid of "the descriptive
     trappings of the story form," are projections of the delusions of
     the characters.

8   HOWARD, RICHARD. "'Urgent Need and Unbearable Fear.'"
     <u>Shenandoah</u> 24, no. 2 (Winter):44-47.
          Review of <u>Presences</u>: by making connections with the fic-
     tion which so often suggests separation and absence[s], these
     dramatic pieces "suture together" what has been sundered. Not
     the masterpiece of Taylor's career, these are experiments wherein
     he works out what is implicit in the fiction. This range of ex-
     periments shows us the missing parts and demonstrates that in
     Taylor's vision all life is haunted.

9   KAZIN, ALFRED. <u>Bright Book of Life: American Novelists and Storytellers from Hemingway to Mailer</u>. Boston and Toronto: Atlantic-Little, Brown & Co., pp. 38, 46-49.

      Taylor is listed as one of the Southern authors read with growing interest in the postwar years. Representing a different school from "the big-writing Southern novelists," with their inflated styles and sensational subject matter, Taylor depicts, quietly and indirectly, "the executive middle class," whose assurances and values are collapsing around them. The climax in a typical Taylor story is marked by illumination and sudden awareness rather than by violence and distortion. A mild disturbance is evident in many women characters who discover their husbands have abandoned them to a world no longer shared by the male, except in his insistence on its preservation.

10   OLSON, RICHARD D. Review of <u>Presences: Seven Dramatic Pieces</u>. <u>LJ</u> 98, no. 1 (1 January):83.

      Unfavorable review: "about the most uninteresting ghosts to be encountered in fiction," for fiction is what these "skeletal literary exercises" are. The mystery and tension necessary for drama is absent; Taylor's followers will be disappointed as will drama buffs too.

11   THEROUX, PAUL. "Old-Family Vapors." <u>BW</u>, 25 February, 13.

      Although ghosts and fantasies require "'too much artifice when presented in fiction,'" the ghosts are central to virtually all of the seven plays in <u>Presences</u>. All, including the stunning and shattering "The Whistler," have used the ghost/fantasy in a technically and dramatically superb manner by "giving voice and shape to what is most private in our mental lives."

12   YARDLEY, JONATHAN. "The New Old Southern Novel." <u>PR</u> 40, no. 2 (Spring):286-93.

      Review-essay of novels by Doris Betts, Harry Crews, Charles Gaines, Madison Jones, Cormac McCarthy, Flannery O'Connor (<u>Complete Stories</u>), Walker Percy, Peter Taylor (<u>Collected Stories</u>), Eudora Welty, James Whitehead, Calder Willingham. Queries "What Comes Next?" now that the sense of place, of community, and of history are being replaced by the levelization of the Southern culture into American facelessness. New Southern writers are interested in writing about their South. Compares Welty and Taylor, the "last authentic practitioners of the tradition," for their stress on place and community, especially the family. Percy provides the definitive portrayal of the New South, but manages to hold to the values of knowledge, tradition, diversity. New Southern fiction is still drawn to the great themes, but must try to give new form to them. See also Walker Percy <u>Guide</u> (1973.24).

1974

1   FUSSELL, B.H. "On the Trail of the Lonesome Dramaturge."
    HudR 26, no. 4 (Winter):753.
        Brief comment within this essay-review about Presences:
    the condensed form of the drama works against "the delicacy of
    relationship that Taylor handles so well" in fiction. The weak-
    ness of these "playlets" is that they show too much artifice.

2   MERIWETHER, JAMES B. "A Peter Taylor Checklist." In South:
    Modern Southern Literature in Its Cultural Setting. Edited by
    Louis D. Rubin, Jr. and Robert D. Jacobs. Westport, Conn.:
    Greenwood Press, p. 425.
        Meriwether lists Taylor's works which had appeared through
    1959, concluding with Happy Families Are All Alike. The only
    critical work noted about Taylor is by Kenneth Clay Cathey
    (1953.1). Reprint of 1961.1.

3   OVERMYER, JANET. "Sex and the Fancy Woman." NConL 4, no. 4
    (September):8-10.
        Because of Taylor's careful portrayal of inconsistencies in
    Josie's character, he avoids presenting a stereotype of a prosti-
    tute, but rather presents a living person aware of her age in
    relation to others. Because she is essentially a passive per-
    sonality, one "easily manipulated," her awareness of the sexual
    colors how she interprets events in the story.

4   SULLIVAN, WALTER. "The Continuing Renascence: Southern Fic-
    tion in the Fifties." In South: Modern Southern Literature
    in Its Cultural Setting. Edited by Louis D. Rubin, Jr. and
    Robert D. Jacobs. Westport, Conn.: Greenwood Press, pp. 385,
    389-91.
        Taylor is listed as one of the young Southern writers,
    along with Shirley Ann Grau, Truman Capote, James Agee, and
    William Styron, who in their writings seem "to depart most pur-
    posefully from the old tradition." His technical skills, crafts-
    manship, and depth of perception, however, distinguish Taylor
    from the other writers of his generation and invite comparisons
    with Frank O'Connor, Chekhov, and Joyce. Taylor should be cred-
    ited as the first Southern writer to discover the Southern city
    as appropriate subject matter for fiction. His interest in con-
    temporary Southern life prompts him to explore social issues, but
    never as ends in themselves. The race question is considered in
    "A Long Fourth," but only as a part of the story's larger con-
    flicts. The recent Southern past is recalled in "A Spinster's
    Tale," but for the purpose of creating the story's frame and
    plot credibility. Sullivan suggests that in "The Guests," a
    terrible triumph is achieved not only by the country cousins over
    the city cousins, but also by each wife over her husband. Re-
    print of 1961.2.

<u>1975</u>

1   ANON. "Peter Taylor." In <u>Contemporary Literary Criticism</u>.
    Vol. 4. Edited by Carolyn Riley. Detroit: Gale Research,
    pp. 542-43.
        Taylor, Peter. "Taylor is an American short-story writer,
    novelist, and playwright. Considered a master of the short story,
    Taylor is usually associated with the so-called Southern Renais-
    sance." Excerpts from the following: Albert Griffith (1970.4),
    <u>Virginia Quarterly Review</u> [Anon] (1971.1), Paul Theroux
    (1973.11), <u>The Antioch Review</u> [Anon] (1973.3), Alfred Kazin
    (1973.9), and B.H. Fussell (1974.1).

2   ANON. "Taylor, Peter (Hillsman)." In <u>Contemporary Authors</u>.
    1st rev. ed. Vols. 13-16. Edited by Clare D. Kinsman.
    Detroit: Gale Research, pp. 794-95.
        Biographical sketch, list of writings, and "sidelights"
    quoted from the following sources: <u>Western Review</u> (1953.1),
    <u>Chicago Sunday Tribune</u> (1959.7), <u>South: Modern Southern Litera-
    ture in its Cultural Setting</u> (1961.1-2; 1974.2, 4), <u>Sewanee
    Review</u> (1962.1-3), <u>Fiction of the Forties</u> (1963.2), <u>New York
    Times Book Review</u> (1964.3), <u>Critique</u> (1967.2, 4-6), <u>Georgia
    Review</u> (1970.8), <u>Peter Taylor</u> (1970.3), <u>Southern Review</u> (1971.3),
    and <u>Contemporary Literary Criticism</u> (1973.2; 1975.1).

3   COWSER, ROBERT G. "Peter Taylor and Trenton." In <u>River
    Region Monographs: Reports on People and Popular Culture</u>.
    Edited by Neil Graves. Martin: University of Tennessee at
    Martin, pp. 17-24.
        Taylor's Trenton, Tennessee background was discussed within
    a National Endowment for the Humanities sponsored discussion
    group which met in Trenton in 1974. Stories set in Trenton,
    Taylor's birthplace, appealed to the group, and various persons
    (including two of Taylor's cousins) thought that "What You Hear
    from 'Em?" used persons from Trenton as a basis for the character
    Aunt Munsie. Similarly, "Their Losses" seems to incorporate
    anecdotes which relate to Mrs. Kitty Clark, a resident of Trenton.
    Taylor's mother who had a gift for story telling must have talked
    of eccentric Trentonians after the family moved to Nashville.

4   MAIOLO, JOSEPH. "<u>Presences: Seven Dramatic Pieces</u>." In
    <u>Masterplots 1974 Annual</u>. Edited by Frank N. Magill. Engle-
    wood Cliffs, N.J.: Salem Press, pp. 324-27.
        Taylor's playwriting is developed here; these stories are
    centered around the "real and imagined" ghostly presences of
    characters. As dramatic pieces, it is remarkable how Taylor
    succeeds, for it is as if he has hit upon something common to
    human experience. In several of the stories, the presence pro-
    vides a focal point for the conflict "that exists, or comes to
    exist" between characters. These pieces are ultimately about the
    confines of family and the fact that the living cannot protect us

from the dead, or the reverse. While there may be some weakness
in Taylor's "typecasting," his work provides an "extended definition of the spiritual world."

5   RUBIN, LOUIS D., Jr. "Southern Literature: A Piedmont Art."
     In William Elliot Shoots a Bear: Essays on the Southern Lit-
     erary Imagination. Baton Rouge: Louisiana State University
     Press, pp. 195-212, esp. 199.
         While not directly treating Taylor's art, the essay pro-
     vides valuable insights into the shift from the Low Country to
     the Up Country. Rubin maintains that all the "really major"
     Southern writers of the 1920s and 1930s "were raised above the
     fall line, and Reynolds Price, Peter Taylor, and Randall Jarrell
     are all inland folk."

6   SULLIVAN, WALTER. Introduction to A Requiem for the Re-
     nascence. Athens: University of Georgia Press, pp. xxii-
     xxiii.
         Assesses Taylor as a writer who seems both "fresh" and
     "anachronistic"; his vision is compared to an old maid aunt
     "endowed with angelic powers of perception." Nevertheless since
     the 1960 publication of "Miss Leonora When Last Seen" Taylor's
     work has "sagged."

1976

1   ANON. "The Short Stories of Peter Taylor." In Masterplots.
     Edited by Frank N. Magill and Dayton Kohler. Rev. ed.
     Englewood Cliffs, N.J.: Salem Press, pp. 6024-26.
         Reprint of 1968.1.

1977

1   ANON. Review of In the Miro District and Other Stories.
     Booklist 73, no. 15 (1 April):1146.
         Taylor creates a "comfortable familiarity," then twists the
     situation to a "startling conclusion." The eight stories differ
     widely: Taylor is an innovative storyteller.

2   ANON. Review of In the Miro District and Other Stories.
     Choice 14, no. 8 (October):1056.
         Favorable review of stories about characters who are
     "lonely," "misunderstood," and "resentful," most of whom find it
     difficult to know why it is better to live than die. Reinforces
     the claim that Taylor is the "finest living writer" of the short
     story.

3   ANON. Review of <u>In the Miro District and Other Stories</u>.
    <u>Kirkus</u> 45, no. 3 (1 February):121.
        Taylor's "virtues are most evident" in "The Throughway,"
    which conveys a "pervasive sense of belonging to a special ambit
    which is slowly losing its lien on the past." Four of the sto-
    ries, "a kind of free verse," are "otherwise conventional."

4   ANON. Review of <u>In the Miro District and Other Stories</u>. <u>PW</u>
    211 (7 February):90.
        "Beautifully put-together" stories; Taylor's stylistic
    mastery allows him to probe corners of the soul and psyche which
    are both "surprising and frightening."

5   BAILEY, PAUL. "Small Is Beautiful." <u>Observer</u> [London],
    2 October, p. 26.
        Peter Taylor, unlike many "over-reachers" on the American
    scene, presents his audience with a "subtle and delicate art"
    that has too often been ignored. "Venus, Cupid, Folly and Time"
    is "one of the indisputable small masterpieces of contemporary
    fiction." <u>In the Miro District</u> is equal to Taylor's art at its
    most assured and resonant. Although he writes about the Tennessee
    of his youth, he does not suffer from the excesses of a Southern
    writer. His prose possesses a "classical elegance" that is both
    "calm and measured and continuously informative." "The Instruc-
    tion of a Mistress," of <u>In the Miro District</u>, manifests a new
    quality in his fiction--"an element of barely controlled dis-
    dain," an element as appropriate as the ironic tone of the title
    story. The "galloping, unforced free verse" of "The Instruction
    of a Mistress" makes it the best story of the collection. In
    addition, Taylor's narrators move "as calmly as ever" from posi-
    tions as "elegist" to that of "sardonic recorder."

6   BEAVER, HAROLD. "The Shadow of the South." <u>TLS</u>, 30 Septem-
    ber, p. 1097.
        Review of <u>In the Miro District and Other Stories</u>. It is
    not difficult to see why Taylor's fame has not matched his criti-
    cal acclaim since his stories are at odds with usual opinion
    about the South. His well-made tales contain "whole worlds of
    tension," and resist the "rhetorical swell" of Southern prose.
    The finest piece is the title story, one not just about one ado-
    lescent, but of an entire society.

7   BOATWRIGHT, JAMES, ed. "A Garland for Peter Taylor on His
    Sixtieth Birthday." <u>Shenandoah</u> 28, no. 2 (Winter):5-85.
        This issue of <u>Shenandoah</u> is dedicated to Peter Taylor on
    his sixtieth birthday. The garland is composed of some seventeen
    pieces--poems, critical essays, reminiscences--paying tribute to
    Taylor as writer, teacher, delightful friend and companion. The
    contributors include: Robert Lowell (1977.25), Robert Penn
    Warren (1977.38), Allen Tate (1977.33), Andrew Lytle (1977.26),
    John Thompson (1977.34), Richard Howard (1977.21), Brainard

Cheney (1977.11), Mary Jarrell (1977.22), David McDowell
(1977.27), Herschel Gower (1977.18), Ashley Brown (1977.8),
Stephen Goodwin (1977.16), Thomas Molyneux (1977.28), Albert J.
Griffith (1977.19), John Casey (1977.10), Robert Wilson (1977.39),
and J.F. Powers (1977.31).

8   BROWN, ASHLEY. "Peter Taylor at Sixty." Shenandoah 28, no. 2
     (Winter):48-53.
         This essay, written as a tribute to Taylor on his sixtieth
birthday, succinctly reviews his career as dramatist, short-story
writer, and creator of verse narratives. The central theme of all
Taylor's work is "the slow dissolution of the family." As a play,
A Stand in the Mountains reads beautifully and confirms Taylor's
reputation as "our Southern Chekhov." In Presences, a collection
of short plays, Taylor approaches the Noh "in which the super-
natural permeates the naturalistic." However, Taylor's latest
short story, "In the Miro District," returns to the Nashville
scene. The verse narratives in Ploughshares, though written in
irregular blank verse, are really stories with a narrator at the
center. "The Megalopolitans" in this collection "is the most
powerful thing Taylor has written."

9   BROYARD, ANATOLE. Review of In the Miro District and Other
     Stories. NYTBR, 3 April, p. 14.
         Comparing Taylor's "The Captain's Son" to the "Southern
syndrome" of writing which produces characters lacking personali-
ties and having only traditions, the reviewer asserts that Taylor
offers "sentimental generalities in the place of individual
anguish." While the title story "succeeds," Taylor seems not to
have noticed that current fiction "has seen fit to complicate
itself."

10   CASEY, JOHN. "Peter Taylor as Merlin and Mr. O'Malley."
     Shenandoah 28, no. 2 (Winter):71-79.
         Tribute to the master on his sixtieth birthday from a
former law student at Harvard, transformed into writer by the
magic of Taylor's presence and influence. The article reveals
Taylor's talents as a writing teacher and his unflagging commitment to his students and their work. Unlike Jean Stafford and
John Updike, he has not spurned the role of teacher, but has com-
bined it successfully with his life as a writer.

11   CHENEY, BRAINARD. "Peter's Nashville Producer & a Southern
     Senator from Maine." Shenandoah 28, no. 2 (Winter):24-27.
         Account by a long-time family friend of the fiasco result-
ing from his efforts to produce Tennessee Day in Saint Louis before a Nashville audience on March 3, 1958. Against the good
advice of Andrew Lytle, the old Southern Senator is woefully mis-
cast, and disaster ensues. Cheney notes that The Early Guest and
A Stand in the Mountains have been successfully produced, and he

compliments Taylor's talents as a playwright, especially as evidenced in Presences.

12 CUSHMAN, KEITH. Review of In the Miro District and Other
    Stories. SSF 14, no. 4 (Fall):420-21.
        The volume is "decidedly uneven," and four of the stories
    are not exactly stories. However, the longer ones are valuable
    and especially the title story, "high-spirited, moving, rich in
    human understanding," is Taylor's usual high level of achievement.

13 DEEMER, CHARLES. Review of In the Miro District and Other
    Stories. NL 60, no. 12 (20 June):19-20.
        Critical reception of In the Miro District has varied
    widely, yet examination of these stories reveals a skilled
    craftsman's work. Taylor demonstrates that he can produce stories with a variety of narrative strategies. One technique is
    his proven method of the suggestion of an oral story-teller;
    another technique uses prose-poetry to produce formality. Taylor
    always writes in his own voice without regard for current
    fashions.

14 DURRANT, DIGBY. "Cruel and Comic." London Magazine 17, no. 5
    (November):92-96.
        Review of In the Miro District and Other Stories. Taylor's
    "wonderfully written and absorbing" stories are full of the kinds
    of actions he admires within the rich "provincial family life" of
    Middle Tennessee. While much of what he sees is "cruel, decadent, and violent," his gaze is affectionate and unjudging.

15 EDWARDS, PAGE. Review of In the Miro District and Other Stories. LJ 102, no. 7 (1 April):836.
        "Thoroughly delightful and solid collection." The "prose
    poems" possess a "quiet textured flow."

16 GOODWIN, STEPHEN. "Like Nothing Else in Tennessee."
    Shenandoah 28, no. 2 (Winter):53-58.
        Tribute to Taylor on his sixtieth birthday by a former
    student in his creative writing class at the University of
    Virginia. The essay reveals Taylor's devotion to his native
    state of Tennessee and its continuing influence on him. Most
    importantly, Taylor is presented as an inspiring teacher, marked
    by a personal generosity expressed in and out of the classroom.

17 GOODWIN, STEVE. Review of In the Miro District and Other
    Stories. NewR 176 (7 May):33-34.
        These stories are not repetitions of Peter Taylor's former
    work, but are "varied and innovative, even rebellious," although
    the author seeks to preserve, even in this collection, the vanishing Tennessee of his past. "For Taylor the story is itself a
    way of knowing, of shaping knowledge; though it cannot restore

the past . . . , it nevertheless reconciles us to that vanished
world and to the present. . . ." Unlike much new fiction written
under the influence of Borges, Taylor's stories are not atemporal
but rather are obsessed with time.

18 GOWER, HERSCHEL. "The Nashville Stories." Shenandoah 28,
      no. 2 (Winter):37-47.
      "Who, then, are Taylor's people--characters--individuals--
the blood and flesh of the stories?" Gower suggests they are a
good deal like Taylor's own family. Having recently moved from
plantation, farm, small Southern town, they attempt to bring
their formal eighteenth-century manners with them. This attempt
to transplant agrarian attitudes and mores in an urban environment results inevitably in conflict. These conflicts are relatively mild, however, and unlike the characters John Updike,
Philip Roth, and Walker Percy create, "Taylor's Nashvillians are
human beings who elicit compassion from us but do not strike us
with terror." If one objects that Taylor's vision is too narrow,
limited only to the ironic depiction of this new urban upper-
middle class, Chekhov and Turgenev could be subjected to the same
criticism. What is the fate of this recently urbanized class of
Southerners who still retain "Happy Valley" as the wellspring of
their values and manners? Will their descendants, discarding
their inherited agrarian ways, be assimilated entirely into the
life of the Super-City? Although his characters do not speculate
about the future, Taylor may have "recorded a fragile company
just in the nick of time."

19 GRIFFITH, ALBERT J. "Presences, Absences, and Peter Taylor's
      Plays." Shenandoah 28, no. 2 (Winter):62-71.
      Written as a tribute to Taylor on his sixtieth birthday,
Griffith's essay examines the seven one-act plays in Presences
(1973), which were not available for his full-length study in
1970. Griffith finds Taylor "sufficient" as a playwright, but a
finer artist in fiction. Much can be learned about the fiction,
however, by examining the drama. Many of Taylor's recurring fictional themes reappear in the plays: the individual in conflict
with his family and/or society, the continuing influence of the
past on the present, and the complex, ambivalent nature of family
life which both nurtures and suppresses. Conspicuously absent in
the plays are those fictional devices so often associated with a
Taylor story: central-consciousness point of view, the
digressive-progressive narrative development, and the textual
richness, especially in regard to place and character. One
Jamesian influence far more discernible in the plays is Taylor's
tendency to allow his dramatic characters to become manipulated
abstractions in a formula-like pattern.

20   GRUMBACH, DORIS. Review of In the Miro District and Other
      Stories. Los Angeles Times, 24 April, p. 14.
            Of the eight stories, four are masterpieces: "In the Miro
      District"; "The Hand of Emmagene"; "The Captain's Son"; and "The
      Throughway." Each is discussed and analyzed briefly as the work
      of a Southern writer. The first-person narrator's irritation at
      the influence of the past on the present is reminiscent of
      Katherine Anne Porter's Miranda. Because Taylor has truths to
      tell us about our human condition, his is "a voice worth strain-
      ing to hear."

21   HOWARD, RICHARD. "A Letter from the Sorcerer's Apprentice."
      Shenandoah 28, no. 2 (Winter):23-24.
            A poem in which the poet acknowledges Taylor as his liter-
      ary master and mentor. He admonishes Taylor to return to the
      prose medium for his stories and to turn away from the verse
      stanza of "the four tales," presumably "The Instruction of a
      Mistress"; "The Hand of Emmagene"; "Her Need"; and "Three
      Heroines"--recently published in In the Miro District.

22   JARRELL, MARY. "Peter and Randall." Shenandoah 28, no. 2
      (Winter):28-34.
            Mary Jarrell "recaptures" the period of the friendship be-
      tween her husband, the poet, Randall Jarrell, and the fiction
      writer, Peter Taylor. It was a friendship based more on differ-
      ences than similarities, as both men differed widely in personali-
      ties, temperaments, tastes, and interests. Summer vacations, in-
      cluding both families, at Buonassola, Monteagle, and Antioch are
      warmly and vividly evoked. Though friendship, like love, must
      forever remain a mystery, Mrs. Jarrell speculates that her hus-
      band's and Taylor's mutual interest in literature; the fact that
      one wrote poetry, the other fiction; "the temperature of their
      friendship," which guaranteed "nobody was ever a pest and nobody
      made a scene"--all contributed to the rather long relationship.
      A blessed time when "two people saw the best and not the worst in
      each other."

23   KUEHL, LINDA. Review of In the Miro District and Other Sto-
      ries. SatR 4 (14 May):35.
            Taylor is the greatest writer of stories in English. He
      creates "compressed novels" rather than short stories. The new
      volume contains work "distilled through a style that is transpar-
      ent yet opaque." His craft provides work "in delicate balance"
      with both strong authority and "transforming grace."

24   LONGLEY, EDNA. "Crocheted Castle." New Review 4, no. 43
      (October):59-60.
            Review of In the Miro District and Other Stories. Although
      Peter Taylor's credentials as a short story writer are acclaimed,
      he is not Chekhov. His narrators assume many roles, but they
      never develop beyond "rather unvarying and uninteresting

persona[e]." The free-verse form of four of the stories reflects
more outline than "poetic flesh." The outline is an integral
part of a Taylor short story. Predictable irony, paradox, or
simple conflict are elements upon which Taylor builds. Despite
his weaknesses, Taylor brings an innate and "cumulative power" to
this collection.

25   LOWELL, ROBERT. "Our Afterlife." Shenandoah 28, no. 2
      (Winter):5-7.
          Tribute in verse to Peter Taylor on his sixtieth birthday
      from his Kenyon classmate and longtime friend. The poem cele-
      brates a shared literary life and an enduring friendship. ("Our
      loyalty to one another sticks like love. . . .") The last stanza
      of the poem is prophetic in predicting the poet's imminent death.

26   LYTLE, ANDREW. "On a Birthday." Shenandoah 28, no. 2
      (Winter):11-17.
          Andrew Lytle, lifetime friend and mentor of Taylor's,
      evaluates his fellow Tennessean as "one of the best short story
      writers in English. . . ." Tracing a source of Taylor's art to
      his family background in Tennessee politics, Lytle half-facetiously
      suggests that Taylor's "purity of style" is a reaction to his
      grandfather's florid oratory. He sees, however, a clear thematic
      relation: Bob Taylor's hopeful message to Reconstruction Era
      Tennesseans that the family might yet be restored; this failing,
      Peter Taylor's fictional depiction of the family's subversion,
      following the emigration from community to city. Though Taylor's
      stories are saturated with Tennessee manners and mores, they
      transcend their locale by their universal themes, the two most
      prominent being human betrayal in all its manifestations and
      the capacity to perpetrate the most heinous crimes against our
      fellow man. In his examination of "Whistler"; "The Throughway";
      "The Hand of Emmagene"; and "The Captain's Son," Lytle finds
      Taylor's pervasive irony Christian, as the author's charity
      towards even his most monstrous characters contains "the quality
      of grace," while avoiding a false or easy compassion.

27   McDOWELL, DAVID. "The Year without Peter." Shenandoah 28,
      no. 2 (Winter):34-36.
          Taylor's classmate, friend, and future editor/publisher de-
      scribes the events leading to Ransom's leaving Vanderbilt in
      August, 1937, for Kenyon College, accompanied by his students,
      Robert Lowell, Randall Jarrell, and McDowell. In deference to
      his father's wishes, Taylor returns to his home in Memphis, not
      joining his illustrious teacher and classmates for a year.
      McDowell has produced an informative memoir, written with warmth,
      humor, and affection for the occasion of Taylor's sixtieth
      birthday.

28   MOLYNEUX, THOMAS. "Peter." Shenandoah 28, no. 2 (Winter):
     59-61.
          Taylor's enormous charm and abundant social grace were in
     special evidence during an evening spent with Jean Stafford. His
     addiction to story telling is frequently observed in his social
     life as well. His refusal to desert the short story for the
     essay, review, or memoir is revealed in his response to Harper's
     request for a piece of nonfiction: "I told them life was too
     short for that."

29   PHILLIPS, ROBERT. Review of In the Miro District and Other
     Stories. Commonweal 104 (19 August):540-41.
          Greets this addition to Collected Stories that "takes
     risks" and "succeeds often." Cites major content areas: family
     relationships, home as microcosm, marriage as catalyst. Consid-
     ers stories set typographically as poems the least successful of
     the volume.

30   PINKERTON, JAN. "The Vagaries of Taste and Peter Taylor's 'A
     Spinster's Tale.'" KanQ 9, no. 2 (Spring):81-85.
          Taylor's story has not received much critical attention
     perhaps because the subject matter of frigidity is old-fashioned,
     and that fact constitutes an objection which critics are not
     likely to admit. Yet if critics wanted to establish Taylor as a
     writer of the first rank still other elements could be emphasized.
     The story might be analyzed as the "case history of a spinster";
     the heroine's story may even coincide with a shift from female
     fear of the male to male fear of the female.

31   POWERS, J.F. "Peter Taylor's New Book." Shenandoah 28, no. 2
     (Winter):84-85.
          Tribute to Taylor on his sixtieth birthday and to his
     recently published book, In the Miro District. Taylor possesses,
     with Fitzgerald, the genius for recreating the period and loca-
     tion he wishes to evoke. Only "The Instruction of a Mistress"
     fails to strike the right tone, and this may be because it is not
     set on native soil. Taylor's stories combine "a mixture of
     gravity and comedy that gets about as close as a writer can to
     life without spoiling it."

32   ROBINSON, CLAYTON. "A Tennessee Boy in St. Louis: A Note on
     Peter Taylor's A Woman of Means." Interpretations 9, no. 1:
     74-78.
          Often criticism focuses upon the "woman of means," yet if
     one assumes that Taylor's choice of narrator was carefully
     planned, the novel can be studied as reflection of a larger pat-
     tern in his work: "the countryman's attachment to place . . .
     set against the rootlessness of urban life." Quint's love of
     Tennessee, and his attractiveness to his stepmother grow out of
     associations with his rural world. Hemingway, Anderson, and

Twain use similar boy observers. Seen this way, the novel is the story of someone who carries with him the influence of his country background.

33 TATE, ALLEN. "Peter Taylor." Shenandoah 28, no. 2 (Winter):
    10.
        A brief tribute to Taylor on his sixtieth birthday from his first college English teacher at Southwestern in Memphis. Taylor was already too precocious at the age of eighteen to learn anything about poetry from his professor, but Tate did have the distinction of introducing "our Southern Chekhov" to his wife-to-be, Eleanor Ross, a gifted poet in her own right.

34 THOMPSON, JOHN. "A Man's Estate, by P-t-r T-yl-r."
    Shenandoah 28, no. 2 (Winter):17-22.
        A humorous assault on Taylor's Agrarian principles and his well-known real estate activities by a fellow classmate of the Kenyon class of 1940. Although this essay can be appreciated somewhat by the uninitiated, it is intended primarily for the inner circle, who can fathom the oblique references and private jokes.

35 TREGLOWN, JEREMY. Review of In the Miro District and Other
    Stories. New Statesman 94 (23 September):418.
        Brief mention: the best of these stories are "about rich adolescents in prohibition Tennessee." Some pieces are "mysteriously printed as if they were blank verse," yet even if they are sometimes overwritten they are "deft in their psychology," and factually interesting because of particulars of time and place.

36 TYLER, ANNE. "Farewell to the Story as Imperiled Species."
    National Observer, 9 May, p. 23.
        Review of six collections of short stories, including Taylor's In the Miro District. "For really classical short stories--tightly structured, finely controlled, with a pure clear tone--no one can surpass Peter Taylor." After completing Taylor's "elegant, jewel-like stories," the reader can be assured that the short story as a form is alive and well.

37 _____. Review of In the Miro District and Other Stories. BW,
    4 December, p. E3.
        Anne Tyler briefly reviews several 1977 novels. In the Miro District might be called "'Southern'" because of a sense of place, history, and its graceful manners, but beyond this "Taylor is a superb craftsman," whose stories are complete, fully rounded, and nourishing.

38   WARREN, ROBERT PENN. "Two Peters: Memory and Opinion."
      Shenandoah 28, no. 2 (Winter):8-10.
         A tribute to Taylor on his sixtieth birthday from his
      former graduate professor at L.S.U. and one of his early editors
      (in The Southern Review), Warren warmly remembers Taylor as a
      diligent student and a charming fellow. His opinion of him as an
      artist is that Taylor should be included with "the few writers of
      our century who have captured a true and original world in the
      story form. . . ."

39   WILSON, ROBERT. "A Sixty-Year-Old Smiling Public Man."
      Shenandoah 28, no. 2 (Winter):80-84.
         A former creative writing student at the University of
      Virginia and assistant-editor of Shenandoah pays homage to his
      teacher on his sixtieth birthday. Taylor's courteous manner, his
      generous encouragement, and his penetrating critical insights en-
      dear him to his classes. Outside the classroom, he is remembered
      for his host of friends, his love of cocktail parties and good
      conversation. Despite a heart problem, Taylor is a man of great
      physical energy, who appears to be aging both gracefully and
      comfortably.

40   YARDLEY, JONATHAN. "Discovering an American Master." BW,
      10 April, p. E7.
         Review of In the Miro District and Other Stories. Although
      a writer of the first rank, he is unknown by the general reader
      because he has been willing to publish in journals with small
      circulations. "The Captain's Son" reveals a story of compassion
      and fullness of detail unequalled by most other writers. This
      and other stories of marriage reveal "what is happening inside
      that most intimate of human arrangements," and these revelations
      are seldom fully known by the participants themselves. In all
      human relationships he watches his characters "struggle against
      entrapment and . . . observes the accommodations they make. . . ."
      In a time when much of our fiction is self-consciously relevant,
      his fiction "comes to us durable, rooted and solid."

                                    1978

1   ANON. Review of In the Miro District and Other Stories.
     Listener 98, no. 2537 (1 December):734.
        Brief mention: Taylor's stories are effective because they
     demonstrate more restraint than one might expect from "Faulkner's
     literary descendants." Taylor does not exaggerate eccentricities
     even when he brings his characters to moments of confrontation.

2   CASEY, JANE BARNES. "A View of Peter Taylor's Stories." <u>VQR</u>
     54, no. 2 (Spring):213-20.
     The tension created by the opposing forces of order and
disorder in human affairs has preoccupied Taylor from the beginning of his career. His real theme from his earliest volume to
his most recent, <u>In the Miro District</u>, has been "the great modern
problem of how to incorporate the most vital, but also the most
archaic urges into civilized life." These urges, originating in
man's sexuality, are opposed as destructive forces in "A Spinster's Tale" and "A Long Fourth." Later stories such as "At the
Drug Store," recognize the dynamic power of man's erotic, anti-
social drives, but end with their repression for the sake of
family life. Only in the stories of his last volume ("Daphne's
Lover" and "In the Miro District") does Taylor discover the
proper counterbalance to these dark impulses. The delicate
equilibrium is effected not by social restraints but by each
individual's unique "built-in restrictions," which exert their
own pressures on behavior.

3   GARRETT, GEORGE. "Coming Out of Left Field: The Short Story
     Today." <u>SR</u> 86, no. 3 (Summer):461-73.
     Essay-review of <u>In the Miro District</u> in which the general
atmosphere attendant to the production of serious short stories
is discussed: quality of recent writing is high, and Taylor's
<u>In the Miro</u> "seems . . . to be his most adventurous and exciting
work in many years." Taylor's work is "daring" because all
things work "to make a writer repeat successes." Taylor's ex-
periments in drama, teaching, and interchange with younger writers seem to support this new collection.

4   PEREZ, GILBERTO. "Narrative Voices." <u>HudR</u> 30, no. 4
     (Winter):612-13.
     <u>In the Miro District and Other Stories</u> briefly discussed
within essay-review. While approving of the irony in the title
story, objections are raised about other stories and the new
"verse prose" which seems inappropriate to a story such as
Emmagene's; however, elsewhere, such as in "The Captain's Son,"
Taylor remains an "able writer" and "master craftsman."

5   SIMS, BARBARA B. "Symbol and Theme in Peter Taylor's 'A Wife
     of Nashville.'" <u>Notes on Modern American Literature</u> 2, no. 3
     (Summer):Item 22.
     The automobile and Helen Ruth's inability to drive; her
maid, Jesse McGehee's teaching the sons of the family how to
drive; and the fact that automobile driving was considered below
the dignity of a "lady" are themes that combine to reenforce the
loneliness and isolation of Helen Ruth, who is relegated to a
nonproductive role in her society.

6   WILLIAMSON, ALAN. "Identity and the Wider Eros: A Reading
     of Peter Taylor's Stories." Shenandoah 30, no. 1 (Fall):
     71-84.
          As a tragicomic writer, Peter Taylor has had a great deal
     to say in his fiction about an emotional phenomenon, earlier
     labeled by Freud as "the wider eros," which often poses a threat
     to the individual identity. As a force of social cohesion, the
     wider eros frequently encounters those opposing forces of the
     individual psyche--jealousies and taboos, for example--which
     impede its expansion. The conflict which results illustrates
     that as hard as it is for people to control their aggressions and
     hatreds, "it is almost as difficult and frightening . . . to man-
     ifest the breadth and depth of their loves." Rather than stress
     class, location, or changing customs, Williamson chooses those
     stories "in which some person, or, more commonly, some feeling or
     human potentiality, is excluded or killed in the dangers ensuing
     from the wider extensions of love": "Dean of Men"; "Venus,
     Cupid, Folly and Time"; and "Daphne's Lover." Those stories are
     also discussed which "adumbrate oneness or transcendent love" as
     a response to the operations of the wider eros: "1939"; "Three
     Heroines"; and "Knowing."

7   WOOD, SUSAN, and WILSON, ROBERT. "Charlottesville's Five--
     Writers on the Ridge of Fame." WP, 7 May, "Style" sec.,
     p. H-1, passim.
          Feature story on five Charlottesville, Virginia, writers:
     Peter Taylor, James Alan McPherson, Douglas Day, John Casey, and
     Mary Lee Settle. In response to the often asked question as to
     how he accepts his lack of broad public recognition, Taylor com-
     ments that he has had no interest in personal fame or fortune and
     that many other interests--"teaching, farming, traveling . . .
     and 'keeping a hand in real estate'"--occupy his time. When
     asked about his interest in writing a novel, he indicates his
     preference for the "'tightness and drama'" of the short story,
     although he suggests that his long play, A Stand in the Mountains,
     may become a novel. Taylor is seen as the product of his own
     Southern upper-middle-class background, and his knowledge of
     Nashville family life in the 1920s and 30s as the wellspring of
     many of his finest stories.

                              1979

1   BINDING, PAUL. Separate Country: A Literary Journey Through
     the American South. New York: Paddington Press, pp. 33, 84,
     113-21, 156, 200, 204, 209, 213.
          Essay based upon an interview with Taylor at the University
     of Virginia. Recounts in some detail Taylor's association with
     Tennessee and the facts of his literary and family background.
     Taylor is described as being "in a nonpejorative sense a gossip."
     Gossip can be considered creative when it is used by the artist

to learn about humans and the communities in which they exist.
In his creative use of gossip, Taylor is like his contemporary
English colleagues, Anthony Powell, Angus Wilson, Barbara Pym,
and Kingsley Amis, who have found English society, like the society in the American South, still cohesive enough for artistic
exploration. Several of Taylor's stories are discussed briefly,
and Taylor's account of the historical basis of "The Hand of
Emmagene" is presented. Binding quotes Thomas Daniel Young of
Vanderbilt as describing "In the Miro District" as one of the
most significant pieces of Southern fiction in the last decade.
It is a story concerned not only with a conflict in sexual codes,
but with the deeper cultural conflict between the liberal element
in Southern society and "a certain hardness and narrowness in the
ways of the Old South."

2   BLOOM, LYNN Z. "Peter Hillsman Taylor." In Southern Writers:
     A Biographical Dictionary. Edited by Robert Bain; Joseph M.
     Flora; and Louis D. Rubin, Jr. Baton Rouge and London:
     Louisiana State University Press, pp. 448-50.
        Basic information about life, education, and teaching
     career. Robert Penn Warren's views which introduced A Long
     Fourth, "became the prototype for the dimensions and tone of much
     subsequent criticism." Critical commentary about the plays indi-
     cates reservations. Works are listed through 1977.

3   BRAUDY, LEO. "Realists, Naturalists, and Novelists of Man-
     ners." In Harvard Guide to Contemporary American Writing.
     Edited by Daniel Hoffman. Cambridge, Mass.: Harvard Univer-
     sity Press, p. 128.
        Taylor cited, along with Anne Tyler, Ann Beattie, Santha
     Rama Rau, and Sylvia Townsend Warner, as an example of the New
     Yorker's commitment in the 1970s to publish short fiction by
     regional and even foreign authors. This search for quality fic-
     tion by regional and foreign writers "provides an emblem of the
     gradual decentralizing of American culture that characterizes the
     post-Vietnam period."

4   DULA, LUCILE N. The Pelican Guide to Hillsborough: Historic
     Orange County, North Carolina. Gretna, La.: Pelican Publish-
     ing Co., p. 63.
        Peter Taylor's former home in Hillsborough, North Carolina,
     located at 157 East King Street, and now called "Seven Hearths,"
     is pictured here.

5   HALIO, JAY L. "Persons Placed and Displaced." SoR 15, no. 1
     (Winter):250-56.
        Review of In the Miro District and Other Stories includes
     some of his best work and several "highly successful examples of
     a new technique." Taylor's work transcends region, while he pro-
     vides a real sense of place and persons. His new "colloquial

free verse" proves to be an ideal instrument for getting to the
heart of a situation or character.

6   SCOTT, NATHAN A., Jr. "Black Literature." In Harvard Guide
     to Contemporary American Writing. Edited by Daniel Hoffman.
     Cambridge, Mass.: Harvard University Press, p. 287.
          Taylor is listed, along with Katherine Anne Porter, Robert
     Penn Warren, Eudora Welty, Flannery O'Connor, and William Styron,
     as one of the great literary talents to appear in the South after
     1945, whose recognition was hastened by "the towering genius" of
     Faulkner and the interest regenerated in Southern fiction.

7   SIMPSON, LEWIS P. "Southern Fiction." In Harvard Guide to
     Contemporary American Writing. Edited by Daniel Hoffman.
     Cambridge, Mass.: Harvard University Press, p. 186.
          Although Taylor's range is narrow, limited primarily to the
     upper-middle-class families of the urban South, he proves in The
     Collected Stories that he is unsurpassed "in portraying the crit-
     ical moment when an ordinary person has an inner revelation of
     the fallibility of social order. . . ."

8   STAFFORD, JEAN. "Some Letters to Peter and Eleanor Taylor."
     Shenandoah 30, no. 3 (Spring):27-55.
          A dozen letters from Jean Stafford to Peter, and sometimes
     Eleanor, Taylor, which span the years June 1940, to 28 September
     1943. The letters are written from Baton Rouge, Louisiana; New
     York City; Monteagle, Tennessee; Yaddo, New York; and Damariscotta
     Rills, Maine. The letters are filled with personal matters and
     everyday events but do, on occasion, include literary gossip.
     The binding thread between the letters is Stafford's growing con-
     cern about her husband, Robert Lowell, and his status as conscien-
     tious objector. From the letters, Stafford emerges as a loving,
     devoted wife, and Taylor as a loyal, committed friend. Despite
     the fact that Stafford and Taylor are both short-story writers,
     there is little literary talk or theory included. There is an
     interesting comment by Stafford in the last correspondence: "I
     was delighted, also, that you want to write an autobiography,
     because the same thing occurred to me not long ago." Following
     the letters, is "A Commemorative Tribute to Jean Stafford," given
     by Peter Taylor, on 13 November 1979, at the National Academy and
     Institute of Arts and Letters, New York City. See 1979.9.

9   TAYLOR, PETER H. "A Commemorative Tribute to Jean Stafford."
     Shenandoah 30, no. 3 (Spring):56-60.
          This tribute to Jean Stafford, who died 26 March 1979, was
     originally delivered on 13 November 1979, before the National
     Academy and Institute of Arts and Letters, New York City. In his
     tribute, reprinted as part of a memorial issue of Shenandoah mag-
     azine, Taylor contrasts the private Stafford, who avoided teach-
     ing, lecturing, and reviewing as invasions of her privacy, with
     the public Stafford, the artist who sent her works out into the

world to be judged on their own merits. Despite, or because of, her personal need for privacy, "the public life of her literary work" was enormously successful, culminating in the Pulitzer Prize for Fiction in 1970. See also 1979.8.

10   YARDLEY, JONATHAN. "The State of American Fiction."
        <u>Commonweal</u> 106, no. 9 (11 May):265.
            Review of <u>The Collected Stories</u>. Within a discussion of current American fiction and its relationship to family, Taylor's work is compared to other major writers. John Cheever, John Irving, and Eudora Welty have been widely read, yet "a good case can be made that Taylor is the greatest living American writer of the short story." His stories "are simply unmatched."

<u>1980</u>

1   ANON. "4 Current Paperback Fiction Books Reviewed." <u>BW</u>,
        6 July, p. 8.
            Review of <u>The Collected Stories</u>. A traditional story-teller often compared to Chekhov, many of Taylor's stories derive from his listening to tales as a boy, or directly relate to personal experiences. For example, "1939," records a train journey that Taylor and Robert Lowell made to New York to visit their girlfriends, in Lowell's case, his future wife, Jean Stafford. <u>Collected Stories</u> is "a splendid introduction to a fine writer."

2   RICHMAN, ROBERT. Review of <u>The Collected Stories</u>. <u>Village</u>
        <u>Voice</u>, 28 April, p. 42.
            This volume, while eleven years old, should appeal to readers who have lately come to Taylor's work, for these stories bear a significant resemblance to his more recent fiction. "Dean of Men"; "The Other Times"; and "1939" are discussed as examples of how Taylor treats the past. These "stories seem refutations of the notion that moral ardor must inform good fiction, but they raise the question anyway." Taylor's "sober prose" also is successful in suggesting nuances of racism: in "Cookie" he reveals truth, but also a disturbing conformity to conventional attitudes.

Master's Theses on Peter Taylor

HOLBROOK, NANCY LU NICHOLS. "Violence and Order in the Short Stories of Eudora Welty, Flannery O'Connor, and Peter Taylor." Vanderbilt University, 1961.

BRANTLEY, JULIA A.R. "The Past in the Present: A Major Theme in Six Short Stories of Peter Taylor." Vanderbilt University, 1965.

WOOD, GERALD E. "Major and Minor Themes in the Works of Peter Taylor." Vanderbilt University, 1965.

McMASTERS, SUSAN. "'This petted Sward': Peter Taylor's Agrarian Characters." Winthrop College, 1973.

Indexes

Andrew Lytle

Wade, John Donald, 1968.3;
    1980.2
<u>Wake for the Living: A Family
    Chronicle, A</u>, 1973.4;
    1975.1-8, 9-10, 12-13;
    1976.2-3; 1977.1-3
"Walls of Mortality, The," 1970.9
Ward, C.A., 1958.14
Warfel, Harry R., 1951.1
Warren, Robert Penn, 1935.1;
    1969.3; 1971.6-7; 1974.7;
    1978.1
Watson, Sterling, 1973.9
Weatherby, H.L., 1970.11; 1976.3
Weaver, Richard M., 1963.8
Welty, Eudora, 1958.4
Weston, Robert, 1970.12; 1972.13;
    1978.3
Wharton, Don, 1931.7
"Whole and the Parts: Initiation
    in 'The Mahogany Frame,'
    The," 1970.7
Wilson, Edmund, 1947.8
Wimsatt, Mary Ann, 1980.8
Wolfe, Thomas, 1957.4
"Word Made Flesh: Andrew Lytle's
    <u>The Velvet Horn</u>, The,"
    1968.9
"Working Novelist and the Myth-
    making Process, The," 1971.4
Wright, Scott, 1975.12
<u>Writer in the South, The</u>, 1972.11
Wyeth, John A., 1960.8

"Yankees of the Race: The
    Decline and Fall of Hernando
    de Soto," 1973.2
Young, Thomas D., 1971.3; 1974.3;
    1975.13; 1980.9
Yu, Frederick Yeh-Wei, 1972.14

Walker Percy

Abádi-Nagy, Zoltán, 1973.1

"Absurd Insurrection: The Barth-Percy Affair," 1969.1

"Adam in Extremis: Die Romane Walker Percys," 1973.19

"Additions to the Galaxy," 1967.15

Aesthetics, 1977.44

"Afternoon with Walker Percy, An," 1971.15

"After the Faulkner," 1972.9

"Afterword: Wonder and Alienation--The Mystic and The Moviegoer," 1965.2

Alienation (theme in Percy), 1966.11; 1967.1, 4; 1968.6, 9; 1972.13; 1973.19; 1975.34; 1976.3, 28; 1977.10, 47; 1980.43

"Alienation on the American Plan," 1968.9

All the King's Men, 1971.44

Alterman, Peter Steven, 1974.1

Alvarez, A., 1973.8

"America, America," 1966.18

"Americanness of The Moviegoer, The," 1979.32

"American Novel, A Survey of 1966, The," 1967.11

American Romance, An, 1977.27

"American Romances: Fiction Chronicle," 1977.27

Amis, Kingsley, 1966.22

Anderson, David C., 1971.1

"Angels and Beasts: Gnosticism in American Literature," 1976.4

Answer from Limbo, An, 1963.1

Anti-Death League, The, 1966.22

"Apocalypses and Other Ills," 1971.13

Appleyard, J.A., 1976.2

Arrington, Robert L., 1976.3

"Art as Symbolic Action: Walker Percy's Aesthetic," 1980.43

Arthurian Legend, 1977.37

Art of Walker Percy, The, 1979.4

Atchity, Kenneth John, 1980.5

Atkins, Anselm, 1968.1; 1971.11

Atlas, James, 1980.6

Auer, Michael J., 1976.4

"Author-as-God View Flaws Second Coming," 1980.11

"Authors that Bloom in the Spring," 1971.37

Avant, John Alfred, 1971.12

"Bad Catholic Stars in Crazy Plot," 1971.36

Baker, J.F., 1977.8

Baldwin, James, 1967.7

Balliett, Whitney, 1980.7

Barnes, Julian, 1977.9

Barthelme, Donald, 1976.23

Barth, John, 1969.1; 1975.7, 12

Barthes, 1976.9, 19

"Basking in the Eye of the Storm: The Esthetics of Loss in Walker Percy's The Moviegoer," 1975.27

Batchelor, John Calvin, 1980.8

Bates, Marvin Randolph, 1978.3

Bates, Randolph, 1980.9

Becker, Tom, 1978.4

"For a 'Hostile Audience': A
    Study of the Fiction of
    Flannery O'Connor, Walker
    Percy, and J.F. Powers,"
    1975.19
Ford, Richard, 1977.23
Fox, William Henry, 1979.8
"Freedom, Fate, Myth, and Other
    Theological Issues in
    Contemporary Literature,"
    1971.11
Freisinger, Randall R., 1975.12
Fremont-Smith, Eliot, 1980.22
French novel (influence upon),
    1967.4; 1968.12
French, Philip, 1977.24
Friedman, Bruce Jay, 1975.12
"From Malasian to Saint: A Study
    of Walker Percy," 1973.13
"From Moviegoing to Moviemaking:
    Rhetorical Progression in the
    Walker Percy Fictive Pro-
    tagonist," 1980.47
"From Mr. Percy, a Temptation
    Play for Folk-Rock Age,"
    1966.15
"From Physician to Novelist:
    The Progression of Walker
    Percy," 1977.54
"From the Delta . . . ," 1968.11
"From the Realistic to the
    Fantastic: Walker Percy's
    Expanding Vision," 1978.17
Frye, Northrop, 1971.11
"Fugitive Group, The," 1973.7
Fuller, Edmund, 1975.13; 1977.25;
    1980.23

Gallo, Louis Jacob, 1973.13
Gann, Daniel H., 1980.58
Gardiner, Harold C., 1961.8
Gardner, John, 1977.26; 1978.1,
    14
Garvey, John, 1975.14
Gass, William, 1975.21; 1976.23
Gaston, Paul L., 1972.8; 1974.6;
    1976.12
Gates of the Forest, The, 1966.37
"Gentleman and Fornicators: The
    Last Gentleman and a Bisected
    Reality," 1979.6

"Gentleman Without a Past,"
    1966.29
Gilder, Joshua, 1980.24
Glassman, Peter, 1977.27
Gnosticism, 1976.4; 1977.12;
    1978.22; 1979.33
"Gnostic Vision in Lancelot,
    The," 1978.22
"God and Man in Louisiana,"
    1977.46
Godshalk, William L., 1974.7;
    1979.9
Golding, William, 1974.1
"Good and the True, The," 1966.16
Goodman, Walter, 1966.19
Goodwin, Stephen, 1972.9
"Good Word: Walker Percy
    Redivivus, The," 1971.43
Gordon, Caroline, 1979.10
Grau, Shirley, 1977.27
Gray, Paul, 1976.13; 1977.28;
    1980.26
Gray, Richard K., 1978.15
Greeley, Andrew, 1977.29
Greene, Graham, 1974.9
"Greening and the Crumbling,
    The," 1971.32
Griffith, Thomas, 1977.30
Grumbach, Doris, 1966.20
Guerard, Albert J., 1967.7
"Guidebook for Lost Pilgrims,"
    1965.1
Guidry, Frederick, 1977.31

Hall, Constance, 1978.16
Hammond, John Francis, 1979.11
Hardy, John Edward, 1975.15;
    1980.27
Hawkes, John, 1975.7
Hawthorne, N., 1973.21
Haydel, Douglas Joseph, 1978.17
Hayes, Richard, 1967.8
"Headiest, Happiest Holiday
    Gifts: Books, The," 1971.50
Heidegger, 1967.4; 1971.11;
    1972.13; 1978.9
Heller, J., 1967.4; 1975.7, 12
Helterman, Jeffrey, 1978.18
Hemingway, Ernest, 1976.4
Hendin, Josephine, 1973.14
Henisey, Sarah, 1968.5

Kiley, John, 1971.30
King, Barbara, 1974.8
King, Richard H., 1975.18
Kirby, Jack Temple, 1978.20
Kirby, Martin, 1976.14
Kirkeby, Marc, 1980.31
Kisor, Henry, 1980.32
Kissel, Susan S., 1975.19;
    1977.33; 1980.33
Kitching, Jessie, 1966.24
Klein, Marcus, 1967.10
Kline, Edward A., 1976.15
Knipp, Thomas, 1966.25
"Knowing the Noumenon," 1968.12
Kosinski, Jerzy, 1971.41
Kostelanetz, Richard, 1965.1
Kreyling, Michael, 1978.21

"Ladies in The Last Gentleman,
    The," 1978.16
"Lady and Her Business of Love in
    Selected Southern Fiction,
    The," 1976.7
Lambert, Gavin, 1966.6
Lancelot, 1977.1-9, 11, 13-32,
    34-41, 43, 45-46, 49, 50-53,
    55-59; 1978.1, 4-5, 7-9, 12,
    14, 19, 21-23, 27-29; 1979.1,
    3, 7, 11, 15, 22, 26-28, 30-
    31; 1980.12, 43, 62
"Lancelot and the Medieval Quests
    of Sir Lancelot and Dante,"
    1980.16
"Lancelot and the Search for
    Sin," 1979.7
"Lancelot: Sign for the Times,"
    1980.13
Lancelot, Sir, 1980.16
Language, 1975.1-5, 11, 17, 21-
    22, 24-26, 31, 34; 1976.2-3,
    21, 26, 32; 1977.44; 1978.3-
    4, 30; 1979.21-22, 30, 31;
    1980.10, 23, 52
Lanterns on the Levee, 1970.3, 5;
    1979.16
"Lapsed from Grace," 1971.2
"Lapsometer Legend," 1971.24
Lardner, Susan, 1977.34
Last Gentleman, The, 1966.1-5, 7,
    9-38; 1967.1-5, 8-15;
    1968.3-4, 6-8, 12; 1969.2-3;

1970.2, 6; 1975.30, 34;
    1976.24, 31, 33; 1977.35;
    1978.7-9, 16, 24; 1979.2, 6,
    12, 14, 21, 23, 26, 29, 33;
    1980.8, 27
"Last Gentleman, The," [Essay in
    Masterplots 1967 Annual],
    1967.13
"Last Gentleman, Authority, and
    Papa Hemingway, The," 1966.13
"Last Man in America Who Believes
    in Love," 1977.16
Lathe of Heaven, The, 1978.6
Lauder, Robert E., 1974.9
Lawson, Lewis A., 1969.4-5;
    1970.2-3; 1972.11; 1976.16;
    1978.22; 1979.15-18; 1980.34-
    36
"Lay Preacher," 1980.15
"Lead Us into Temptation, Deliver
    Us Evil," 1977.52
LeClair, Thomas, 1972.12;
    1974.10; 1975.20-21; 1977.35;
    1979.19
Lee, Hermione, 1978.23-24
Lee, Robert E., 1979.16
LeGuin, Ursula K., 1978.6
Lehan, Richard, 1967.11; 1968.6;
    1973.17
Lehmann-Haupt, Christopher,
    1977.36
"Lesions of the Dead: Walker
    Percy's The Last Gentleman,
    The," 1979.12
Lessing, Doris, 1971.28
Levi-Strauss, C., 1975.22
Lewis, C.S., 1975.14
Linguistics, 1975.3, 31; 1976.14,
    16, 21-22, 26; 1980.57
Lischer, Tracy Kenyon, 1978.25;
    1980.37
Locke, Richard, 1977.37
"Logos and Epiphany: Walker
    Percy's Theology of
    Language," 1977.10
"Loss of the Creature, The,"
    1976.32
"Lost Cause: Myth, Symbol, and
    Stereotype in Southern Fic-
    tion, The," 1978.11
"Lost Souls," 1980.40

Love and death (theme in Percy),
1967.2; 1971.51
"Love and Marriage in Walker
Percy's Novels," 1976.17
Love in the Ruins, 1971.1-10,
12-13, 15, 18-28, 30-34, 36,
38, 50, 52; 1972.1, 3, 6-14,
18; 1973.1-3, 6, 12, 17, 21,
24; 1974.1-3, 7, 9-10;
1975.7, 14, 16, 30, 34;
1976.24, 30-31; 1977.34-35,
48, 55; 1978.6-10, 24, 27;
1979.2, 9, 26-27; 1980.12, 62
"Love in the Ruins: Thomas
More's Distorted Vision,"
1979.9
"Lucid, Sympathetic Study of
Walker Percy, A," 1979.35
Luschei, Martin L., 1970.4;
1972.13; 1974.5; 1979.20;
1980.9
Lyons, Gene, 1980.38

McCleary, William, 1961.10
McGuane, Thomas, 1971.31
Mack, James R., 1976.17
MacKethan, Lucinda, 1980.39
McLellan, Joseph, 1976.18
McMurtry, Larry, 1975.22
McNaspy, C.J., 1966.26; 1975.23;
1977.39
McPherson, William, 1971.32
Mailer, N., 1976.34; 1979.32
Malaise (theme in Percy), 1968.1;
1969.5; 1972.13; 1973.20;
1980.21
Malamud, B., 1967.4, 11
Malin, Irving, 1977.39
"Man on the Train, The," 1969.5;
1972.4; 1975.18, 30
"Man the Symbol-Monger," 1976.9
Marcel, Gabriel, 1966.23; 1968.2;
1969.1; 1970.4; 1972.13;
1973.7; 1975.34; 1978.9;
1979.12
"Marriage of Two Minds," 1979.25
Marsh, Pamela, 1971.33
Massie, Robert, 1961.11
"Master Class: From the Corre-
spondence of Caroline Gordon
and Flannery O'Connor, A,"
1979.10

Maxwell, Robert, 1967.12
Media-Made Dixie, 1978.20
"Melted into Air," 1967.10
Melville, Herman, 1973.21
"Memorable Madman," 1977.21
Merkin, Daphne, 1980.40
"Message in the Bottle, The"
(1959), 1967.12
Message in the Bottle, The,
1975.1-5, 8-11, 13-14, 17-18,
21-26, 30-31, 33; 1976.2-3,
5-6, 8-10, 12, 14-16, 18-22,
26, 28, 35; 1977.44, 50;
1978.30; 1979.22, 30-31, 53;
1980.42
"Message in the Bottle, The," [in
Masterplots 1976 Annual],
1976.21
Michaels, Walter, 1975.24;
1976.19
"Middle-Landscape Myth in Science
Fiction, The," 1978.6
Miller, Nolan, 1976.20
Milton, Edith, 1977.40
"Minor Novelists in the Active
Mode," 1970.7
"Mr. Percy's Look at Chaos,"
1971.22
"Mr. Percy's Positive Statement,"
1971.1
Mitgang, Herbert, 1977.41
"Mode of 'Black Humor,' The,"
1973.21
"Monomythic Quest: Visions of
Heroism in Malamud, Bellow,
Barth, and Percy, The,"
1979.11
Moore, Brian, 1963.1
"Moral Fiction," 1978.14
"Moral Tales For a Depraved Age,"
1977.30
More, Saint Thomas, 1973.3;
1974.12; 1977.48
"More than One America," 1963.5
Morgan, Berry, 1966.27
Morning and the Evening, The,
1961.4
Morse, J. Mitchell, 1966.28;
1971.34
Moviegoer, The, 1961.1-14;
1962.1-4; 1963.1-6; 1964.1;
1965.1-2; 1966.6, 8, 11, 21;

(Moviegoer)
    1967.2, 5-6, 9-10, 12;
    1968.1, 5-6, 9-10, 12;
    1969.2, 5; 1970.3-5;
    1971.11, 14, 16, 18, 29, 44,
    51; 1972.4, 7-8, 11, 13, 15;
    1973.8, 17-18, 20; 1974.8;
    1975.27, 30, 32, 34; 1976.7,
    24, 27, 31; 1977.35, 47, 59;
    1978.7-9, 14, 25, 31;
    1979.2, 13, 16, 20, 26, 30,
    32, 34; 1980.21, 24, 27, 45,
    56-57, 62
"Moviegoer, The," [Essay in
    Masterplots 1962 Annual],
    1962.1
"Moviegoer and the Stoic
    Heritage, The," 1979.16
"Moviegoer as Dissolve, The,"
    1979.20
"Moviegoer of the 1950's, The,"
    1968.10
"Moviegoing and Other
    Intimacies," 1962.4
"Moviegoing in The Moviegoer,"
    1980.34
"Movie Magazine: A Low Slick,
    The," 1972.4
Muggeridge, Malcolm, 1971.43
Mulligan, Hugh A., 1977.42
Murray, Albert, 1971.35
Murray, James G., 1980.41
Murray, John J., 1975.25
Murray, Michele, 1971.36
Muther, Elizabeth, 1980.42
"Mysteries and Movies: Walker
    Percy's College Articles and
    The Moviegoer," 1972.4
"Mystery of Language, The,"
    1976.3

Nagel, Thomas, 1975.26
Naming, 1975.28; 1976.11; 1980.52
"Naming as Disclosure: A Study
    of Theme and Method in the
    Fiction of Walker Percy,"
    1976.11
"Narrative Triangle and Triple
    Alliance: A Look at The
    Moviegoer," 1978.31

"Narrative Triangulation in The
    Last Gentleman," 1979.33
National Book Award, 1962.2-4;
    1974.2; 1976.31
Neilson, Keith, 1976.21
"Neither Far Out Nor in Deep,"
    1976.14
"Neo-Romanticism in Contemporary
    American Fiction," 1976.34
"New American Fiction, The,"
    1965.1
"New Breed: Walker Percy's
    Critics', A," 1980.63
"New Fiction," 1963.3
"New Lancelot Seeks His Knight-
    hood, A," 1977.22
"New Novels," 1967.14
"New Old Southern Novel, The,"
    1973.24
Night Visitor and Other Stories,
    The, 1966.37
1984, 1971.13
"Notes for a Novel about the End
    of the World," 1975.30;
    1977.16; 1979.9
"Novelists as Preachers," 1977.37
"Novelists of the Madhouse,"
    1977.29
"Novel of Powerful Pleasures, A,"
    1980.45
"Novel's Ending and World's End:
    The Fiction of Walker Percy,"
    1973.11
"Novels of Walker Percy, The,"
    1967.2

Oates, Joyce Carol, 1966.29;
    1977.43
O'Connor, Flannery, 1971.15;
    1972.15; 1973.19; 1975.18;
    1977.50; 1978.27; 1979.8,10;
    1980.33
O'Donnell, Roy, 1976.22
"Oh, You Know Uncle Walker,"
    1971.17
"On Man the Sad Talker," 1975.17
"One of the Roaming Kind,"
    1966.21
Open Decision: The Contemporary
    American Novel and Its Back-
    ground, The, 1971.14

"Walker Percy," [in Contemporary
Literary Criticism], 1975.6
"Walker Percy," [in Contemporary
Literary Criticism], 1978.2
"Walker Percy," [in Contemporary
Literary Criticism], 1980.4
"Walker Percy," [in Separate
Country], 1979.2
"Walker Percy," [in Southern
Writers], 1979.17
"Walker Percy," [in Twentieth
Century American Litera-
ture], 1980.49
"Walker Percy," [Mississippi
Library Commission], 1976.31
"Walker Percy: A Checklist,"
1973.10
Walker Percy: An American
Search, 1978.9
"Walker Percy and Gabriel Marcel:
The Castaway and The Way-
farer," 1975.34
"Walker Percy and Modern
Gnosticism," 1977.12; 1979.3
"Walker Percy and Post-Christian
Search," 1968.1
"Walker Percy and the
Archetypes," 1979.27
"Walker Percy and the Novel of
Ultimate Concern," 1980.29
"Walker Percy and the Resonance
of the Word," 1980.10
"Walker Percy and the Search for
Wisdom," 1973.7
"Walker Percy and the Self,"
1974.11
"Walker Percy: A Pragmatic
Approach," 1979.30
Walker Percy: Art and Ethics,
1980.55
"Walker Percy as Martian
Visitor," 1976.16
"Walker Percy as Satirist:
Christian and Humanist Still
in Conflict," 1980.62
"Walker Percy, A Sign of the
Apocalypse," 1980.28
"Walker Percy Bibliography, A,"
1980.58
"Walker Percy--En udda amerikan,"
1972.2

"Walker Percy: Eschatology and
the Politics of Grace,"
1980.20
"Walker Percy: Not Just
Whistling Dixie," 1977.23
"Walker Percy Novel Puzzles over
the Farce of Existence, A,"
1980.60
"Walker Percy Prevails," 1974.8
"Walker Percy Redivivus," 1978.26
"Walker Percy's Bicentennial
Message," 1975.30
"Walker Percy's Christian
Vision," 1974.7
"Walker Percy's 'Consumer-Self'
in The Last Gentleman,"
1976.33
"Walker Percy's 'Conversions,'"
1977.33
"Walker Percy's Devil," 1977.36;
1979.19
"Walker Percy: Sensualist-
Thinker," 1972.7
"Walker Percy's Fancy," 1967.12
"Walker Percy's Funhouse Mirror:
More True than Distorted,"
1977.59
"Walker Percy's Indirect
Communication," 1969.5
"Walker Percy's Ironic Apology,"
1978.3
"Walker Percy's Kierkegaard: A
Reading of The Moviegoer,"
1978.25
"Walker Percy's Knights of the
Hidden Inwardness," 1974.12
"Walker Percy's Lancelot,"
1977.31
"Walker Percy's Lancelot:
Secular Raving and Religious
Silence," 1978.12
"Walker Percy's Language of
Creation," 1978.30
"Walker Percy's 'Larroes,'"
1973.18
"Walker Percy's Profoundly
Satisfying Novel," 1980.23
"Walker Percy's Sci-Fi," 1971.38
"Walker Percy's Silent
Character," 1980.35

"Walker Percy's Southern Stoic,"
1970.3
Walker Percy's 'The Last
Gentleman,' (Ellen
Douglas), 1969.3
"Walker Percy's Wonder-Working
Powers," 1979.18
"Walker Percy Talks about
Kierkegaard," 1974.4
"Walker Percy Talks of Many
Things," 1966.22
"Walker Percy Tells How to Write
a Good Sentence," 1980.46
"Walker Percy: The Last
Gentleman," 1968.8
"Walker Percy, the Man and the
Novelist: An Interview,"
1968.2
"Walker Percy: The Physician as
Novelist," 1972.11
Walter, J., 1980.57
Warren, Robert Penn, 1971.44;
1977.27
"Watcher, a Listener, a Wanderer,
A," 1966.9
Watkins, Floyd C., 1970.6
Watkins, Suzanne B., 1977.54
Waugh, Evelyn, 1971.43, 46;
1972.10; 1977.38
"Way Back: Redemption in the
Novels of Walker Percy,
The," 1968.6
Webb, Max, 1979.34
Weber, Brom, 1973.21
Weinberg, Helen A., 1970.7
Weixlmann, Joe, 1980.58
Welty, Eudora, 1972.3
Westendorp, T.A., 1973.22
West, Nathanael, 1963.6; 1968.10
"What Language Reveals--And What
It Conceals," 1975.22
Whitehead, Alfred North, 1976.31
Whitman, Walt, 1976.4
"'Why Does Man Feel So Sad?,'"
1975.23
"Why Is 20th Century Man So
Sad?," 1975.9
Wiehe, Janet, 1980.59
Wiehe, P.L., 1977.55
Wiesel, Elie, 1966.37
Wilkie, Brian, 1966.38

"Will and Allison," 1980.7
"Willard Huntington Wright Murder
Case, The," 1972.4
Will, George F., 1977.56
"William Alexander Percy, Walker
Percy, and the Apocalypse,"
1980.36
Williams, Joan, 1961.4
Williams, Mina G., 1973.23
Williams, Thomas, 1980.60
Wills, Garry, 1972.18
Wineapple, Brenda, 1976.34
"With Manic Laughter: The
Secular Apocalypse in
American Novels," 1975.7
Wittington, Mary J. Garrard,
1968.11
Wolfe, Peter, 1968.12
Wolff, Geoffrey, 1977.57
Wood, Ralph, 1976.35; 1977.58;
1980.61-62
"Words, Words, Words," 1976.15
"Writings about Percy," 1980.9

Yagoda, Ben, 1979.35
Yardley, Jonathan, 1971.52;
1973.24
"Year in Books: A Personal
Report, The," 1971.39
Yeats's "The Second Coming,"
1971.23
"Yoknapatawpha Blues," 1976.13
Young, T.D., 1976.24; 1980.63
Yount, John, 1977.59

Zaidman, Bernard, 1975.33
Zeugner, John F., 1973.10;
1975.34

Peter Taylor

Agee, James, 1974.4
Agrarianism, an influence on
    Taylor's work, 1948.8;
    1959.6-7; 1960.1; 1963.1;
    1964.7; 1977.18, 26, 32, 34
Amis, Kingsley, 1979.1
Anderson, Sherwood, 1964.5;
    1977.32
Anna Karenina, 1959.3
Arnold, Matthew, 1971.7
"As a Boy Grows Older," 1950.2
"Assessments of the Finely
    Aware," 1959.6
"At the Drugstore," 1965.1-2;
    1967.4; 1970.7; 1971.5;
    1978.2

"Bad Dreams," 1954.6; 1965.1
Bailey, Paul, 1977.5
Baro, Gene, 1959.2; 1964.3
Baumbach, Jonathan, ed., 1965.1;
    1968.2; 1973.2
Beattie, Ann, 1979.3
Beaver, Harold, 1977.6
Betts, Doris, 1973.12
Bibliography, 1961.1; 1967.6;
    1970.3; 1973.2; 1974.2;
    1975.1-2; 1979.2
Binding, Paul, 1979.1
Biography, 1948.8; 1952.1;
    1967.7; 1970.1-3; 1972.3;
    1973.6; 1975.3; 1977.8,
    10-11, 16-18, 22, 25-28,
    33-34, 38-39; 1978.3, 7;
    1979.1-4, 8-9; 1980.1

"Black Literature" [in Harvard
    Guide to Contemporary Ameri-
    can Writing], 1979.6
Blackman, Ruth, 1959.3
Bloom, Lynn Z., 1979.2
Blum, Morgan, 1962.1
Boatwright, James, ed., 1977.7
"Books in Brief: Current Books
    in Short Compass," 1973.7
Borges, Jorge Luis, 1977.17
Brace, Marjorie, 1948.3
Bradbury, John M., 1963.1
Braudy, Leo, 1979.3
"Brief Lives," 1969.9
Bright Book of Life: American
    Novelists and Storytellers
    from Hemingway to Mailer,
    1973.9; 1975.1
Brooks, Cleanth, 1969.5; 1971.2
Brooks, Jeremy, 1960.6
"Brothers in Loss," 1967.8
Brown, Ashley, 1962.2; 1977.7-8
Broyard, Anatole, 1977.9

Caldwell, Erskine, 1960.1
Capote, Truman, 1954.7; 1964.5;
    1969.10, 18; 1974.4
"Captain's Son, The," 1977.9, 20,
    26, 40
Casey, Jane Barnes, 1978.2
Casey, John, 1977.7, 10; 1978.7
Cassill, R.V., 1969.6
Cather, Willa, 1950.5; 1964.8
Cathey, Kenneth Clay, 1953.1;
    1974.2